I never intended to write a book. The Laugh A Minute Clinic began as a series of anecdotes about fun things that I encountered during my career as a veterinarian. However, it quickly evolved into a humorous, but serious book with the underlying theme of how to succeed. First, in college, then in vet school, then in a career and, finally, in life.

It began as a small amorphous thought in the back of my brain and over a number of months grew into an almost physical entity that worked its way forward and began pounding on the inside of my forehead as it attempted to enter our world.

My first several attempts at putting it on paper were futile. Just before I started writing successfully I received an email with a quote from GK Chesterton: "You should not write anything until you can no longer not write." It was timely and providential. I feel very strongly that this is not my book....I simply put to paper what was put in my head. I hope that you reap the benefits of what He has sown.

Gregg T. Greiner DVM

**The Laugh a Minute Clinic**
2010 Kelmscott Communications Paperback Edition
Copyright 2010 by Gregg T. Greiner DVM
All rights reserved.
Published by Gregg Greiner Properties

Printed in the United States of America
by Kelmscott Communications, Inc.
Aurora, Illinois

Cover design by Janet Abramic
ISBN 987-0-9845065-0-7

Website available spring 2011 via link on burrridgevet.com.
Look under 'our partners'.

Discounts available for bulk orders by contacting website.
(be sure to tell the neighbors)

Roger —

Love to learn.

Learn to Love!

All my best

10-12-22

Praying for your
success

KELMSCOTT
COMMUNICATIONS

# The Laugh A Minute Clinic

*Fun Loving*

*Fun Living*

*Fun Learning*

By Dr. Gregg T. Greiner DVM

# Acknowledgements

There are so many who have contributed to the making of this book that I cannot begin to mention them all. I fear that I will omit many names, therefore, I will not name any. Please know that you all remain in my heart and that even the least of you played a role in the formation of my thoughts. Sometimes it was the smallest word of encouragement that kept me going. Sometimes it was a major gaffe that became part of the book. I thank God daily for the wonderful people that have been sent to me, especially those that were sent when I needed them most. I thank you all for responding to my needs in ways that exceeded all of my expectations. I am a better person for knowing each of you. May you be blessed seventy times seventy times over.

# About the Cover

When photoshop software became widely available my second brother, Keith, decided to give me a personalized calendar for Christmas. He developed an elaborate story about my 'secret mission' in veterinary school. I was performing genetic experiments involving the insertion of human genes into animals and he had the pictures to prove it. For each month of the calendar he had a picture of me with my face added to whatever animal was in the original picture with me. This one was my favorite. I was holding Jackie and Kelly's last puppy.... unaware of the future events that would cement our friendships for eternity.

# Dedication

*Glen and Grace Greiner on their wedding day, Dec. 15, 1951*

This book is dedicated to my father.
A man of few words, he meant what he said.
His passing has left a deafening silence in my soul.

# Contents

# Preface

Where does one start when giving an audience a glimpse of his life? What message should be left in their minds and hearts? What lessons can be learned from my experiences that a wider audience would appreciate? These are the thoughts that enter my mind as I embark on this adventure. I can answer the first question directly. The others may remain unanswered except in retrospect by each member of my audience. I hope that each of you relates to my story in a unique fashion as I have always tried to relate to every patient and client as unique individuals.

I am filled with anticipation as this comes together because I have no clear idea of the size of my audience (more than ten, I hope) or the reactions you will each experience as I expose a portion of my life, mind and soul to you. I hope that I can remain on task as this book progresses because my mind does tend to wander. Fortunately, it is too weak to go far.

That, by the way, is how my mind tends to wander. Odd thoughts pop up without warning. Some are profound. Most are just random access words often in the form of puns. The pun center in my brain probably occupies two thirds of my frontal lobe. Apparently, there is a large chute resembling a water slide which shoots those puns right out of my mouth without warning, usually without the water, and often at the most inopportune moments. In order to control the direction of this project I have limited some of these random rest stops on the highway of life to the bottoms of pages in this book. Otherwise, we may never get to where we are going.

My journey into veterinary medicine began before I knew it. I came to that realization after 20 years in practice. I was speaking to a group of third grade students as part of a career day program. One of them asked me when I decided to become a vet. I gave them my usual spiel that deciding upon a career path involves many factors including life experience, educational success, personal strengths and weaknesses and your level of motivation and willingness to work.

As I kept talking and looking for the real answer I found that I had none. Picking a major in college certainly puts a stamp on it, but when did I decide to become a vet? As I often do in moments of doubt, I went to my personal guru, Mom.

I asked her when she had the first clear signs that I wanted to become a vet. Her answer: "When you were 4 or 5...that's all you ever wanted to be. Every once in awhile a fire truck would pass by and you'd want to be a fireman or you would see a baseball game and want to become a ball player for a time. But, the next week you'd be right back to being a vet." So that was it! I was born to be a vet. Fortunately, I was also born into a very supportive family that gave me a good work ethic and the determination to fulfill my dreams. I admire people that succeed in life without a good support network. I had enough trouble succeeding even with a lot of support on the home front.

My family has always played a vital role in my life so that is where I have elected to start my story. I did promise not to divulge any family secrets, but certain members of my family have taught me valuable life lessons. Special mention has to be made of my dearest sibling and first dog, Mittens. She was the ninth child in our family and the one with whom I could communicate the best (unless slugging it out with your brothers counts as communicating....in that case we really got our messages across).

Proceeding somewhat chronologically from Mitts I will share some of my educational experiences....what it takes to get into veterinary school and how to succeed once you get there. I hope that this will benefit both prospective students and their parents who may be sharing the emotional and financial burdens associated with a long educational process. Much of what you will read will pertain to getting any college level education, so please don't think you should skip that portion of the book just because you are attending another part of campus.

Next, I will share some of my early work experiences with you. Again, I hope that much of this has universal appeal since my position as a new graduate seeking employment was not unique. After many years of no appreciable income it was exciting to put school behind me and, yet, it was sad that my insulating cocoon was being removed never to return. Butterflies can spread their wings, but at appreciable risk. I was very fortunate to be in the small minority who immediately landed in nectar and stayed there. If you can't find clover follow the bees. Just be sure they aren't really yellow jackets.

The rest of this onus, er opus, will be somewhat random selections of events that occurred throughout my life as a practitioner in a busy small animal general medical and surgical referral practice in the western suburbs of Chicago. I have tried to address some of the myriad changes which have occurred in veterinary medicine over the past twenty five years. Most have been positive, but I haven't spared you from some of the negative.

My professors did a terrific job of preparing me for practice, but they couldn't begin to make me appreciate the level of commitment and attachment that I would develop towards my patients and clients. I was very reluctant to start this project as I feared it would detract from my service to them. It wouldn't have happened at all except as a tribute to my clients, my patients, my associates, my staff and my family. I pray that I may continue to deserve their respect and trust as I proceed with my professional and personal life. They have always been an inspiration to me; may they be the same to you. If their stories change the direction of your life may it always be in the right direction even if it isn't towards a career in veterinary medicine. It is a long and difficult road to become a vet. It requires a lot of sacrifice to make it through school and to be successful in practice, but the destination is well worth the effort of making the trip. If you are called, answer. And try to enjoy the journey every step of the way.

*The author with Mittens, the mountain dog, on the roof of Dad's house January, 1974.*

# CHAPTER 1

## *Hat, Scarf, Gloves and Mittens*

It was difficult being an animal lover while growing up in a large family. Space was always at a premium. Money never seemed to be tight, but that was an illusion created by Mom and Dad. They never discussed finances in front of us children unless it directly impacted one of us. If there was a particularly inviting toy or a piece of sporting gear that caught your eye then it was up to you to earn it. As a result, entry into the work force was as early as you developed a desire to accumulate 'wealth' in the form of 'stuff'. Getting an allowance in exchange for doing chores and hawking golf balls at the nearby golf course became inadequate for my needs by the time I was 15 years old. I didn't need a lot of stuff, but I knew college wouldn't be far off and I wanted to pay my own way as much as possible.

I am the oldest boy in a family of eight children so I was always a bit more serious about life than my peers. I must temper that apparently lofty position by admitting that I have three older sisters with whom I competed for attention. That lasted a few short years because my first brother, Geoffrey, came along two years after me.

He became my main comPAINion as we were soon beating on each other as only loving brothers can do. Keith arrive next, then another girl, Lynn, and finally, David. The firstborn of the family, Gail, kept her siblings on a pretty short leash. When Mom left her in charge Gail ruled the house. It was not a benevolent monarchy. Her main strategy for dealing with the pack was force. It worked. We toed the line for fear of facing the consequences. Marsha was next. She was always calm and kept the peace by reasoning with us. She let us help her bake cookies when we were good. By the way, what is the point of baking that delicious cookie dough anyway? The littlest of the big sisters is Janice. She was never really called upon to be in charge until her late teens. By then 'the boys' weren't the challenge that we once were. Her looks of exasperation usually made us feel guilty. Tears were sure to work.

As you might imagine, another motivating force to start working outside the house was a certain sense of self preservation. Sanity seems much more precious when you're on the brink of losing it. Yes, my mother needed us to get out of the house. Therefore, she, er, I stretched the truth about my age as I applied for a job at Burger King. Marsha was already working there so I would be able to ride with her. Since she was such a good worker they took a chance on me. That first paycheck was a thing of beauty...$74.00! I signed the back of it and gave the check to Mom. She cashed it in for me at the Lincoln Savings and Loan. After taking out rent and the money I had borrowed from her, she gave $40 back to me. That was a bit of a surprise. I thought that she would keep it all in order to manage the money for me. That would have taught me nothing. It was up to me to guard my treasure. I couldn't just leave it lying around as a temptation to my brothers. Therefore, I opened my first savings account.

Shortly after starting my busy new work schedule another opportunity would enter my life and change it permanently. Mom sent two of the girls to the grocery store for some emergency supplies. That usually meant milk and pasta. This day it was milk and bread. You could bet on it being milk and something.

Today's shopping cart would include a bit of a surprise.

Motto's supermarket was just a mile from our house. Janice would eventually meet her future husband while working there. Our family was on a first name basis with everyone in the store as Dad impressed them every week with his cart full of supplies. The special of the day, however, was found in front of the store. There was a little girl sitting outside with a box of puppies. She was miserably sad because her mother was making her give the puppies away. The story varies as to how the selection process took place, but the little black one with white feet and a small patch of white on her chest was the clear winner. They weren't exactly sure if it was a male or female at the time. They didn't ask many questions and the puppy probably picked them, truth be told. (Note to all puppies reading this....be cute and aggressively friendly. That will give you the best odds of getting a good home; this is the equivalent of winning the doggie Lotto)

While presenting their surprise to Mom (they knew Dad wasn't home yet...this definitely plucked their courage) they made sure that us youngsters were present in order to get the full effect of the oohing and aahing. We were ready to add any necessary sound effects to promote our cause. Whining is definitely the most effective means, particularly after whole-hearted oohing and aahing. Mom pulled her usual stalling technique by announcing that we would have to wait for *father* (<u>Dad</u> would have left us with more optimism) to come home so she could discuss it with him.

Well, you've never seen chores get done so quickly. The entire house was cleaned up and all of our homework was done before Dad walked in. For the benefit of those reading this that can't remember anything prior to 1970 I should tell you that Dad walked in the door at 5:10 every night. This was the custom of most dads in the good ole days. He dutifully greeted us each day, went through the mail and read the Chicago Sun-Times as he enjoyed his dinner. He then took a short nap before playing with us kids and dealing with the issues of the day. There was only one issue this day. I was a bit concerned that we may have blown it by playing our hand before dinner, but how can you keep from bursting with the news of a new pup in the house?

We made all of the usual promises. 'We'll feed her; we'll clean up after her; we'll train her to tap dance if we have to. She is so small she won't even shed!" Dad had a little gleam in his eye as he held our little treasure and said, "Let me talk this over with your mother." Oh, no! When the two of them communicated about anything you could bet that they were going to make a practical decision that made perfect sense and could withstand a nuclear blast of emotional pleading. It was time to start bargaining.

Since my allowance was likely going to end and was small in comparison to that big $74.00 payday it could go towards feeding the dog. I failed to mention the first half of that sentence during the negotiations; I did my best to look pitiful. My brothers showed willingness, however short lived and insincere, to do their chores and homework without complaining. We would skip college and become professional athletes if that's what it took to keep this poor unwanted pooch. We were completely surprised and ecstatic when Mom simply announced that we would need a box for a bed if the pup was going to spend the night with us. Gosh, the humiliation of begging hadn't even begun in earnest.

The next thing Mom did was to lay out the conditions for our continued good fortune. The future of the puppy would depend on our behavior more than hers. "After all, she is just a pup and she needs to be taught the rules since she doesn't know them yet." Any accidents were the fault of us kids. Anything she chewed was our fault. Being on the good furniture was our fault. If she passed gas it would be our fault. Actually, we had that one covered by blaming it on Geoff.

The first order of business was to name our newest family member. After all, you can find a new home for a dog, but it is much more difficult to give away a family member. I know because I had several attempts with my brothers. We set to the task, our heads spinning with ideas. Each of us wanted to be the one to come up with the perfect name. She didn't look like a Mabel or Annie. Spot seemed trite as we had all read See Spot Run in our primers. I wanted a famous name from literature. I was afraid to mention Beelzebub as she might live up to it. The name finally emanated from the mouth of a babe (she still is), my only little sister, Lynn. Those little white feet fascinated her. She looked at them and kept saying, "Mittens, she has mittens." It stuck. Mittens it was. Everyone liked it. I was a bit disappointed, but the fact that I finally had a dog made up for any shortcomings in the name.

Mittens was her formal name, but she will always be Mitts to me. None of us ever called her Mitsy except for my old Aunt Sis. Her advanced age and gentle demeanor brought her privileges not enjoyed by most of the family. We never corrected her. A sure sign that Mitts was definitely in with Mom is that the only time Mom used her full name, Mittens!, was when she was in trouble. Just like me when I heard "Gregg Thomas!" Mitts knew she was in for it when Mom used more than one syllable and an exclamation point.

The first night passed uneventfully as the poor thing was simply exhausted from all of the handling and chaos she had endured. The next night she wasn't nearly as content to be away from her littermates and she let the entire house know about it in no uncertain terms. She wailed pitifully and relentlessly. Not wanting her to nix our deal by keeping Dad awake, I crept downstairs to the basement and carried her box up to the rec room. I placed it next to the couch and settled in with a pillow and blanket. Whenever I removed my hand from the box she would become restless and start whimpering. I eventually drifted into sleep face down with my hand still hanging over the side of the couch touching Mitts.

She slept through the night very nicely, but the next morning I couldn't feel my hand and my fingers were swollen (dependent edema I was to learn much later). I shook it off as quickly as possible and put the box back in the basement. I felt relieved that my parents weren't up yet. I took Mitts outside where she went to the bathroom almost immediately. I brought her back in to the kitchen just as Mom was coming down from her bedroom. Of course, I immediately boasted that Mitts had been a good girl all night and that her box was dry. Mitts helped advance her cause by giving Mom about 30 licks on her toes; right on cue!

The following night was a bit more challenging. The old hand in the box trick wasn't good enough. She wanted real company this time. Ten minutes passed with no break in the whining. It seemed like an hour. I finally relented and took her under the blanket. I figured that she would be like a baby. I could let her fall asleep and then move her back into the box. She curled up in a little ball and nestled against my stomach. As I started to pet her she wagged the end of her tail just a bit, took a deep breath and let out a contented sigh. I did the same and awakened 8 hours later with Mom sitting next to me on the couch. Busted! And yet, amazingly, not! Mom seemed very understanding about my concerns and she decided that perhaps Mitts should be allowed to sleep with the rest of the family so long as she behaved.

No dog was ever housebroken so quickly. Mittens had more attention than she knew what to do with. She was passed from one loving set of hands to the next. She was lucky to hit the floor let alone have an accident on it. We often joked that she thought her name was 'Put-the-dog-down' because every time Mom saw her that's what she said. We would later determine that Mitts was actually training us. All she had to do was look cute and someone would run to do her bidding.

Mitts learned tricks about as fast as we could come up with them. She fit in well with our family because she loved to learn new things just like us kids. She paid attention to each of us. She would look into our eyes as we spoke to her as if every word was important. I sometimes felt that she was trying to read my mind; it's pretty slow reading so I think she got bored with it quickly. She had complete trust in us and she wanted to be part of the action at all times. Whatever we were doing, she was in.

We often carried her up into our tree fort when she was little. When she was about one year of age I taught Mitts how to climb ladders. That led to her ability to climb our willow tree and get into the tree house once you boosted her up to the first branch. We would always be there to catch her if the need arose, but she never missed a step on the sturdy branches. She loved to survey her domain from the heights. She rarely barked or paced up there. She simply enjoyed the company and the scenery.

Getting down was another matter. She couldn't negotiate even the first step down nor would she consider trying it. We had to hand her down from one set of hands to the next. Once you had a secure footing you would get Mitts; then the hander-offer would climb down, get a secure foothold and the process would be repeated. Mitts would practically go limp as she patiently waited to reach *terra firma*. I think she knew we would rather fall ourselves than drop her. Mom knew that, too. She would shake her head as she averted her eyes from the impending disaster that miraculously never happened. I suspect our guardian angels did the same.

Years later, I went into our attached garage to get my baseball equipment. I heard a faint whimper, but shrugged it off as my imagination as there was nothing breathing in the garage but me. I turned to leave and heard it again. I looked up at the ladder leading into the attic and was startled by a pair of eyes looking back at me! At first I thought it was a raccoon. But, as soon as ours eyes met, Mitts started barking at me. Her message was loud and clear; "It's hot up here and I can't get down. Hurry up!" I did. Apparently, she thought that the ladder had been placed there for her entertainment.

The neighbors were all fond of our new dog. Most of them were families with several children although none of them were as large as ours (except for the Hendersons on the next block...they had eleven kids. We couldn't understand why Mom and Dad didn't try to catch up with them). Everyone liked dogs and now they could basically have one without any of the responsibilities that came with it. As a result, when things got a bit slow around our place Mitts would go visiting.

We lived just outside of town. The lots were half an acre each. The houses behind ours faced a golf course. Oops, a country club; they were a bit snooty about that at times. Those houses were much bigger and yet contained almost no children. The lots to our sides weren't all occupied...a couple of them were mowed in order to give us play areas and others were unkempt fields. Across the street was an abandoned farmer's field with a small forest of maple trees that had taken up residence. Beyond that was a mile of forest preserve. The big houses behind us were off limits to us and Mitts, but the rest of it was fair play. Mitts became the star of the neighborhood. She would actually get invitations for dinner. The Fitzsimmons would call from three lots over and ask if Mittens had eaten dinner yet. If not, she would be let out the back door. Mrs. Fitz would give a holler and off Mitts went.

I don't want to give the impression that Mitts the Mooch didn't earn an honest living. She worked hard for her treats. Her tricks were many, varied and well polished. She did the usual things like sit, stay, shake, the other paw, down, roll over and sit-pretty. However, she also added to the effects by having the stage presence of a Shakespearian actress. When you wanted her to play dead you simply had to point a finger at her and say, 'bang!' She would go into a down position and then tilt her head to the side and slowly fall over onto her side as she scanned the room for the upcoming treat. She wouldn't completely die until she heard a second shot, 'bang!' Then she would go limp and stay limp until she heard the OK.

My brothers and I taught Mitts how to say her prayers. It wasn't the actual incantations but she did assume the proper posture. She would put her feet up on your knee and then bow her head and touch her nose between her paws. Her eyes would never leave the biscuit. If you suggested that she should 'pray harder' she would then bury her head between her paws and stay there until the OK was sounded. This was indicated by someone saying 'Amen'. If she could, in fact, pray I think it would have been that Geoffrey would lose his appetite so that she could get more leftovers, especially on liver night.

My personal favorite was when Mitts smiled. She came by it naturally. When greeting someone new or when she was being apologetic for doing some bit of naughtiness, Mitts would lower her head and show her teeth. I would later learn that this is a very submissive behavior. Many people thought she was growling or snarling when she was actually trying to say, "You're not going to kill me, are you?" Taking advantage of this tendency, I would lift her lips and ask Mitts to smile. Well, she learned that one in half an hour! It became an instant hit and it was one her best tricks. If smiling didn't get your attention she would follow it with a big sneeze. I never did figure out the meaning of that one.

When she wanted attention Mitts would go through her routines. She would start with speaking....bark, bark, bark, bark, bark. When that didn't work then it was time to shake. She would give paw and give paw and give paw. Then, it was on to smiling. Sometimes she would try other things like playing half dead. If she was determined to get some attention her tactic was to steal something and then parade it in front of you. At that point you had better pay attention or your personal item was about to become a chew toy. She usually grabbed a tennis shoe, but anything with your scent on it would do.

Whatever we were doing, Mitts was in. You couldn't rattle the car keys without her running at you with a crazed look on her face: A CAR RIDE! A RIDE IN THE CAR! RIDING IN THE CAR! I'LL DRIVE IF YOU WANT! You had to literally sneak out of the house. I'm certain that Mom used Mitts to help keep tabs on our comings and goings, especially when we were teenagers.

In the fall of the year, Dad would help us plug the drain for the empty lots two doors north and east from us. They would flood and freeze into an ice skating rink by mid winter. We grew up playing ice hockey in the winter and field hockey in the summer, Mittens was no exception. One of her favorite games was to grab onto your hockey glove so that you could skate backwards and pull her. She would skeech along the ice on all four feet. When her feet got cold she would pick one person and start barking at him while looking him right in the eyes. She wanted the hat off your head to warm her feet! We would take turns putting our hats on the bench that Dad had built for us. She would jump up, put all four feet on the hat for a few minutes and then go back out and try to grab somebody's glove, puck or anything else that would result in a chase. When we went out in the winter weather Mom made sure of two things. Dress warm and bring the dog with you. We were all sure to be tired that night.

One summer day Mitts went missing. Not just visiting, missing. After calling all of her usual haunts, we came up empty. We spread out through the neighborhood in an organized fashion: "You guys go that way and we'll go this way and if you find her come and get us!" We searched for over an hour. Our friend, Eddie, even brought out his walkie-talkies. (They were fun when you were in sight of each other. Other than that you could yell with more range than those dang things.)

An hour is nearly eternity for a kid. She was nowhere to be found. We even checked the busy street to look for her body as that seemed to be the only place on our little earth that we hadn't checked. As we neared home, dejected though somewhat relieved at not finding her carcass, the walkie-talkie crackled to life. "We found her, we found her. Over." (Even with momentous news such as this you have to maintain protocol.) "Where the heck is she? Over."

"You'll have to come and see for yourselves! Over."

Well, we ran that last half a block and found a small crowd gathering in the backyard. They were all looking up at the roof. And there she was. The queen was looking down on her subjects with a wag in her tail. She actually looked like a queen as the brick chimney behind her had the appearance of a throne. Of course, she was actually there for the shade as it was hot up there. She was no dummy.

We had no idea how she had gotten up on that roof. There was no visible means of climbing. No windows granted access to

10

the roof. No climbable branches came close to it (believe me, with us boys around Dad kept the trees trimmed). She couldn't have flown up there since Mom wouldn't let us build that airplane like we wanted to. What the heck! Scratching our heads, we hauled out the ladder from the garage and got her down.

Later that day we learned the truth. Dad had been cleaning the gutters when he received a call from the oil refinery where he worked. While he was on the phone, Mitts decided to see what he had been working on. Up the ladder and onto the roof she went. Since he had to leave for the office, Dad took down the ladder and put it away, not realizing the impending anguish he had unleashed. In fairness to Dad, it was a very safe bet that our ball would have landed on the roof in need of repeated retrieval if he had left that ladder up. With kids around you take nothing for granted.

*Showing no fear, Mittens climbs the ladder to join me on the roof. Notice the casual position I have taken; I had no qualms about her being on a ladder.*

*A client brought his two year old male Labrador retriever in for his annual wellness visit. I commented on the exceptional condition of the dog. As he was explaining that the dog had been swimming at the family lake house at summer his young son interrupted exclaiming, "Yeah, and he goes all the way under water. And I know he almost even caught a fish!"*

*"What kind of fish was it?" I queried.*
*He was straining his little brain to come up with an answer. I suggested one: "I'll bet it was a catfish. Dogs love to chase cats."*

*That was it. It made perfect sense to him. Dad thanked me for clearing that up for his son. His mother was certain to hear of it. I cemented our friendship with a piece of candy for the boy and a biscuit for his brave dog.*

*Donna, a longtime client, named her new puppy Barley. It was because he was Barley qualified to be a dog, not because he was a wheaten terrier.*

*During the first wellness examination of an eight week old border collie its owner asked three different times if I thought it was indeed a purebred dog. I replied that he was a fine example of his breed and asked if she had some concerns about the dogs' heritage. "No," she replied, "but I walked him around the perimeter of the yard three times and he still wants to leave it!"*

# CHAPTER 2

*Seizure Salad...Petit Mal with a Side of Valium*

So there I was; a boy and his dog. Life was good; a little school, a little work and a lot of fun with my new best friend. Then one day it happened. The disease that Mitts would carry with her for most of her life came down like a lightning bolt.

We were playing in the backyard when Mitts quit for no apparent reason. She was acting a bit strange, disoriented. It was as if she was seeing or hearing something that I couldn't. I called for Mom. She came out instantly as she heard the distress in my voice. She didn't have to ask what was wrong. Mitts was now wobbling and falling over as she tried to walk towards Mom. "What's wrong, Mitts?" Mom asked as she tried to pet her and give her some comfort.

Mitts couldn't focus on anything. She continued to shake and stumble, but now she seemed to have some purpose. She seemed intent to get to the grass. She pulled away from Mom and swayed like a wind chime as she walked past me about 10 feet. Then she started vomiting. The only thought I had was that she must have eaten something in the garden and gotten food poisoning, or worse. Perhaps Dad sprayed some chemical in the garden! (DDT in the environment was in the news at this time and we had recently talked about chemical pollution in school.) I wasn't going to let her go without a fight! I ran into the house and came back in a flash with an old blanket. I threw it over Mitts and told Mom: "Get us to the vet!"

I'm sure Mom was doing her best to put a positive spin on Mitts' condition as we sped towards the vet. Perhaps she said nothing. I don't remember hearing anything. I just remember praying and asking Mitts to hang on because we were going for help. I hoped I wasn't suffocating her, but I was afraid to loosen my grip. I wondered if it was her tremors or mine that I felt.

When we got to Dr. Hagenburg's office it must have been immediately apparent that we had a problem because the nurse took us straight to an exam room. She left and a moment later the vet came in. I told him exactly what happened in a very controlled manner and finished with; "I think she has food poisoning and that she may be dying."

As I finished speaking I unwrapped the blanket from around Mitts. She promptly stood up and started wagging her tail and licking my face! Puke breath! What a wonderful surprise! I couldn't have been happier. I held her at arms' length and stammered: "You, you were dying! Bad dog!"

Dr. Hagenburg had the biggest smile you've ever seen. He proceeded to tell me all about epilepsy in dogs. He suggested that we return for a fasting blood sample to make sure that there wasn't an underlying cause for the seizure and that we keep track of her seizures to determine their frequency and severity as that would determine the course of treatment. He ended by saying, "Congratulations, you have an attack dog." That became a running joke in my family. If I yelled 'Attack', Mitts would have one. Fortunately, the epilepsy didn't affect her longevity and the joke ran for many years.

Dr. H, as he would become known, seemed such a nice man that I pestered him for three years before he finally hired me to clean cages. I owe him a tremendous debt of gratitude not only for being a good vet, but also for being a wonderful person. I must also admit that I didn't put all of my eggs in one basket. I called every vet in the phone book every six months for those three years. Many of them wanted me to volunteer my time to come in and get a feel for what goes on in a vet clinic. I knew that I couldn't afford to do that as I needed to save money for my education. I sincerely hoped that it would be more than four years of college.

During that time I switched jobs. I felt I had mastered everything at Burger King. The job was becoming dull routine and the pay wasn't what I had hoped to work into. I still loved those Whoppers, but an opportunity arose to work at a mailing service. One of my counselors met me in the hall and said that the family of a fellow student was looking for someone reliable to work in their business. I went on an interview and was hired on the spot. For any youngsters reading this, the lesson to be learned is that you will develop a reputation based on your behavior. It will be a good one or a bad one, and believe me, it is better to have people help you up the ladder to success than to have them stepping on your fingers. Guard your reputation by living up to your responsibilities.

The Imhoff mailing service was a small family operation. In the two and a half years that I was there it was bought by a larger company. My hard work paid off as I was not only asked to continue working with the new company, but I was given more responsibilities and a raise. It was mostly factory work. The inserting machines were my favorite. They were very complex with gears and vacuum lines and levers and suction cups. I could hear a leak in a vacuum line from 10 paces after awhile. I would volunteer for anything as most of the jobs were very repetitious once you mastered a few of the quirks that each machine seemed to have.

The new owners were brothers. They were both married, but neither had children. They were very forthcoming with fatherly advice to us young employees. The finest pearl of wisdom from them was this: "There are only two kinds of people in this world: ones who make interest and ones who pay it. You know which one you want to be! There are certain things you will need to go into debt for; your education, a car, a house. Those are necessities and that's OK. Never go into debt for your lifestyle. My wife and I could barely afford our house payment when we were first married. We had just started the business and we were lucky to have enough for a down payment on a modest house. We ate off of a cardboard box for a month. Then we got a card table. Finally, after 3 years, we were able to afford a dining room set for which we paid cash. I look back on those years with great fondness. Working towards a common goal brought me and the misses very close together. We are still close and we could still go back to eating off of a cardboard box if we needed to." Wow! Live your life like that and you can't go far wrong.

They treated me with great kindness and in return got a full day's effort for a fair wage. I was allowed very flexible hours as I had started my undergraduate studies by now. On every school break I was allowed to work as many hours as I wanted. During one such break I worked from 7:00 p.m. to 7:00 a.m. six days a week for four weeks. The money was great and I was too tired to spend it! However, the handwriting was on the wall.

There wasn't a job there that I couldn't handle. Some of the employees had been there for thirty years and couldn't do more than a handful of duties. If they were five minutes late for a break they were ready to explode. They came to work not a minute early and left not a minute late. I thought to myself, 'If I ever quit school and come back to this, somebody please shoot me. Otherwise, I'm likely to do it myself someday.'

During my stint at the mailing service I discovered that my next door neighbor was good friends with the owner of a veterinary hospital near our home. They were both small aircraft pilots. They owned property near each other in Texas and would vacation there with their families. When the girl next door started helping out with kennel work I became interested in checking it out even

17

though I knew that they weren't hiring any more help.

Dr. Boosler was rather intimidating. He was kept busy with clients and didn't have much time to spend with me. I didn't get to know him very well partly because I was more interested in the animals than I was in him. In spite of their numbers the place was clean; noisy, but clean. I was told in no uncertain terms not to get in the way or touch any animals; we did have liability even back then. Never being one to watch others work, I pitched in where I could....mostly empty cages. They were empty of animals that is. They did manage to leave behind some presents....made them themselves by the looks of them. No really big messes though since I was a guest.

As fate would have it, there was an emergency that day. A dog came in with an infection in the uterus and she would need surgery immediately. I didn't get to see much of the actual surgery as the doctor's back was to the window I was camped at. The atmosphere seemed strangely unhurried, but a sense of urgency was definitely there. I was doing my best to be invisible. I didn't want to cause a catastrophe. I wasn't nervous, but I was very tense as I did my best to see what was happening. Suddenly, the door of the surgery room was opened and in came the other vet, Dr. Royce. I thought that Dr. Boosler must have had his hands full and needed an assistant. Suddenly everyone started laughing and Dr. Royce left the room as quickly as he had come in. On closer inspection I noticed that he had found a baby's bib left behind by a client in the waiting room and that he was wearing it as a surgical mask!

That was my first exposure to veterinary surgery. It made a great impression on me. I realized that even in moments of stress you sometimes need to laugh. You can be very serious and still have fun. The secret is in being confident and competent. As it turns out, pyometra (pus in the uterus) is very common in unspayed dogs. The surgery is basically a hysterectomy (spay) and Dr. Boosler probably had several hundred under his belt at that point in his career. He certainly could take a moment to laugh.

Energized by this experience, I made what would turn out to be my final round of calls. Perhaps it was a sense of urgency or more maturity on my part, but this time I met with success. In fact, I received two job offers on the same day! Both clinics were near my house, but Doctor Hagenburg's office was directly on my way to school and he just seemed nicer. He was.

A few years later I would discover that the other vet was flat out dishonest as well as incompetent. Being nearby, we saw many of his mistakes as the owners sought a second opinion. Even as the wheels of justice slowly bore down on him, Dr. X (I won't use his name) never changed. He lost his license in Illinois, but not before suing our local association for defamation and winning an unfair amount of money. He was found practicing in Wisconsin a few years later. Another long process revoked that license. Finally, an employee of the Illinois Department of Professional Regulation found him practicing back in Illinois without a license. The find was accidental. While he was vacationing with his family and their dog, the professional reg employee took the dog to a local veterinary hospital for emergency care. There, to his surprise, was Dr. X practicing. Worse, so was his son who had never gone to vet school! At this point the charges were criminal. However, the case against Dr. X wouldn't be pursued as he passed away shortly after he was discovered. It gripes me to know he wasn't made to pay for his crimes. I never heard what happened to the son. This would later become a motivation for me to become active in organized veterinary medicine. Fortunately, one of the benefits of the information age is that this type of thing is unlikely to recur. States now share information, including disciplinary actions taken against professionals.

*As I was shoveling the snow from my neighbor's driveway another neighbor, 6 years old, came over to supervise. She asked why I was doing the shoveling instead of Mr. McGrath. I told her that he was having some heart problems so I thought I would try to help him out a bit. She replied, "That's OK if he has a heart attack. I can baby sit his dog."*

*A client was complaining loudly at the front desk. The waiting room was filled with people. He was insisting that we charged one dollar more for a heartworm test than the clinic by his house and, therefore, he should get an entire years' supply of heartworm pills for free (about a $50 value at the time).*

*At first, all I could muster was a weak 'Excuse me?' He went bravely on. "You call them. You will see. You charge one dollar more!" He was very animated and he was certain that he was correct.*

*"First of all," I responded, "it is illegal for me to shop around to see what other clinics charge. That is price fixing. Secondly, this would be like me going to a grocery store and insisting that they charge two cents more for a can of corn than the store down the street and, therefore, I should get my steak for free."*

*"Yes! Yes! This is so!" Ah, I was finally getting it.*

*I apologized for not being able to accommodate his desires and gave him a copy of his pet's medical records. I offered a list of referrals to other clinics if he would like to try his luck with them. I ushered him out the door and made sure that it closed securely behind him. I turned around to a standing ovation from the rest of the clients.*

# CHAPTER 3

## *The Road Scholar*

Most students have some idea of the type of career path they should seek.  Whether they follow their heart or not depends on a lot of factors.  I grew up in the age of sex, drugs and rock 'n roll.  I was fortunate that none of those things became much of an influence on my life.  I was surrounded by activities and parties, but I didn't allow them to become a thing to live for.  I had a vision of where I wanted to go, but I wasn't exactly sure that I would ever get there.  There seemed to be a lot of obstacles in my way.

The first was high school.  I had a choice of two schools.  Since I lived in unincorporated Cook County nestled between two towns I could have attended either Bremen High School which was having a problem with drugs and race riots for several years running or Oak Forest High School which was brand new with only one class ahead of me.  Also, I would have to take a bus to Bremen or walk to Oak Forest.  Not much of a decision there.  I became an Oak Forest Bengal.

Continuing my good study habits there was easy.  My parents always rewarded good grades with high praise and money.  They punished bad grades by....by...hmm I never wanted to face the consequences so I'm not really sure, but I'm certain it would have been appropriately awful; probably no sports. That threat always worked.

As I neared the end of my junior year I had the obligatory visit with the guidance counselor. I had several previous visits as required in order to register for classes each year, but this one was different. I seemed to be taken more seriously as if somehow I was more of an adult. We were talking about colleges and careers and being realistic with goals and achieving those goals in a stepwise manner. As we progressed in our conversation I sensed that I was being pushed away from my goals. She felt that a career in mathematics would suit me best.

I actually ran out of math classes in high school. They didn't offer calculus at that time so I was forced to turn to Math Club if I wanted to stay involved with the subject during my senior year. That seemed to be the goal of our current discussion....keeping Gregg busy in math. I had other ideas such as a shortened school day senior year so that I could work. I suppose my counselor was truly sincere. After all, I did score in the 99th percentile in math. I just couldn't see what kind of a job that meant....it wouldn't involve animals; that's for sure!

As I began to look into colleges I was beset on all sides by people trying to give me advice. Most of it was negative on my dreams and positive on theirs. All of the college counselors focused on my math skills and wanted me to pursue a math major. "After all, look at your math scores. You're a natural." None of them seemed to know what types of jobs were attainable with said math major. The next step after attaining that degree was graduate school. Then you would specialize into a career; probably teaching. That seemed a million years and a million miles away from where I wanted to go.

My parents weren't sure what kind of advice to give me. Mom had never set foot on a college campus. Dad had two years of junior college and lots of night school. Neither of them wanted to discourage me from getting into vet school, but they both knew the odds of getting accepted were only about one in twenty. Dad was Mr. Practical in that he insisted on an alternate plan if I didn't get into vet school. Since he worked at an oil refinery he was strongly suggesting that I get at least a minor in chemistry. I could always finish that major and go on to chemical engineering. I wanted to major in biology since that was the best track to take to get into vet school with the possible exception of majoring in animal science at the University of Illinois. I ruled that out because of my age. I was only 17 when I started college and I felt that I wasn't ready to move to the big U. where I would be one of the faceless, nameless masses. I wanted something smaller and closer to home where I could get personal attention if I needed it.

During this period of decision making my guidance counselor did provide one wonderful piece of advice for me. She suggested that I take the CLEP test.....College Level Examination Program. It was a program designed to identify college prospects. You could use it to find your weaknesses and try to focus on improving them before starting college.

I have always been a B student in English. In fact, I am amazed that I am sitting at my desk writing this book. The reason I ran out of math classes in high school is that I transferred from parochial school to public school in seventh grade. My test scores put me into advanced math classes and literature classes. The last grammar and structure class I took was back in Catholic school. I thought I should take that CLEP test to see what I needed to work on before I got into College Writing. So I did and I am glad of it!

My scores weren't stellar, but the admissions office at Lewis University felt that I had done well enough to comp out of two semesters of College Writing. All I had to do was pay for the credits and they would be granted with no grade towards my GPA (grade point average....it is everything when you're an undergraduate student with any intentions of staying in school beyond a baccalaureate). That was the solution to all of my problems! I would start my freshman year as a math, biology and chemistry major. I had to sneak in some humanities to satisfy the registrar, but I wouldn't take any class that required writing anything resembling a major paper. At least I didn't have to worry about a bunch of busywork that might drag down the GPA!

I can't emphasize this enough to students interested in a college career....try to comp out of a class in your worst subject. Not only will it save you from facing a semester in that dreaded subject, but it may make or break your career. It ended up saving me a year of college.

After my freshman year I decided that advice from my counselors was just that...advice. I took it with a grain of salt. I knew that *they* wanted me to become a well-rounded citizen. I knew that I wanted out of there as quickly as possible. Therefore, I would meet with the first available counselor and get a list of recommended classes. I would then wait for the last hour of registration before going in to sign up. I would also carry with me the list of required classes that I needed to apply for vet school. When I was notified that Religion 101 was booked up (Lewis is a Catholic University) I asked how Calculus 3 was looking...wide open! Gee, so is Organic Chemistry and so is Physiology. I did manage to sneak in two semesters of Latin American History that year. It turned out to be a surprisingly refreshing break from the sciences.

So there I was, getting along with a triple major and no one taking me to task for it. I was carrying 18-hour loads and working 30 hour weeks. I had just started my new job with Dr. Hagenburg.

The weeks were flying by. I had a strict schedule of driving to school with one of my friends who lived down the street from me. We used his car and I paid for his gas plus a bit of wear and tear allowance. We left for school at 7:20 and were there by 7:55. Just in time to take a seat and get ready to learn. We left at 2:00 or 3:00 depending on our schedules. When his classes ran later than mine I would study or do some lab work to kill the time. He would do likewise for me. On the way home Larry would drop me off at work. I would clean cages and bathe pets until everything in the kennel would pass inspection perfectly. Then I went to the middle portion of the clinic where the real action was. I would do anything the doctors needed from me. That usually meant holding a dog or cat while the doctors were working on it. That never bothered me because I was always watching and learning. Everything was clean and secure before I left for the night.

On one of my days off of school, it may have been during Thanksgiving break, I was able to work the morning shift. As I was to discover, that is when the fun stuff happens. Dr. H invited me to 'assist' in surgery. I held the dog for him as he administered the anesthesia intravenously. At the time that consisted of a barbiturate in a syringe taped to the patient's leg. Once asleep, the dog had a tube with an inflatable cuff put down its trachea to ensure an open airway and to administer inhaled gas anesthesia to maintain unconsciousness. The level of anesthesia was controlled by a simple knob. You merely turned it to the desired setting between 0 and 5%. At the time I was allowed to vacuum the hair clippings for the nurse as she shaved the abdomen in preparation for spaying the dog. Otherwise, I was trying not to get in the way.

I admit that I was a bit apprehensive as the nurse was scrubbing the area. I had pictures of bloody everything dancing through my head. I had no idea what came out when you spayed a dog, but I didn't think it would be pretty. Much to my amazement the incision (actually, I expected a cut, a BIG cut) was only a couple of inches long and it barely bled! I really expected it to bleed. I mean, I would bleed if you cut me like that! When I asked Dr. H if that was normal he said, "Yes." Then he explained why.

When your body develops in the uterus the spinal column develops first. As the tissues grow around to the front they meet in the middle and fuse. This results in a line of tough connective tissue called the *linea alba* (white line for you non-Latin speakers). He pointed it out as he spoke. It was very distinctive. There are few blood vessels or nerves here. That makes the surgery easier and less painful for the patient. Fortunately, we don't need to hide the scar like human surgeons, otherwise we would have to make a bikini incision which is much messier. I was entranced by the surgery. I wanted to know what everything was and where it was and why it was there and how to know you were taking out the right stuff. I knew that this is what I would be doing for the rest of my life.

Near the end of the surgery Dr. H asked me to turn down the dial on the anesthetic machine. As I stepped away from my position near the wall I suddenly grew light-headed and slowly slumped to the floor. Dr. H told me to drop my head between my knees. The nurse took over my duties as she handed me a glass of water. Dr. H just laughed and said, "You're going to make a great surgeon some day!" I replied, "Doc, I think I forgot to breathe! That surgery was awesome!"

Much later I was to learn that when you stand in one spot long enough the blood tends to pool in your extremities. When you try to move there is too little blood for your brain and out you go. My brain has enough trouble as it is even when it is hitting on all eight cylinders. Take away a couple and I fade fast.

At any rate, watching my first real surgery combined with Calculus 3 convinced me to officially switch my major to biology with a minor in chemistry. I knew that I would do whatever it took to get into vet school and survive it. My focus and resolve were now one hundred percent on a successful entrance into vet school.

This is probably a good time to point out to all undergraduate students a few of the little details about going to college. Your educational experience will change your life for the better if you stay focused on the tasks at hand, but surely for the worse if you lose control.

None of my high school friends went to college. They went to work right out of high school. They had more money than they had known in their whole lives although it wasn't so much when you look back on it now. They each had a hot car and one or more girlfriends. They wanted me to go out and party every weekend. I didn't have the time or the money. So I eventually ended up with new friends. Many of the old gang are still perched on the same bar stools they planted themselves on those many years ago. There is so much more to life....stay in school.

The colleges and universities currently encourage students to take general education courses during freshman year. The idea is that you can always declare or change your major in midstream. Although this sounds enticing don't fall for it. They want you to stay in school for five or six years to get a degree. That means more money in their pocket and MUCH less in yours. Worse yet, many colleges don't give you a course in your major until junior year. By the end of that year you are totally reluctant to change majors because you ideally have just one year remaining. What if you don't like it? You're stuck with that major or spending extra time in college!

If you take your tuition and fees and add that to what you would earn in a year of working it comes out to an incredible sum of money. Now, compound the interest on that for your lifetime and it is in the hundreds of thousands of dollars! Finish it up in four years or less; it will look much better on a resume if you finished on time. It shows initiative, organization and determination. What employer wouldn't like that?

*Dr. Hagenburg, whom I now call Roger, insisted that I include a particular anecdote about me that he has related to many people over the years. Roger was always great about giving me hours to work. He didn't care what I was doing so long as it was productive. I did a lot of cleaning. Roger always wanted the clinic to be spotless. He checked for dust all the time. I don't think he would even allow a dog named Spot on the carpet. I decided to get to the source of the ever accumulating dust.*

*It was quite slow one snowy winter day. Roger came back to check on what I was doing in the kennel (he should have known better). He saw me standing on a ladder with only my legs exposed below the ceiling tiles. The hose from the central vacuum was running up into the ceiling. I explained that I had found the source of our dust problem…I was vacuuming the tops of the ceiling tiles!*

*During the Presidential campaign in 2000 a woman came in to the office to pick up some prescription food for her dog. It was near closing time and election day is usually a bit slow. As it happened, I greeted her at the desk and struck up a conversation. She excused herself because she was anxious to get home and "See what happens with the erection. I mean election, election!"*

*I once worked the early shift at a shoe factory. I like to rise and shine.*

*A friend of mine had company coming from out of town for a Christmas visit. Their trip was complicated by a snowstorm. Instead of stopping at a motel they decided to push through the storm. After their arrival they were relating the details of their perilous trip. The Mrs. said that she counted 46 cars in the ditch. My friends teenaged daughter excitedly asked, "How big was the ditch!?"*

# CHAPTER 4

# *Into the VAT*

The application process for veterinary school has changed somewhat since I applied. The pool of applicants has shrunk on a per-position basis and the breadth of opportunity has widened in that you can now apply to any of the Colleges of Veterinary Medicine in addition to the one in your home state.

I once sent a letter to Michigan State University inquiring about their application process. This was well before I would have even applied for admittance to veterinary school. I have a lot of family in Michigan and it would have been possible for me to change residency by moving and working there for six months. I received a very polite but firm letter suggesting that I should stay home since I was fortunate enough to have a wonderful vet school in my home state. The non-resident applicants from states without a vet school were definitely given preference to non-residents who had access to one. I still think they didn't want an Illinoisan on campus. After all, being from the Chicago area I might be some relation to Al Capone. The campus wouldn't be safe or sober. As if it ever was.

With that slap on the wrist I set my sights firmly on Champaign-Urbana. The dean's office was very helpful. The more applicants, the better. For them. They are already in the profession in one way or another. Their goal is to select from the best candidates available. The more that apply, the more likely you are to encounter some winners. By that I mean those who are of good moral fiber and ability-- people who will succeed educationally and professionally and become a credit to the profession. I must admit that the system seems to work.

The easiest way to get information about applying to vet school is to contact someone who has done it....a vet! Veterinarians have access to referral centers. Some of the best are at the university teaching hospitals. Since I lived at the University of Illinois small animal clinic as a student intern, I know the U. of I. phone number by heart. Even if I practiced out of state (hint: I have a Michigan license) I would recommend contacting the U. of I. I'm sure that other vets may have a view different than mine and steer you to someone with whom they feel comfortable. Another wonderful resource is the American Veterinary Medical Association. They have a lot of information on the various careers available to vets, although none could be better than mine. There are also a lot of opportunities in the profession as an assistant. The AVMA has an informative brochure on becoming a veterinary technician... the right arm of a vet. The contact information for the AVMA is available through any veterinarian. A list of veterinary schools in the United States as well as outside of the country is available from the AVMA.

The odds were definitely in favor of it, and yes Dr. Hagenburg turned out to be a graduate from Illinois. He was very encouraging as he helped me deal with the details of mapping out a plan. He was very insistent that school come first. He had my coworkers cover my hours if I needed time off around final exams. Since finals were always followed by a break I made up for lost time (i.e. wages) by working 60 hours a week whenever possible. After only a week or so of extra hours everyone was glad to see the return of the kennel dude. (I was promoted from kennel boy once I had proved my worth.)

Towards the end of first semester junior year I decided to take the Veterinary Aptitude Test (VAT). This is a comprehensive test of your knowledge in several subjects (mathematics, chemistry, biology) as well as your ability to read, retain and apply new knowledge. The reading comprehension test allowed you to read an article and keep it in front of you during the test. In the study reading test, you were given an article to read for a period of time and it was taken away before the questions were given to you. As a final poke in the eye, one of the sections was repeated. Supposedly, this is similar to the tests taken to apply to medical school, but I am unfamiliar with those. I didn't take the MCAT (Medical Careers Aptitude Test) because I didn't want to jinx my karma by putting eggs in other baskets so early in my odyssey.

My reasoning for taking the VAT in my junior year was two-fold. First, I wanted to see what it was like so that in the probable event of my failure I would know what to study and how to be better prepared for it in round two; academically and emotionally. You can take the test as often as it is offered without penalty although there is a fee each time. The scores aren't reported to anyone else unless you request it. I didn't. Second, if I did get a decent score I could apply to vet school and start to get my name in front of the appropriate people. I felt they might take me more seriously if I applied early and often. I figured that the only moat around the building was the one I would dig myself. You can knock on the door and someone will open it every time. In fact, they are likely to invite you in!

Dr. H was very enthusiastic about the VAT. He graduated in 1970 so he had taken it not so long ago. (It still seems like last week to me!). He knew exactly where the test was to be administered. He had a map of the campus in Champaign, but it didn't have any of the surrounding town. He was adamant that I should stay at a motel in Champaign the night before the test so that I could get a good night of rest before the ordeal. He didn't want me to be up at

5:00 a.m. and then drive two hours and then look for somewhere to eat breakfast and then look for the right building and the right classroom. There was only one thing to do. We needed a dry run to the big U.

Two weeks later Dr. H and I were on the road to Champaign. I had never been south of Kankakee before. I was eager to see some of my home state. Suburbia quickly faded into corn fields. Then there appeared some soy bean fields. Then some corn. Then some soy beans. Corn. Beans. Ooh, a creek with trees and brush! Interstate 57, like most of our fast, efficient highways, has taken the charm out of travel by car. I understand that I-80 is actually worse, but the trip to Champaign is really boring. At least it was only two hours and I was enjoying good company.

Roger, as I can now call him, regaled me with stories from vet school. There were the awful schedules, the tons of work, the tests, the professors, clinical rotations....it sounded wonderful!

As we exited onto I-74, Dr. H was explicit in his directions. You can go a long way without realizing you're headed the wrong way. I joked that he probably knew from prior experience. He did. I counted the exits and watched the mile markers and surrounding buildings for landmarks. I am a very visual learner and I wanted to be sure of my route on the return trip.

Our first stop was the Ramada Inn. We weren't leaving anything to chance. We went inside and made a reservation for my room the night before the VAT. We were informed that we were lucky in that it wasn't a football weekend since no rooms are available for miles around when the game is on. As it turns out, there is very little business going on during football weekends since staff is hard to come by...they're at the game. The date wasn't accidental.

From the hotel we drove straight to Gregory Hall where the test was to be administered. I really felt that the building being named after my patron saint was a good omen. The lecture hall was immediately facing the entrance of the building. After the classrooms at Lewis U. it seemed more like an auditorium, but somehow it seemed comfortable. The acoustics were good. There would be ample room for the hundred or so sweating test takers. I did notice the absence of a pencil sharpener....what a nerd...Dr. H made sure I was aware of that. He suggested that I bring a red pencil with me so that I could draw little hearts on my answer sheet and write my name in two tones so that it would get noticed. Now who's the nerd? Besides, I didn't want to stand out. I just wanted to get in and blend in with a class of 82 students. I also noticed that the seats were very comfortable. I knew I wouldn't have any trouble staying awake for the VAT. Lectures might be another story, if I am accepted into the program.

After becoming familiar with the room I needed to locate two more necessities for a test that would last all day. The bathrooms were located right next to the testing room and the water fountain was right between them. No food would be necessary. I would bring a candy bar in case I felt tired, but I would definitely be too nervous for a lunch. I was ready. I had a room a five minute drive away. I was comfortable with the directions to and from home. What now? Did we drive two hours for only twenty minutes of excitement? Doc had plans.

We drove to the basic sciences building where I would spend most of my first two years doing laboratory work and sitting in lectures. Since it was Sunday there wasn't much going on. The labs were closed but not locked. Students have access to them at all hours. It felt strangely intrusive as Roger opened the door to the anatomy lab and turned on the lights. It seemed that we were sneaking into someone's bedroom at first, but then my senses were assailed by a wall of formaldehyde that was palpable on my cheeks. No, wait a moment. That was tears coming down from my unaccustomed eyes. Covered cadavers hung in inhuman shapes as he lifted the shrouds to reveal hooves and hides and muscles. It brought back a flood of memories to him, but the thought of how little I knew about anatomy filled me with apprehension. Roger assured me that I would come to appreciate the subtle odors of vet school.

Another short drive to the teaching hospital resulted in pay dirt. Since animals are in the hospital at all hours so are some students and staff. After being buzzed into the building and making some introductions a vet student offered us a tour. We eagerly accepted even though Roger knew his way around. He was somewhat disappointed that more of his old professors weren't there, but they do deserve some time off, too. The few that we did meet were enthusiastic about seeing him. They were quite interested in where he was practicing, how his family was doing, how business was going and if he had seen any interesting cases of late.

I was impressed with the facility and equipment, but the most lasting impression was how friendly everyone was. Roger kept introducing me to each of the staff and doctors: "This is Gregg Greiner, my kennel help. He'll be going to school here next year." I would quietly mention that I hadn't even taken the VAT yet and Roger would say, "Yeah, but you're going to do great on it." I can't begin to tell you what a confidence booster that was!

After our guide departed we were allowed to wander on our own. We spent a couple of hours checking out both sides of the building; the large animal clinic and the small animal clinic. I expressed some concern about working with the horses and food animals since I had no experience with them. Roger pointed out that he had never touched a horse in his life until vet school. He was sure I would do fine with them.

I don't really recall our ride home. I had so much information racing through my mind and so many questions coming out of my mouth that we seemed to make the trip in ten minutes. I couldn't (and can't) thank Dr. H enough for taking the time out of his schedule to help me. I knew I couldn't let him down...he cared too much for me to let that happen.

When the day came for me to head back to the Ramada Inn I packed up a bunch of text books intending to page through them the night before the VAT. I arrived in the late evening after eating a fast food hamburger. I recall it had no taste. I was nervous; really nervous. A bunch of awful scenarios raced through my head. Of course, I was going to oversleep. I would forget my pencils. I wouldn't know any answers. The person next to me would try to cheat and I would get kicked out. I would forget how to read! "Holy smokes, I have to stop this," I said to myself. I started to page through Organic Chemistry. I had no concentrating ability at all. I pictured the cleaning staff finding my dead body the next morning and remarking, "Oh, another one of those VAT students died of a heart attack. I guess his worries are over."

That was it. I went for a walk. As I cleared my head it dawned on me. I couldn't know everything. I knew what I had learned in school thus far and that would have to do. I decided that a good night's sleep would be of much more value than cramming. I was right. After a long, tiring walk I took a long, hot shower. I did a crossword puzzle to clear my head and fell asleep wondering about the answer to 84 down.

The courtesy call disrupted my dreamless sleep the next morning. It was followed by the alarm clock set for ten minutes later, but I was already up and moving. I decided to check out of the hotel and not return rather than having any remaining tasks to think about during the test. I stopped for coffee and a donut and went to Gregory Hall where my fate awaited.

I was relieved to find assigned seating. No guessing who to sit next to...you don't want a fidgeter or heavy breather or something worse sitting next to you, but this way you weren't responsible for the choice. Everyone else seemed equally nervous. That was a relief. Once we got underway I think you could have dropped a bomb next to me and I wouldn't have noticed. I was focused.

First came the rules and the Draconian steps that would be taken for cheating. Then came the instructions for the test and the order in which it would be given. The last section was a surprise as to which section would be repeated.

The math and chemistry sections were a breeze. I did start as a math major and I loved chemistry....lots of math in that subject as it turns out. The reading comprehension was fair enough. They asked questions that I comprehended (!) based on the articles they gave us. I did need to go back and review a couple of things, but time permitted it despite the limits.

Next came biology, my declared major. What could go wrong here? Everything. Most of the questions were on things I either hadn't studied or didn't care to study. There were lots of questions on invertebrates. Vets don't work on mollusks, do they? I became so worried about the things I didn't know that I was having trouble remembering some things I was sure I knew. I took a deep breath and double checked that I was at least marking the right column of dots on the tally sheet. I didn't want a complete disaster.

The study reading test was in three sections. The test monitors distributed a lengthy and detailed article that had to be read in only fifteen minutes. It was taken away and the test questions were then handed out. I recall that the first two articles were very interesting to me although I don't recall the subjects. The questions seemed mostly answerable although I guessed at a few. The third article was sent from heaven. It was on red blood cell morphology. It was long. It was filled with technical terms. I had just finished studying the subject the week before! I breezed through it and looked up to see the looks of consternation on a lot of faces. I must confess that I enjoyed a feeling of empowerment. I was putting a puck into an empty net. Game, Set, Match; at least on this section of the test.

Next up was the announcement of the subject for the final section. And the winner is.........MATH!!! What a relief. I couldn't take another round of that biology. The second section on math was even easier than the first one. It seemed like the consolation round. I knew the biology brought me down, but that last math section had brought me back up. Where would I end up in the final rankings?

The waiting seemed interminable, but I was still in school and working so the day that I received the VAT scores caught me by surprise. The envelope was perched on the counter awaiting my return from work. I looked at it. It beckoned me. I looked at it. It mocked me. I started to open it, but I couldn't. I decided that Dr. Hagenburg should be with me when I did. He shared my trials as he relived his own. I felt my heart pounding as I put it in my backpack. I would have to wait one more day.

I showed the unopened envelope to my classmates and professors at school the next day. They couldn't believe it was intact. They were dying to know. They offered to look and not tell me. No, my mind was made up. It would wait until after I had cleaned the kennels. If it was awful, then I could go straight home to face my demons.

By 4:15 I had all of my work done. No one seemed to notice my somber mood as I kept myself sequestered back in the kennel. When Dr. H had a lull in the action I handed him the envelope. "How did you do?" he queried unaware that it hadn't been opened. "You'll have to look for me, Doc. I couldn't open it myself."

He made no hesitation as he quickly tore into the cellulose messenger. He paused for an eternity without saying a word. "What does it say?" I finally asked.
"It says you're going to vet school." he replied.
"It can't say that, I haven't applied yet."
"Well, you shouldn't have much trouble with a 98 percentile!"

I couldn't believe my ears followed by my eyes. I had scored in the 99th percentile in every subject except that darn biology. At least it hadn't dragged me to the bottom of the charts.

For my younger readers I would like to spell things out a bit for you. When you go into a big test, whether it is the ACT, SAT, VAT, MCAT, GRE or whatever, be prepared. For example, I don't know anyone else who actually visited the test room ahead of time. That was a big edge for me. I was comfortable. Your best weapon is your wits. Keep them about you. Get a good night of rest because thinking will be more valuable than recall. Don't get flustered when you hit a bad stretch. If you feel like you're losing your composure take a brief mental break to regain it. Then jump back into the game. It is a game after all, but you are playing for some serious marbles.

You will need to guess at times. Chance will play a role, but remember that chance favors a prepared mind. If you can rule out one or two wrong answers on the questions you don't know for certain then chance will smile upon you more often than not.

Set a goal and do what it takes to accomplish it. I was fortunate to do well on my first stab at the VAT. I planned on at least two more years of trying if I failed the first time. I also planned to learn from that failure if and when it occurred in order not to repeat my mistakes. In the immortal words of my grandfather, 'Plan your work. Work your plan.'

Play sports. Any sport. You will learn strategies on how to compete and win. You will learn how to interact with competitors. Your mind will work better and faster with physical exercise. You will learn that hard work and perseverance pay off in the end. You won't get that from computer games.

The class size at most of the universities has increased over the years. The University of Illinois is currently accepting 120 students for the 2011 entering class. The pool of applicants is expected to number about 900. About a one in 7.5 chance of getting in. That is about twice as good as the odds I faced back in 1978; my class was near the peak in applications per position. Those numbers are subject to change so be sure to check them out ahead of time.

I do have a bit of bad news. The VAT is no longer administered. The current test scores come from the GRE; the Graduate Record Examination. That means a larger population of students taking the test and less of a focus on subjects and abilities specific to potential veterinary students. However, remember that all of your potential rivals have the same obstacles to overcome. Keep your eye on the prize and work hard; you'll get there.

*As I pulled apart a bran muffin it crumbled into a thousand dry little pieces. It was one of those new diet muffins made with sawdust for added fiber. They're known as stud muffins.*

*If you suffer from low self esteem perhaps you should see an I doctor.*

*Is a priest considered an altar ego?*

*Was reconstructive surgery developed after the Civil War?*

*I saw a dog that was so fat that his tail was a wagon.*

*After a trip to Florida I came down with a respiratory infection. I told my doctor that I had probably caught it on the airplane. After running some tests, it turned out to be a terminal illness.*

*There are plenty of openings in proctology.*

*If you suffer from erectile dysfunction, should you really see a shrink?*

# CHAPTER 5

## *Apply Liberally*

The application requirements for veterinary school have changed very little over the years, but the process has been updated to keep pace with our rapidly changing technology. It seems that anything electronic is looked at more favorably. I'm certain that this makes handling information much easier for the selection committee. It can be transmitted with the touch of a few keys and a mouse click or two. No more stacks of paper to handle and mail and sort through. However, I can't help but feel that this makes the process more sterile, less personal and more hazardous for the applicant.

The academic requirements are spelled out clearly in the information available from any of the veterinary schools. I will not go into detail about them for fear that you might use this as a guide. Standards and requirements may change in the future (which is now from when I applied) and I wouldn't want to mislead your efforts. If you attend a small school for your undergraduate studies *you must be certain* that the credits will transfer and be applicable to the prerequisites laid out in the application packet.

Attending Lewis University gave me some concern over my

laboratory experience. The lecture portion of the sciences followed the standard textbooks. I counted on that being universally taught at nearly every school; it was. The laboratory facilities might have fallen short of the bigger schools, but the personal attention I would receive more than made up for any lack of equipment. I had no trouble keeping up with my classmates in veterinary school.

Of course, the GRE is going to count as a large portion of your academic achievements, but the committee realizes that some people don't take tests well and they will look at other aspects of your application to form an opinion of you. One of the biggies is the dreaded GPA. Yes, those non-science classes have come back into play.

One of the most important aspects of picking a humanities class (besides how much work will be involved) is the professor. I talked to classmates about each of my prospective teachers. Sometimes you don't have a choice of professor, especially in your major. In elective classes a poor lecturer can spell disaster so I was more alert to the teaching style of the professor than the actual course content.

The shining example of this was Latin American History. My professor was a Cuban exile who fled his country just before Fidel Castro came to power. He had a very unique perspective on all of Latin America and he embellished an otherwise boring text with personal stories that made the people much more real. Their struggles were his struggles. As a result you felt their pain. Suddenly, their names were much easier to remember. There was a solid context in which you could place them. I could appreciate my life and my country much more profoundly. We are truly blessed....be sure to spread that around as you go through life. Now that is the kind of class worth taking! It is very easy to do well in such a learning environment. Pick your profs well.

The next requirement is work experience. This was the single most important factor in my success. It made me aware of the many challenges that would confront me in practice after I graduated. It gave me skills that would make vet school much easier for me. It taught interpersonal skills as I learned how to be compassionate and how to communicate with people that are distressed by a sick or injured pet. Most importantly, it built a strong bond between me, Dr. H and *our* patients.

Dr. H never was much of a *boss*. He led by example. His caring attitude spread throughout the clinic. His patients became my wards when they stayed in the hospital. I was always alert to any changes in their condition. His training guided me through my mission. I took ownership of the practice in a very personal way. He repaid my efforts in many ways, but by far the most embarrassing was the letter of recommendation he wrote for my application to vet school.

You will need three of these to apply. They can't be from a biased source such as a family member. They should ideally be from veterinarians that have known you for a respectable period of time or from your professors. The more detailed the letter the better. It should include what you have experienced and accomplished during your time at the clinic. Most importantly, it should describe your personal qualifications as they pertain to becoming a good vet. That is where Dr. H exceeded all of my expectations.

He piled it on so thick that I was blushing as I read the letter. I couldn't read it in front of him....I felt as if I was standing there naked. He detailed my personality so well that I thought he had a peep hole to the kennel area or a hidden camera placed inside the hospital cat. I couldn't believe he knew me so well just from working with me. He finished with such glowing recommendations that they might have made me king if the position was available. I feared that the heat pouring from my face would scorch the paper it was written on! Needless to say, my work experience was priceless, whether I continued on in school or not. I must also add that his partner, Dr. Adkins, wrote the second letter of recommendation for me. His was much more clinical and focused on my actual work and work ethic. It complemented Dr. H's letter nicely.

The necessary documents in hand, I compiled a nice packet of information about myself. I thought of it as my dossier. However, I didn't wish to present myself as a man of mystery. I was a man on a mission. To fully launch the mission I decided to write a cover letter that would list the contents of the packet. More importantly, it also laid out some of the reasons why I was intent on a career in veterinary medicine.

I briefly mentioned my long time love for animals. I assumed that everyone applying would have that same interest so I didn't dwell on it. More significantly, I mentioned how my interest was piqued at watching my first surgery and that I felt compelled to pursue this career as the ultimate goal of my life. After reading Dr. H's letter I had little left to be embarrassed about so I placed my passions out there for all to see.

I finished with a sincere request that if the committee needed any additional information to *please* (I wanted to drip honey on the word) contact me and I would provide it as quickly as possible. That may sound like puckering up to the ole back side, but, well, it is. What the heck, it's your career on the line.

Off went the packet in the mail. I enclosed a self addressed, stamped postcard with a request that it be returned to me so that I would know that it had been received. I can't take credit for that gem. Mom saw how much effort I had put into the application and she suggested it as some assurance that it fell into the right hands. What a relief when it was returned in just a few days with a brief note on it…received in good condition.

Most of the information that a current applicant will send is electronic. That holds an advantage in speed and in convenience. You can send the information to several vet schools with ease (apply liberally). However, it definitely lacks a personal touch. It also increases your risk of making a mistake. I had my entire packet in front of me when I sent it off. I had everything in the order that I wanted it seen. I inspected it a hundred times. The VAT score was sent separately by the testing company, but I included a copy of the letter I received with my score on it just in case it wasn't received or some error had been made. You could hold the entire bundle and see the work that went into assembling it. As they say in the old WWII movies, my papers were in order. You don't see that on a computer screen.

They were also neat; even my writing (my staff will not believe this). Yes, I hand wrote my cover letter. I also insisted that my letters of recommendation were hand written. I wanted to give the impression that I cared. I also wanted it to be clear that the doctors had written the letters themselves and had not merely signed off on the work of someone else. As embarrassing as it was to read them, I had earned those letters. I wanted them to have full effect. You don't get that from an email.

The next step involved waiting. When you're young, life still holds a lot of questions about the future and time moves slowly. Despite remaining busy virtually all of the time the wait seemed interminable. In a matter of only a few weeks I received a letter from the admissions office. The wait was shorter than I had anticipated…I knew it had to be good news! I was invited for an interview. No real details other than where, when and why. They wanted to meet me personally to determine my qualifications for becoming a vet.

What the heck does that mean? I ran to Dr. H with a host of questions and concerns. Roger was apparently recalling his admissions interview as he smiled and said, "You'll live through it. Just remember that every one of them sat in that same chair at one time or another. Just try not to picture them in their underwear. That never works!"

As he coached me along I began to realize that the main focus of the interview wasn't what I knew. They already know what you know from the packet in front of them. They want to know what you're made of. They may want to verify a few things that were submitted with your packet to be sure that your integrity has remained intact while compiling the application, but otherwise they want to learn about you.

Again, I was prepared. I went in with a clear conscience. I hadn't exaggerated anything I had submitted. In fact, I had learned a few new things that I could add to the resume if the opportunity arose. Dr. H coached me along in a number of things. I would like to do the same for anyone seeking my help in similar circumstances.

The interview was designed to be intimidating. A chair was placed in the middle of the room in front of a long table with seven or eight people seated behind it. I don't recall the exact number because I was so nervous. I expected the lights to go out followed by a single bright bulb shining in my eyes. Interrogators would start yelling questions and if they didn't like my answers I would fall through a trap door or get ejected through the ceiling. The floor felt solid as I walked to an apparently normal chair.

Some of the interviewers observed my demeanor as I entered the room and took my seat. Others were doing some last minute homework as they looked over my file. I wonder to this day if some of them were doing crossword puzzles. That would have been ironic as I would later work puzzles during some of their lectures. I cleared my throat as I sat down. That seemed to garner some attention. I introduced myself and stated the purpose of my visit, "I would like to be a member of the veterinary class of 1982." It seemed nice to fire the first shot. Introductions followed. Thank God their names were clearly displayed with large paper placards folded in front of each doctor. I couldn't have remembered a single one.

It quickly became apparent that this would be a case of good cops, bad cops. The good cops started first by verifying some of the information on my application such as where I went to school and the size of my family. (They seemed impressed…thanks go to Mom and Dad.) Then one of the bad cops interrupted at the very end of my answer and asked me in a very aggressive manner, "What makes you think you'd be a good vet?"

Dr. H had warned me that this might happen. Rather than becoming startled I calmly finished my sentence without looking over at 'the intruder' (I had another term in mind at the time). I then turned to him and said, "I'm sorry, could you please restate your question?"

That seemed to catch him off guard. He not only restated it, but he did so in an entirely different tone of voice. I had survived the worst of it. Only one minute into the interview and I knew I had the advantage. Not over my interrogators, but over anyone else who would sit in the middle of that room; the competition. The entire panel seemed to relax and my interview became a discussion. I think that meant more to the panelists than anything I actually said. After all, I was an intellectual child in a room of adults. They just wanted to see if I was ready to wear long pants.

I must advise you to be yourself during the interview. You got yourself this far; so keep it up. You are what they are most interested in. Who are you? We already know you're smart. How well do you interact with people? Animals don't bring themselves to a vet. You will need tremendous communication skills to be a good vet. How well do you respond to pressure? If you think this is tough just wait until a wailing client brings a critically ill patient to you or you have a bleeding abdomen on the surgery table.

That is what they are truly after. They have a very short time to pick you out of the crowd. They take that responsibility seriously. Play their game to win.

*Late one night I rushed to the clinic to help a toy poodle that was suffering from multiple seizures. They sounded mild, but were occurring every few minutes. I turned around to retrieve the medical records when I heard her champing her lips as if in a seizure. A quick examination on the counter revealed the cause of the seizures. They were cured instantly by removing the piece of plastic stuck between the inside portion of the upper premolars.*

*Emergencies are often in the eye of the beholder. I received a call from a client who very calmly described his dog that had just been hit by a car. The dog was confined to his crate and was resting comfortably, but from the description of the injuries I was certain that it had a broken rear leg. I suggested that I needed to see the dog right away, but the owner had other ideas. "It's pretty late and he doesn't seem to be in distress. How about if I just keep and eye on him and come over in the morning?" He did. The left tibia was fractured. The dog was happy as a clam. We applied a cast to the leg. He went home a few hours later. He wore the cast as if he had been born with it and healed uneventfully over the next six weeks.*

*I examined a dog that had a mild rash on its stomach. Rather than taking oral medicine to give her pet the owner requested a tropical (instead of topical) ointment. I suggested cocomutt oil.*

CHAPTER 6

## *Great Expectations*

After the interview it didn't seem to take much time to receive a letter of acceptance from the University of Illinois. There was one little string attached, however. I still needed one more class to have all of my prerequisites; Biochemistry 350. Any of you readers who have taken Biochem350 can probably hear the theme music from *Jaws* just about now. I had the same reaction at reading the course syllabus that I had when the head fell out of the hole in the submerged boat in the movie.

Unfortunately, Lewis U. didn't offer advanced chemistry during the summer. I would have to go to the big U. for this class. In a sense that wasn't such a bad thing. It gave me a chance to get oriented prior to the plunge into vet school. Also, most of the students would be away for the summer so the crowds wouldn't be too bad. I would only have a single class to worry about and it would only last for six weeks....six long weeks.

After enjoying the small class sizes at Lewis, it came as a shock to see how many students were attending biochemistry at the University of Illinois. It occurred to me that the 350 was a reference to the number of attendees rather than the course level.

The lecture hall was a large auditorium with the seats arranged in bowl fashion. There were four large projector screens behind the professor. In front of him was a large desk with a black slate top. His meager stack of notes gave the impression that he would fall far short of the scheduled three hours of lecture. After a brief introduction he raised the first projector screen and revealed line after line of chemical equations. Gulp. The blank expressions of the other screens ominously guarded the complicated formulas hidden beneath them.

The poor T.A.s (teaching assistants) had to come in early or stay late in order to write all of the prof's equations ahead of time. A ladder must have been employed because none of them appeared to be on a basketball scholarship. They also had to handle virtually all of our questions. That was usually by appointment in the evening hours. There was no discussion in class. The professor gave a monologue. It was fast and there was no access to the equations ahead of time. You wrote as quickly as possible in the vain attempt to keep up with the lecture. When, not if, you fell behind you hoped it was at a non-critical point so that you didn't get lost for good. Reading ahead was a must. I wished I had already started. I thanked God this was my only class at that time. I had other demons to face as well.

Since this was my first experience away from home I was taken aback by the sheer size of the school. Biochemistry class was within easy walking distance of the graduate dorm, but the College of Vet Med was a bike ride. I didn't want the expense or responsibility of a car. That turned out to be a good thing as parking was always a problem around campus.

Sherman Hall is located about two blocks off of the quadrangle. I had never lived in anything but a house on half an acre of land. My one room apartment that shared a bathroom with the adjacent room would have been very claustrophobic if not for the large black locust tree that dominated the view from my third floor cell. The large open crown was comprised of many oddly shaped branches. It provided a home for at least one family of squirrels. They quickly learned that there would always be a small pile of treats on the ledge outside my window. Sometimes it would be the remnants of a bag of chips. Usually it was corn 'donated' by a local farm. Two or three ears fit nicely into a compartment of my backpack. After a trip back home I would treat them to some sunflower seeds pilfered from Dad's supply of bird feed. They returned my gesture by providing entertainment and reminding me of home. Dad was constantly trying new techniques to keep those darn squirrels out of the bird feeder. I often pondered how the squirrel war was being waged back on the home front. I might have been charged with fraternizing with the enemy if Pops had found me out.

It is amazing how much stuff you can cram into a dorm room. I had the usual supply of clothes, books, stereo, small refrigerator and a hot pot. Since I was on a budget I decided that I would buy my own snacks at the grocery store rather than buying them from the vending machines. It was also much healthier to buy fresh fruit and snacks rather than go to 'the casino' as it became known.

There are winners and losers at any casino. There are always more losers than winners; they remain in business to make money. So it was with the vending machines. The slots were pretty fair. Those were the soda machines. You usually came away with a cold drink. The poker machines were the snack machines. They came in two varieties; the coiled rod with bags of chips and candy bars that advanced as the rod was rotated and the cold snacks that lay hidden behind the clear plastic doors. You never knew whether you'd get anything at all or whether you might get doubles. Occasionally a tip was left behind in the change slot. Those were the days when a quarter still had value.

The basement of the dorm also housed a laundry room. Mom had coached me on doing laundry. She didn't want my visits home to be punctuated by ten loads of it and I didn't want to carry it back and forth to Chicago. It was really pretty simple. Separate the whites. Add a little bleach to keep them white. Use the same amount and type of detergent for whites or colors. Same water temperature for anything I would need to wash; warm. Sweaters get washed by hand. They stayed home. I owned no delicates.

I would like to share with you some secrets about doing laundry that I managed to discover in the chemistry lab that was the laundry room of Sherman Hall. First and foremost, do not EVER mistakenly place something red in with the whites. You will have pink underwear. Second, don't EVER add extra bleach in an effort to whiten your clothes (or in an attempt to get the pink color out). It will eat them. As you may have surmised, I learned those lessons back to back.

I never suspected that you could actually pull the entire top off of a sock while putting it on your foot. Sadly, it was over a month before I managed a trip home to go clothes shopping. I brought some of the offending evidence to show to Mom. She was rather well informed on the subject of bleach damage. A tip from her: don't let it splash on you or your clothes; watch your eyes (she mentioned that as a routine safety precaution for everything, even clipping your toenails); rinse spills with cold water.

One bit of good did come from my early experiences with laundering clothes. I met my first classmate, Charlene, as I was lugging a basket of clothes back to my room. She was bubbly and energetic. She had a giggly laugh and she used it freely. We shared the common fates of living at the dorm and facing four more years of college. We became friends very quickly. It was nice to know that she was nervous about starting classes, too. It was also nice to meet some of the graduate students at the dorm. Charlene had already formed a small circle of friends due to her outgoing personality and her prior experience of leaving home for undergrad studies. She seemed to have made some good acquaintances. I felt comfortable with them and they helped to ease my transition into postgraduate studies. Sadly, I don't remember their real names because we all had nicknames for each other.

I was DD....short for dog dissector. At first I felt stereotyped.

Yes, I did have to dissect a dog and I did complain about it quite a bit. Anatomy was a tough class. But I also moved on to dissect a cat, horse, cow, pig, chicken and even a fish. DD seemed so limiting. I was much more than that. It stuck like glue. The shoe not only fit, it became quite comfortable over the next three years.

Mr. Wit was one of my favorite companions at meals. As his name implied, he had something to say about everything. Usually it made sense, but he had his moments …thus the name. He had a passion for running. I recall that his feet made almost no sound when he ran. He had a very smooth motion with little wasted energy. His event was the marathon. If you're going to run that far you will need lots of energy in the form of carbohydrates. The best carb on campus is, of curse, oops, of course, beer. That always brought out the best from Mr. Wit.

Chief had black hair and a thick black beard. He was a long-time resident of the dorm as he was already doing post doctoral work when I met him. He got his nickname because he was studying Indian culture. As it turns out he was actually studying the Hindi language, but the name seemed to fit. I do recall his name was Bill, but he seldom answered to it. He had a passion for playing bridge. There would be silence at the card table until the hand was won or lost. Then a commotion would ensue as the bids were reviewed and the play analyzed.

Vinnie was always there for the card games and Murphy's pub. He was sweet on Charlene. He had a quiet calm about him. He appeared to lift weights. Seriously. Some people seemed to be concerned that he carried a baseball bat with him at all times. He was actually quite nice.

Rosebush was an engineering nerd that always seemed lost in thought. He had a prickly beard and a large red nose…thus the name. After every meal he would get a cup of hot water for tea. He would carefully dip the tea bag into the water ten times, squeeze out the extra water with his fingers, sop up any water he spilled around the cup on the saucer and squeeze that into the cup.

He was so regimented about it that we made plans around it. "Are you in a hurry to go somewhere or are you sticking around for the count down to splashdown?" "No, if I see the Rosebush get water I'll be late for class."

The list went on. Some of the faces I saw nearly every day never had a name. Each person had his or her own mission. Some people hung out at the dorm and some were seldom there. I found the dorm to be a nice break from my classmates. I also found my room to be a fortress against the forces that sought to derail my education. There are many distractions to be found on campus, especially large ones like the state land grant colleges. It was much easier to make good decisions without a room mate to deal with.

After sharing a bedroom with three brothers for all of my teen years, it was easy to keep my dorm room clean. So I did. I dusted every other week while my clothes were in the laundry. I never left dirty dishes lying about. I had heard stories of cockroach infestations and I didn't care to bring them home with me. The janitorial service cleaned the bathrooms every week. My room was immaculate.

When Charlene and Chief came to my room for the first time they asked if they had to 'scrub-in' in order to enter. "Why do you keep it so clean in here?"

"Because I grew up with brothers that kept our room a mess." I replied.

"Would you like to see the best thing about having my own room?" I asked. I took a pen from the desk drawer. I set it on the middle of the desk, gave my best *voila* motion and leaned back in my chair with my arms folded. After an appropriate pause I said, "I could come back in a week and that pen would still be there. I've never had that in my life!" It was true. My brothers touched everything I owned.

Being the eldest son does have some advantages, but a decided disadvantage is that your brothers like your stuff. And they get into it. It doesn't even have to be something cool or neato. They just do it because it is yours and you're older. They want to do and have the things that you do and have. Looking back it seems to have been somewhat of a compliment, but it sure wasn't perceived as such at the time. It seemed odd that I didn't have to guard my gear, but I got over it very quickly (before vet school even started!).

As I neared the end of Biochem350 I had settled in pretty well. I knew that I was going to get a B in the class unless I completely bombed the final. Besides, all I really had to do was pass it since I was already enrolled in vet school. I had made friends with some hard-working, fun-loving students. I knew my way around campus. I was ready to get on with the main course.

*Textbook for plastic surgeons:  All Features Great and Small.*

*I once delivered puppies on Christmas day.  I was Santa's whelper.*

*A client came in wearing a  t-shirt that read:  Satan's Helper*

*I was thinking of hiring a ghost writer to finish this book since it lacks substance.*

*There is a new diet program available in some areas.  They throw you in a big fish tank filled with sharks.  It's called Swim Fast.*

*Why did the cat sleep under the car?  It wanted to be an oily riser.*

*My niece had her ears pierced last week.  My sister took her to a hole-sale store.*

# CHAPTER 7

*Reality Bytes*

Orientation for the start of veterinary school remains a blur to me. There were class schedules to organize, books to buy, lab supplies to obtain, rooms to find, people to meet and an incredible angst that made even simple tasks onerous. This was it. This is what I had waited for. Could I handle it?

I had never seen a schedule so crammed full of core classes. Everything was meat and potatoes. No salad in sight. Certainly, there was no dessert on the menu. This was my career in the making. The one consolation was that we would all be in the same leaky boat. We hoped that we would all be survivors. That was not to be the case.

The first day saw two people abandon ship. They both decided that medical school didn't look so bad after all….off they went. Two replacements were pulled from the waiting list. Those must have been exciting calls; "You're in. Get here!" We eventually felt that the two departures had made a mistake although it did seem tempting to join them at times.

Anatomy would be the main focus of study for the first year.

Everything would be based on an understanding of how things are put together and, more important, why things are put together the way they are. Unfortunately, students of human medicine study only human anatomy. As mentioned earlier, we dissected several species in detail. Once you learn the differences in anatomy between species and understand why they are different, then you have that knowledge cemented in your brain. It becomes a firm foundation for future learning both in college and after graduation. Yes, you will still need to continue learning long after you leave college; more on that later.

Histology is the study of tissues and I don't mean Puffs and Kleenex. Rather, bones and muscles and nerves and organs. It was amazing to see how individual cells as seen under the microscope are a part of the whole. How each was designed to have its place and contribute to the smooth functioning of that particular tissue.

It was also amazing to see how dynamic our bodies are. Every slide contained blood vessels which had carried nutrients and oxygen and body defenses to every corner of every slide. They could be seen filled with red and white blood cells and platelets. We would later learn about pathologic changes that occur with various diseases, but for now we needed to learn what was normal so that we could later recognize abnormal.

The tissues we saw during dissections in anatomy came to life under the microscope in histology lecture and lab. Anatomy taught you where things are, what they do and what they are called. Histology taught you what they are made of and hinted at how they do things. This was just a warm up for future classes.

Microbiology, the study of microscopic organisms, didn't pique my interest at first. All of the germs seemed similar, but that impression would change quickly. In fact, bacteria and viruses are resilient forms of life that can withstand a wide range of environmental conditions. Dividing germs into just those two categories is inadequate. What about the fungi, the rickettsials and, as we now know, the prions? Is there no end to what can kill us?

I was humbled by how little I knew. A moment of realization came to me when I was visiting the veterinary library for the first time. As I looked around the room at the thousands of books, each of them probably the culmination of a lifetime of work, I came to know how little I will ever know compared to what can be learned. I had great doubts about how I could ever remember all of this information let alone organize it into a diagnosis.

That is what vet school is all about…cramming information into your head and then organizing it into useful categories. No one can know everything. The secret to becoming a good clinician is to know where to look for a diagnosis and to keep looking if you don't come up with an answer. As time goes by you will develop a sense of when something is amiss with a case. That is called acumen. It is the little voice in the back of your mind that tells you to keep digging. It has always been there. You must be taught to listen to it. That takes considerably longer than they keep you in school. For now, you just keep learning. Fortunately, you don't have much time to worry about the future. You're worried about the endless written exams and practical exams and pop quizzes. You can't remember what you ate an hour ago, but you remember which sugars Salmonella ferments.

Among the stress and chaos of vet school there must stand an island of sanity. For me it was my friends. They were divided into two distinct groups that rarely met. The first group you met in the previous chapter. The second consisted of my classmates. We became friends in the same sense that you become friends with fellow servicemen. We went through the same basic training and fought common enemies side by side. The hills to be taken had names that ended in 'ology'…..microbiology, physiology, anesthesiology. You took one hill and another appeared on the horizon. You were never certain of where or when a trap may be sprung. Foes were on every side.

Fatigue wasn't seen in its plural form, it was felt. It was beaten back with coffee and carbohydrates. Sleep wasn't for Sundays, it was for someday…usually during a school break. Tension and pressure, though opposite in nature, were palpable in the air. There was only one solution. Share the stress. That's what friends are truly for. Anyone can share good times. Tough times become fond memories only through the camaraderie of loyal friends.

Our class had a wide range of backgrounds and personalities. We had a couple of two-year wonders that were accepted into vet school after only two years of undergraduate studies. We had a couple of PhDs that were starting their ninth years of college. We had everything in between. Some had little experience working with animals and others had grown up with a parent that was a vet. We were a cross section of America. It seemed that each of us belonged to the proverbial *other half* in comparison to someone else in the class.

Many of us felt that there were better ways to handle stress besides the usual complaining and commiseration that constantly afflicts students. Jokes were a continual threat. There were the funny, ha, ha, ha, jokes and then there were the practical jokes. I was definitely noted for the former although many felt they weren't necessarily so funny. My jokes tend to be the pun, pain, groan type funny. Practical jokes take some malice aforethought, planning and time. Time was a precious commodity. Puns just pop up onto the radar screen, do their damage and leave without a trace. Practical jokes tend to linger and cry out for retribution. It usually comes, in spades.

We had the usual sophomoric (sophomoronic as we referred to them) pranks such as switching specimens, moving anatomical markers, and placing a cup of water on the door knob. However, some were very inventive. For example, one of the anatomy ponies was given a home made horn turning it into a unicorn. There was also the time that we switched projector slides for one of Dr. Safani's lectures. It showed an African male with a hugely swollen, larger-than-basketball-sized scrotum. Dr. Safani never even flinched. When he turned and saw the picture he immediately went into his lecture on Elephantiasis. He concluded the talk by pointing to the offending structure and remarking, "When someone gets to this stage, all you can do is hand him a wheelbarrow." He then included some questions on the subject for our next quiz.

As the year progressed it became very apparent that cliques were forming. It seemed that most of them were based on similar styles of studying although some had personalities or interests that complemented each other. A few were romantic. Things never did seem to clique with me. I got along well with the entire class, although I did have some favorites. I won't mention Andy names, but I'll be DANged if I didn't have some buddies that got me discomBOBulated at times.

One of our favorite stress relievers was playing cards. If there was a spare half hour the deck came out. Pinochle was preferred, but not many people knew how to play the game. Therefore, Hearts was the usual game and, on occasion, Spades. We had a few Euchre players around as well. It is an oddity of cards that the better you know your opponents the more difficult is to play against them. You learn their tendencies and style of play. Once they know that you know what they are thinking they change strategies. Once you realize that they know that you know what they are up to, and you change your tactics, then it is up to them to change theirs. The circle of deception goes on forever. It really drives you nuts when they do something totally predictable, but you predicted that they wouldn't and played the hand differently.

For example, Andy always tried to 'shoot the moon' in Hearts. You knew that he knew that you were going to pass him cards that made it impossible for him to do so. Therefore, you would pass him cards that DID make it possible. And then he would manage to do it! Argh! The one time all day that you sent him those cards and he used them against you! What a great game. I can still see him grinning these many years later.

Another great pastime for me was intramural sports. The university had a full range of sports which were open to all students. They ranged from baseball to football and everything in between. My personal favorite was ice hockey. I had skated since I was 4 years old. Since I was always small for my size I found the ice to be a great equalizer. A lot of big guys have trouble changing their momentum on a slippery surface. That suited me nicely. The problem was that I was the *only* one on my team who could skate. We had a great goalie and me. That was it. To our credit, although we lost every game it was never more than a two goal deficit. Oops, there was that one game against the tri-delts (delta-delta-delta fraternity) which we lost by three. Their fans filled half of the arena while ours sat at the end of our bench. Each time they scored a goal they had two trumpeters play a riff from the Canadian National Anthem. That was insult to injury. I may have been fortunate that day. Since I had nobody to back me up I was disinclined to initiate retaliation on the ice. I would have to wait for another opportunity to seek retribution.

Unfortunately, time didn't permit me to become involved with some of the other sports. VetMed did field teams in other sports. Each class had its own team in most events. Games played against other classes meant much more that just playing against a frat team. There were bragging rights that would appear in the vet school newsletter. (How anyone had time to put that together is beyond me. I did make time to read it, however.) Mike created quite a stir by winning the hundred yard dash in a university-wide competition. One of his nicknames became step n fetch as a result.

I did manage to maintain a small income despite my busy schedule. I was given the job of class projectionist. I was in charge of setting up the audiovisual equipment for each lecture. It didn't take up a lot of time and it gave me pocket money so that I never had to phone home for money. That was also my connection to the Safani prank. I can still hear the cries of "GREINER" whenever a slide became jammed. A distinct disadvantage of holding the position of projectionist is that you must attend all of the lectures. That removes the temptation to skip out on classes, especially the early ones.

Monday through Friday afternoon was all school. Time after

class was spent eating, studying and then visiting the dorm residents in the common area before retiring at 11:00 p.m. Although the visits downstairs were brief, the trips helped clear my head before falling asleep.

Tuesday was always special because my parents gave me a gift subscription to the Chicago Sun-Times as a farewell present. They came in the mail starting on Tuesdays. I didn't pay much attention to any actual news at the time because what could be more important than me and my troubles? You Gen Xers can understand that, I'm sure. However, I hoarded those New York Times crossword puzzles as if they were gold. I did them during down times in a lecture to help keep my attention focused. It became a running joke that I would get visibly nervous if I finished my puzzle and didn't have a backup. Since they surrounded the puzzle, the comics were a staple at the time, too.

Friday was my favorite day. Rather than eating at the dormitory cafeteria I would treat myself to free appetizers at one of the local establishments. This meant that I had about one to two hours of free time before the happy hour started. I took advantage of that time to do something physically active. That is the time slot when intramural sports were played in due season. Otherwise, I would play racquetball or shoot hoops at IMPE (Intra Mural Physical Education building) or just go for a bike ride. I needed to burn some calories in order to get rid of some frustration and prepare for MY night out.

After dinner I would go back to my dormitory room and study until nine or ten o'clock. That is when the group would gather in the lobby at Sherman Hall. Everyone seemed to know when everyone else was going to get there. If you were going to be late you made sure that someone knew. If there was some change in plans there would be a note left in your mailbox or a call placed to your room. There was never a need. We always went to Murphy's pub on Green Street.

Murphy's was within easy walking distance from Sherman Hall. It was within reasonable crawling distance for the return trip. It was and still is a bar where the graduate students like to go for a relaxing night out. The main attraction was the fact that Busch beer was two dollars a pitcher. Murphy's wasn't a pick-up bar. It was a good place to blow off steam safely. I rarely met my classmates there. The last thing I wanted to talk about was vet school; this was my recharging time.

Saturday morning was spent nursing any hangover (like I *ever* got one) and doing laundry and cleaning. There is a certain comfort in leaning on a warm, tumbling dryer when a tom-tom is pounding on your cerebrum. The patrons at the casino were sparse this time of the day. It was a relief to not talk to them at times. By midday it was back to the salt mines in preparation for Monday. Saturday night was usually spent in the laboratory at vet school. There would undoubtedly be some loud music from the frat house outside my window. Not that it was irritating. I wanted to join in on the fun to the point of distraction.

Sunday morning found me at church. With all of the distractions on campus it is critical that you keep your moral compass intact. Be sure to attend weekly services at the local church, temple or synagogue. I made it a point to focus my mass intentions on my family. This kept them close to me despite the distance between us. It also kept me focused on why I was in school: to get my degree and make my family proud.

I knew that I could find a party on campus almost every night. If you go off to college looking for a good time you will find one. However, you will accomplish very little else. Virtue is doing the right thing when no one is looking. Your lifelong authority figures and role models are no longer watching you when you're away at school. Keep your morals intact so that you have no regrets upon your return home.

There are some really great parties at the big universities. One of the best ones I attended was for Halloween. That is a very big occasion at the U. of Ill. The police close Green St. to traffic and it overflows with costumed students. One of the engineering students was confined to a motorized wheelchair. His friends built a tank around him and the wheelchair. It was complete with a water cannon and turret. I had a great time mingling with the crowd for about ninety minutes. That was enough time to enjoy the experience. I would have liked a late night out, but classes beckoned the next day. The key is to have balance in your life. That won't change at graduation so get used to it now.

*A client brought in a pill vial with a piece of paper taped over the medicine label alerting me to the fact that it contained a stool sample. He was concerned that it seemed rather hard. I opened it to find a little, bitty bar stool that he had made!! (see next page)*

*A FAX came in from the emergency clinic informing us that one of our patients had been seen there with a history of possibly ingesting a door knob. Radiographs showed no evidence of the knob and it was later found by the owner. It was actually a knob from a dresser, but it inspired us to come up with the top ten reasons why Quincy ate a doorknob:*

10. *His thought process had become unhinged.*
9. *It was a part of his Grand Slam breakfast.*
8. *He wanted nutritional support for his knobby knees.*
7. *He is a dead bolt dad.*
6. *He was hungry for some locks.*
5. *He is doorkey.*
4. *He was trying to get a handle on things.*
3. *He had difficulty coming out of the closet.*
2. *He thought it would help him sing on key.*
*And the number one reason why Quincy ate the doorknob:*
1. *He wanted to be adoorable.*

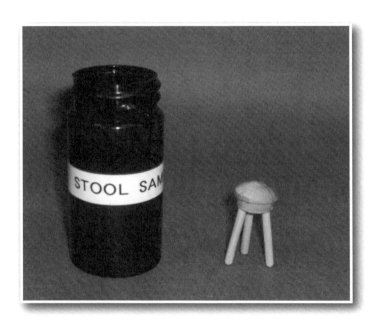

CHAPTER 8

## *Sophomore Jinx*

My first summer break went by in a flash. I was working 60 hours a week at Dr. Hagenburg's practice and spending the weekends working around the garden and house. Throw in some family picnics and a fishing trip to Canada with my father and uncles and I was ready to get back in the academic saddle. This time I was better prepared to face the year. I had my spurs on.

I knew what my financial obligations would be and working all those hours left me with little time to spend the money I had earned. Mom and Dad would contribute to the education fund, but I was happy that their burden would be light as my brother, Geoff, was attending my 'alma mater' (I never actually graduated from Lewis University). Brother number two, Keith, would be joining me at the University of Illinois as an undergraduate freshman the following year.

The class schedule would be extremely packed….38 credit hours over the two semesters. That was misleading because the lab courses would be one credit, but three or four hours of class time. We actually had over 30 hours of in-class time each semester.

This time I knew I could handle the burden. It would simply be a matter of sticking it out. I thought back to the mailing service. I hoped that I would see those people again, but I was determined that I would never work that type of job again.

The semester started out on a couple of positive notes. First, I would again be the class projectionist. Apparently the few pranks we pulled weren't enough to get me canned and the fact that I was always present and never broke any equipment would have qualified me for enshrinement into the projectionist hall of fame if not for the aforementioned pranks. In addition to that lofty position I also obtained a meal job at a sorority.

Most of the meal jobs went to undergraduate students. The servers were mostly good-looking guys that could be a bit flirtatious without crossing the line. They were only supposed to speak when spoken to.....something I have never been able to do. Therefore, I became a member of the cleanup crew. We were the pot lickers. The cook needed two of us to do the cleaning in a reasonable amount of time, but she was kind enough to hire three of us. Amy, Mike and I never abused her kindness. We rotated through and always made sure that at least one of us was there to get the work done. Usually we had a pair. The cook always took care of us. I can't recall eating a bad meal there, although my basis of comparison was dorm food. She even convinced me to try eating liver.

Liver night at home came way too frequently. It was an inexpensive meal for a large family and my parents both loved it and were convinced of the health benefits of eating liver. To this day I hate the taste and especially the texture of liver. Perhaps you think hate is too strong a word. Let me rephrase that. I detest liver in all of its appellations. You can't fool me with pate de foie gras or by wrapping it in bacon and calling it rumake. I don't care if it came from a steer or calf or chicken or deer (Dad's favorite) or even a crappie (Gram's favorite). You can even mash it up with other things and call it Scrapple. I can spot it a mile off.

When I was young and stupid Mom could get me to eat a bit

of it by pointing out how much liver Geoffrey was eating. How could I let my little brother show me up like that? Well, after awhile it was easy. In fact, we worked out a system. We would sit next to each other. I would cut up the liver into rather large, but manageable, bites. Jeff would pile up his veggies on the side of his plate closest to me. As soon as the parental units weren't looking we shoveled off each others' plates as fast as we could. Even better, when we finally got Mittens I was a cinch to clean my plate.

The dinner menu at the sorority was posted the night before. There it was: liver and whatever. Who cared what else was being served…my eyes just stared at the word as flashbacks of nausea and memories of sitting at the kitchen table beyond the limits of human endurance were awakened. I gathered my senses and announced to the cook that I would be unavailable to work the next day. She asked where I would be and I replied; "McDonalds, eating a decent meal!"

In her beautiful southern drawl she laid down her challenge. "Honey, if you don't like the liver the way I cook it then I'll make ya a steak."

"Well, thaw one out and I'll see you tomorrow!" I couldn't lose. I had a glimpse of those steaks in the freezer earlier in the week and they looked yummy!

I must confess that I was both amazed and humbled by that meal. The liver was sliced thin and it was cooked to perfection; it was still just a bit pink in the middle. Smothered with onions to hide the texture, it was actually edible. That remains the only time in my life that I willingly ate a piece of liver. After going through physiology and learning what the liver does, I am convinced that you'd be better off eating the oil filter from your car.

The classes for sophomore year built up from the foundation established during freshman year. In fact, the final exams for pathology included material from histology the year before. That may seem unfair, but you did need to know the normal in order to see the abnormal. Physiology and pharmacology reinforced what you learned in pathology. You discovered *why* those tissues looked abnormal under the microscope and how to effect positive changes with modern drugs in order to alter the course of diseases. Microbiology and immunology taught you what organisms you might encounter in those tissues and what cell types are brought into the region to battle the infections.

Parasitology would be covered in two semesters. Of course, many of the parasites we studied spent a good part of their lives in the intestinal tracts of animals. It didn't take us long to grow tired of looking through poop samples for parasite eggs.

With all these pieces of the puzzle being crammed into your head you would think that a picture would start to emerge. Nope. Not a thing. Just a bunch of facts crammed in from every direction. The big picture was still a long way off.

I had settled into a routine very quickly this semester. Breakfast at the dorm, sack lunch after morning classes, dinner at the sorority after classes ended for the day, study at night, sports on Friday, Murphy's on Friday night. The grades were good; I was just short of an A in every class with the semester half over. What could go wrong? I was about to find out.

I returned to my dorm room from the student union around 11:00 one evening. The phone rang. I picked it up and said; "What's wrong with Dad?"

It was Mom. "He had a heart attack.", she stammered.

"Don't worry about a thing, Mom. Dad's going to be fine." That came out as a statement of fact. For some reason I absolutely knew that would be the case. I had no doubt in my mind whatsoever. He had to be because the alternative was unthinkable. He (we) had too much to live for. I still thank God for that confidence in Dad's recovery.

I was determined to visit him no matter the consequences. I knew I could manage over 70% on my remaining tests. That would still leave me with a grade of B in every class. The problem became transportation. I was usually able to bum a ride from a classmate in order to go home for breaks, but we were up to our ears in work and nobody was going home for several weeks yet.

Necessity is the mother of invention according to the adage. My feeling is that necessity is just a mother. I had only two options.

Public transportation is fine if you're not in a hurry. The bus schedules weren't conducive to getting me home with any time left to visit Dad and I had no idea where I could catch a train. The other option was to let my thumb do the walking.

Despite every evil story I had heard and every warning from my parents, I decided to hitchhike home. It turned out to be a gratifying experience. The longest I had to wait for a ride was ten minutes. The first ride was to the interstate ramp. The second was north. I didn't care how far north so long as I got underway in the right direction. Home was only two hours away and I was determined to get there. However, I wasn't stupid about it. When someone offered a ride I would ask *them* where *they* were going. I didn't let them ask me first. I turned down a couple of rides because I had misgivings about the drivers. I simply said, "Thanks, but that isn't where I'm headed.", and then I would walk away to the rear of the car (it is awkward to back up on an interstate ramp).

After accepting a ride I would explain my situation to the driver. Each of the four times I hitchhiked home I was driven to my front door! It is a shame that our society makes us afraid to help each other. I recently read that one in three hitchhikers meet with some form of foul play. I can't recommend my solution to today's students.

By the time I was able to get home that Saturday Dad had been out of surgery for a couple of days. His triple bypass had gone very well, but I was filled with apprehension as I approached his hospital room. I thought of the irony that I had been born in this same hospital and that my father had been given his second life just a few days earlier. I wasn't sure what to expect. I pictured him as having aged twenty years since I last saw him; frail, weak, in pain.

Not Dad. He was lying up in bed reading a book when I came in. His first concern was me. "What are you doing here? I didn't expect you home for a few weeks."

"Well, Dad, it's customary to visit the people you love when they try dying like that." I later learned that he had initially refused an angiogram because one of the differential diagnoses for chest pain is hiatal hernia. Dad decided that was what he had because he felt 'fine' otherwise and it happened to be the best disease on the list. It wasn't until the guy in the bed next to him died and was resuscitated that Dad decided that he was in good hands. He announced to the doctors that night that he would undergo the angiogram. The other man ended up being released from the hospital before my dad. Fortunately, his tough German stock made Dad too stubborn to die.

As he lay there with his hospital gown unbuttoned my eyes met his incision. That is a shocking sight….your father's sternum split down the middle. I couldn't avert my eyes. I finally said, "Dad, I need to step out of the room for a minute. Button up that gown while I'm gone."

"What? That?" he said, pointing at the sutures. "That doesn't hurt." Then he began touching the incision!

I turned away and said; "Dad, if you want any more visitors you won't be doing that again! Button that up and I'll be right back." He didn't do that again. He threatened to do it, but I threatened to pinch off his IV tubing if he didn't behave!

Ultimately, it was Dad's legs that were to be his biggest problem during the recovery. He had some pain from the incision that was made to harvest the vascular graft and both of his legs would become weak from inactivity. His full recovery would take nearly a year, but he is still with us as of this writing 27 years later. The family still thanks God, Dad's doctors and the staff at St. Francis Hospital for their care of him and his visitors. The owners of several golf courses thank them as well because Dad has kept the grounds keepers busy these many years. Many Canadian walleyes would rue his recovery.

My poor brothers-in-law had the task of driving me back to school. I could fudge a story about getting home with a friend, but getting back to school wasn't as easy. These rides gave us a couple of hours each week to catch up on gossip, tell some jokes and pull some gags on one another. They never complained about the drive despite the four hours it took for a round trip. Mom made sure that they had some gas money and that we all had a meal before leaving.

Perhaps the most touching moment came on the second visit. Dad was home from the hospital, but he wasn't very mobile and he was in constant discomfort. When I came in through the front door Mitts ran up to me wagging her tail, jumping up on me and smiling. She gave me the biggest 'hello' she could muster and then ran back and sat next to my dad. She looked at him then she looked at me. She looked back at Dad, put her foot gently on his knee and looked at me as if to say; "I sure love you, but he needs me more than you do." Mitts never left Dad's side throughout his recovery. It was quite a solace to me to know that she was there to divert his attention from his infirmities.

Once Dad began to heal he started walking and walking and walking. At first, it was to the neighboring driveway, then the next one, and then the next. Eventually, his regular route was about 8 miles. He went to the forest preserve with Mitts at least once a week. Within a very short time Mittens wouldn't let him say 'no' to a walk. She would grab her leash and put it on Dad's lap. It became a big game to them. Dad would throw the leash across the room and say "Not today you rotten hound! No walk for you!" Mitts would run over, grab the leash and throw it back on his lap. The process would continue until she started barking and Mom would yell at them both to go outside. Dad had pretty good nurses watching over him at home.

Fortunately, all ended well. Dad recovered well enough that I stopped coming home every weekend. His timing was great in that the middle of the semester found me settled in my classes and then he recovered well enough in time for me to focus on final exams. The grades didn't suffer at all that semester. My coworkers covered for me at the sorority. I even managed to play ice hockey the following semester.

We had a couple of skaters that season. We even won a game. It was after that game that I received one of the best left handed compliments of my life. One of my team mates brought his girlfriend to every game despite his lack of any ability to play or even stay up on his skates. While we were all at dinner that evening his girlfriend looked at me and said, "You are really amazing out there on the ice!" I was about to thank her as my chest puffed out in obvious pride, but she continued on; "I've never seen anyone who can get up off of the ice as fast as you!" It must have been all of that practice from those years of getting knocked down. Oh well, at least I could still get up.

Second semester flew by; I had an even heavier class load than the first half of the year. One of those classes was livestock management. I began to become interested in production medicine. I had no experience around food animals other than my brother-in-law Bob being a butcher, oops, meat cutter. However, I felt confident that if that was my calling I could answer it. Time and experience would direct me in the near future.

*An elderly client brought his seven year old Irish setter to the clinic on an emergency basis one afternoon. The dog had a distended tick on his foot and it was the cause of great concern for everyone involved. The mister had the misses hold onto the dog while he tried to remove the tick with a pair of tweezers. The normally calm dog became very agitated. The tick wasn't budging. Next, he tried to burn it with a match. The dog actually tried to bite him. Next, he went out to the garage to get a pair of pliers to pull it off. In his absence the misses called the clinic for an appointment which the mister was certain would be a waste of time. She wouldn't let him near the dog with those pliers. The tick turned out to be a rather large, but harmless, skin tumor. No wonder the poor dog tried to bite him! Thank goodness the misses insisted on coming in.*

*At that point, the tumor was a personal affront to the mister's manhood. He wanted it off immediately. I obliged him and burned it off with the help of a local anesthetic. I brought the growth back to the exam room to show the family that what I had removed was NOT a tick. I was holding it in a pair of pliers. The mister felt vindicated!*

*This is an actual message that one of my receptionists wrote for me:*

*Helen McT... called and wanted you to know she didn't believe the advice you gave her but tried it anyway and now Poppy is fabulous. Owner thought Poppy was on her way out but since she has greatly improved she bought her a crystal collar. No need to call.*

# CHAPTER 9

# *Junior Mint*

Junior and senior years of vet school go hand in hand.  As a junior you are required to assist the seniors in the wards.  This is designed to give you an idea of what will be happening when you get direct responsibility for cases and it will help you become familiar with where things are and how the system works at the teaching hospital.  The seniors realize that they were in your shoes just last year and that they are still wet behind the ears themselves…they have the clinical professors to remind them of that constantly.  As a result, the seniors treat the juniors pretty well.

It was an interesting transition from learning about the causes and symptoms of diseases to making a diagnosis.  Our focus shifted from the list of diseases to symptoms associated with organ systems.  Since some diseases affect multiple organs they kept showing up in lecture time and again.  Each disease was gradually pounded into your skull from multiple directions until it became difficult to forget it.  Even years later, it would be possible to detect signs of an unusual disease that you thought you would never see in practice.

At the start of first semester junior year I was offered a job at one of the labs. They were doing a study on the effects of dietary fat on the development of breast cancer in women. They were feeding four diets with differing levels of specific nutrients to a group of very expensive rats which were bred specifically for their tendency to form breast tumors. I was given a quarter-time assistantship to care for the rats, measure their food intake and body weight, and palpate them for breast tumors. Every parameter was duly noted in the records of each rat. If one of them died, I was responsible for performing a necropsy and saving tissues for microscopic evaluation.

This turned out to be a great job. The lab was on the route back to the dorm. The hours were very flexible. I received a tuition and fees waiver and $200 a month in compensation! The quarter-time referred to the fact that it should take about 10 hours a week, which is one fourth of a normal job. I got it down to six to eight hours once I had everything organized and felt comfortable handling the rats.

The mathematics worked out pretty easily. At two dollars a pitcher for beer I was being paid 100 pitchers a month! Add in the meals from the sorority job and I would be living large. I was actually able to accumulate a little money during the year…not quite like having my own mint, but it sure beat going into debt!

Because of my work and school schedule I gradually saw less and less of my dorm buddies. Get-togethers were limited to Fridays at Murphy's. It is a great regret that I didn't obtain addresses to stay in contact with them after graduation. There are no listings in the phone directories under Rosebush, Chief, Mister Wit, etc. I thought I would have another year to spend with these friends, but senior year really put an end to our association as I would rarely get back to my 'home' at Sherman Hall.

I was offered a student internship my senior year. I would receive a free apartment on the upper floor at the small animal clinic in exchange for taking emergency calls at night. There would be six students sharing in the duties….one night a week and every sixth weekend on duty.  Living only footsteps away from classes and rotations was too good an offer to pass up.  After accepting that position I would rarely get back to Sherman Hall.

I had such an intense work load junior year and such a fun time doing it that much of it remains foggy.  I did manage to forge a new friendship with one of my classmates that had heretofore been a shadow.  He remains a dear friend to this day.

Dan had been on the academic bubble for two years.  He really enjoyed his partying and yet he managed to remain in school.  He is very intelligent, motivated and fun-loving.  Emphasis on the latter; so much so, that his grades suffered horribly.  He finally made the decision to change his study habits.  In order to do that, he started to hang out at the vet school.  Of course, that is where the non-genius, nose to the grindstone types hung out as we toiled away at our studies.  That is where I *actually* met Dan for the first time.

He not only needed help studying; he also needed help in making decisions.  His first thought was usually where we could go to unwind.  He never passed a billiards hall he didn't want to investigate.  I must admit that Dan was the ship that followed the wind and I was the anchor that kept him at bay.  When we worked, we worked hard and we worked well together.  When we played we had a blast.  Dan still needed a bit more partying than I was capable of.  He still went out with some of the wild bunch on occasion, but we were the odd couple that succeeded.  When Dan received his diploma he got a standing ovation from the class.  Nobody thought he would survive his own personality.  I sat back in my seat, smiled and wiped away a small tear of pride and satisfaction.

One of the projects we took on together was a stray dog with apparently minor injuries from a car accident.  However, a few weeks later it became apparent that the abrasions on her leg were only the tip of the iceberg.  Her new owners noticed that her right front foot was beginning to turn out.  Radiographs confirmed that the growth plate at the distal (furthest from the trunk) end of the ulna had been injured causing it to stop growing. As the radius continued to grow it was constrained by the ulna and this resulted in a bowstring effect. The treatment consisted of removing a piece of bone from the middle of the ulna. This frees up the end of the radius/ulna and allows the leg to grow straight.

Having done very well in junior surgery and being a prospective student intern had helped me develop a good rapport with the surgery professors. I approached them and told them about the circumstances surrounding the puppy. The owners couldn't afford to pay for the surgery, but they could pay for the supplies. Dan and I would volunteer our time to do the surgery, all of the cleanup and the aftercare. It would give us an opportunity to hone our surgical skills and it would greatly improve the quality of life for the puppy, Mandy. They agreed to our terms. We agreed with theirs and signed a waiver to that effect. The surgery went well and Mandy was discharged the following morning.

Little Mandy did terrific, a little too terrific. She had re-grown the bone we removed within two weeks. We had to redo her surgery. We had learned a hard lesson about placing a fat graft to delay healing of the bony defect. She went on to a full recovery. Dan stayed in touch with the adoptive family and learned that Mandy lived into her teen years with no lameness in the operated leg. That was quite a reward for the hours we put in on her behalf.

A required activity junior year was helping with the annual Veterinary Open House at the teaching hospitals. Both the Large and Small Animal Clinics are opened to the public for one Sunday in April. Everything must be immaculate and the equipment was all on display for the wonderful taxpayers that help provide funding for the school. I volunteered to be the chairman of the poultry committee.

This was no chicken outfit. We had plans to be the best display there…even better than the cow with the window in its stomach! We had the usual chicks hatching during the open house. They were a big hit as they emerged right on schedule. We had the usual display of incubators, feeders and other equipment used in the poultry industry. We had the usual nutritional information and other propaganda provided by some of the local producers. We wanted to go beyond the usual and attract lots of attention.

Plan A: I fed different colored dyes to six hens for a period of 3 to 4 days in succession. I gathered the eggs at the end of the last dye feeding period. I then hard boiled the eggs and cut them in half. The result was a rainbow of colors in the yolk. I must confess that you didn't notice them right away; you had to look closely to appreciate the effect. We didn't have much room for the display and the hatching chicks distracted people from the pretty yolks. It was nice, but not the big bang we wanted.

Plan B: I had heard about someone cracking open an egg and finding a capsule with a note in it instead of a yolk. It was a commercial for some product containing eggs as I recall. We decided that it would be a great idea to do that on camera for the news crew. After lengthy discussions with many professors we decided it could be done.

First of all, we had to make a detailed plan and present it to the animal use committee. We had to include anesthesia and pain management for the chickens. This was quite a deal at the time as animal pain had not yet become an issue in the mind of the profession. We were on the cutting edge of animal care. The process involved surgery since there were no laparoscopic instruments at the time. Surgery on avian patients was an uncommon practice at the time and it gave us another chance to gain valuable experience. We implanted sterile capsules into the oviduct of two chickens and a small sterile rubber ball into the oviduct of a third (imagine being able to bounce the yolk of a raw egg!). Each of the capsules contained a small handwritten note. The chickens recovered from their surgeries uneventfully with no signs of pain. We found the super ball within a few hours. It was too heavy, and it passed through the oviduct so quickly that the hen didn't have time to build a shell around it. The first capsule suffered a similar fate, although you could see that albumin had been deposited around it. The second capsule came out in a perfect, although thin, shell.......and the hen stepped on it. She not only broke the egg; she broke our hearts after all that work. Both of the eggs we had intended to break open for the press would have contained the same message: 'Help me! I'm stuck inside this chicken!'

While we had a great display that year, we didn't best that cow with the window in its stomach. Mom still talks about that one. When she went up to look inside the cow's stomach she didn't realize that the glass wasn't in the window. She put her face right up to it and took a deep breath of methane gas. Thank goodness dad was there to catch her. At least someone in the family was a hit at open house. It went around like wildfire that someone nearly passed out looking at that darn cow. I pretended not to know her until the crowds thinned out.

The workload continued to increase through junior year. We had 42 credit hours over the two semesters with lots of extra laboratory time thrown in. Much of what we covered was going to affect daily life in practice. For example, I knew what type of suture material was required for different procedures. I had learned that from Dr. Hagenburg. However, I had no idea why he selected them. Now I knew. Each type of suture has different characteristics....some are not absorbed, some are absorbed by the body in different ways making them more or less suitable for varying areas of the body and healing conditions. Some have needles, some don't. There are a myriad of things to think about. Seemingly minor decisions that are made at a moment's notice in the operating room will affect the outcome of every procedure. These decisions need to become reflexive and based on sound scientific thinking.

One of the most interesting classes in vet school was radiology, but the scheduling of the class was terrible. We were crammed into a small room in order for us to be close to the images projected on the screen. It was warm and dark. It was right after lunch. The chairs were very comfortable. It was impossible to stay awake. I decided to sit in the front row for one of the lectures. I figured that I would have to stay awake being that close to the lecturer. Nope. I was awakened by the light from the pointer (no lasers in those days) shining in my eyes and the professor telling me to pay attention to this particular slide as it would be on the next test. It was. Thanks for the warning.

Reproductive medicine was interesting. I will never forget the first time I was up to my armpit in the south end of a northbound cow. I might just as well have had my arm in a garbage can. I couldn't feel a thing. I was mostly interested in the consistency of the feces because I had witnessed what could happen when a cow gets nervous about what you're up to. Boots don't help much when the mess starts at the top and works its way down. At some point during my fourth or fifth palpation I finally felt the uterus and fetal membranes. I even managed to palpate the fetus. It was magic.

To this day I miss working on dairy cows. They are bred for temperament as well as milk production as the farmers don't want to risk injury during milking. The cows are handled regularly since they get milked twice a day. They are very curious and they are eager to check you out while you're doing a physical exam on them. Also, the dairy farmers are salt-of-the-earth kind of people. They are very grounded and practical. I miss them and their cows, but I sure don't miss the 5 a.m. starts and pulling calves in sub-freezing temperatures.

Necropsy rotation was nice in the sense that there are very few emergencies when the patients you work on are already deceased. We had one cow presented for necropsy with a history of death. There was nothing else to go on. She died. By the looks of her bloated carcass she had died quite awhile ago although the owner insisted it was recent and sudden. Her severe lack of weight belied the latter claim.

My classmates were insistent that we draw straws to determine who would be the lucky one to deflate the carcass and turn on the fan to ventilate the ward. I suggested that they do it in reverse order. Make sure that the fan is on first and pointing the fumes in the right direction. After much bickering I finally volunteered to do it myself. I had often thought that I was cursed with a poor sense of smell, but it turned out to be a blessing. It paid off that day when the gas came hissing out of the carcass. We ultimately discovered that the cow had ingested a foreign body which perforated the stomach and caused infection throughout the abdominal cavity. The foreign body was a piece of baling wire; 'hardware' disease as the farmers say.

One of the changes in training veterinarians involves junior surgery. I was trained on live animal surgery. Dogs were purchased for the explicit reason that they were to have surgery. The surgeries were considered minor until the last one…a thoracotomy. This final surgery was non-survival….they wouldn't be allowed to wake up from the anesthesia.

I'm sure that many of you are saying that this is cruel. On the contrary, we took very good care of our junior surgery dogs. After all, we became vets because we love animals. Millions of dogs are euthanized simply because they lack a home. The few dogs that were euthanized for our training provided a tremendous benefit to us and our future patients. This was the first time we had to deal with bleeding and suturing live tissues. There is no substitute for teaching tissue handling under duress.

The current curriculum involves teaching with models. If something goes wrong there are no consequences other than saying 'oops'. Currently, most students haven't handled live tissues in surgery before starting their surgical rotation in senior year. At that time, if they are lucky, they will get to do a couple of routine surgeries that the professors, residents and interns let slip through the cracks. That means that they have little or no experience when they start practice. Most general practices are too busy to assign an experienced vet to consult and assist in surgery. I wouldn't want my dog to be the first case for a new graduate. Most of them wouldn't dream of touching an orthopedic or major soft tissue surgery; those would be referred to another doctor in the practice or a specialist in another practice. I still thank God for the experiences I had in junior surgery and for sending Mandy for us to work on. I still have fond memories of those chickens every time I walk down the poultry aisle at the grocery store.

My assistantship went well. A few of the rats in my care died from their tumors. Two died from unrelated causes. My duties included harvesting tissues from the deceased rats for microscopic evaluation, but the study extended beyond my term of service. Thankfully, I wasn't involved with the end of the study when all of the rats were to be euthanized and necropsied. I had become very fond of many of them. They taught me that research would not be in my future and that high levels of fat in your diet are very bad for you.

As always, Dr. Hagenburg was very gracious in allowing me to return to work for my six weeks off of school. I put in my usual 12 hour days, but Dr. H's attitude towards me had changed. He became much more a mentor than a boss. He wanted to challenge my new knowledge. He wanted to help me organize it in my brain. Most important, he wanted me to become successful in my practice life. Sadly, this was to be his last chance to mold me.

My heart sank as Roger broke the news that he had taken his associate as a partner and that the business wouldn't be able to take on another associate for quite some time. I wasn't able to start my career there. However, he did continue to offer help and advice during my senior year as I remained in contact with him throughout my coming search for employment.

*A longtime client rushed his five year old Springer spaniel into the clinic just before closing time one beautiful June Saturday afternoon. I was bringing the records from my last patient up to the front desk when I noticed Ed sitting in the waiting room with the dog sitting on his lap. Ed looked like he was ready to collapse. The dog looked VERY happy.*

*"What's up, Ed?"*

*"Doc, there is something wrong with Georgine's eyes! She can hardly open them."*

*One look at the dog's demeanor told me what was wrong. "Ed. She's buzzed."*

*"What?"*

*"She sure looks like she got into marijuana to me. Is there any chance that she got any?... It does grow wild around here.... Did you take her to the park or the forest preserve?....Ed?"*

*His blank stare slowly turned into a look of determination. He never said a word to me. He stood up with the dog and muttered to himself, "I have to go home." He walked out the door without a good bye or backwards glance.*

*His wife called the following Monday to apologize for Ed's behavior. It seems that a high school graduation party on Friday night had gotten a bit out of hand. Some of the boys had been smoking behind the garage. Apparently, they left their butts on the ground. When Georgine was let out the following morning she found them and ate every one of them. The boys were busted!*

*Dr. Velders had a lab mix, Casey, presented to him with chronic spinal disease. The owners had fitted the dog with a harness in order to support him while walking. As Dr. V was assisting the dog out to the parking lot he quipped, "Look, I have a suit Casey!" I groaned and said, "Get a grip, would ya!"*

*A random thought of mine captured by the artwork of Stacy Hall.*

# CHAPTER 10

## *Senior Moments*

Becoming a senior student marked the beginning of the end of my educational career. The finish line was visible as I limped towards the end of my marathon. I began to feel a resurgence of energy. The year was starting on a chorus of positive notes.

I was in very good shape financially. However, I decided to take on my first student loan. The loan was more of an insurance policy guaranteeing that I would be able to afford my first set of wheels. Yes, my own car! I wasn't expecting to get one until after graduation, especially since I would be living at the vet school. However, my paternal grandma decided that she needed a new car and that I deserved her old one as an early graduation present. There it stood in all its beauty...a yellow Mercury Bobcat wagon with wood panel sides! It wasn't a chick magnet, but it sure beat the Schwinn. Thanks again Gram, may you rest in peace.

Also, I was able to start off the year in small animal surgery. I signed up for an extra rotation as an elective and I got it to start the year. The added bonus was that half of the students were away on their break so that we only had five students on the rotation instead of the usual ten.  Additionally, I lucked out on the draw and ended up on the team with only two students.  Our surgeons and residents had such a workload that they had no choice but to turn over some very interesting cases to our care.  To put icing on the cake, the rotation would be shared with one of my best friends.

I had always been good friends with Bob, but this experience would really put us to the test.  We spent 14+ hour days together.  I even put a mattress on the floor of my room upstairs for him so that he didn't have to go home to sleep.  He couldn't afford the time to drive the thirty minutes home and back.  We would throw a pizza in the oven and run back downstairs to do some treatments.  Run back upstairs and wolf down the pizza, then back to the ward after a quick bite to eat.

We shared all of our cases.  We presented them together in rounds each morning.  The lead clinician on our rotation was Dr. Johnson. He was very enthusiastic and passionate about patient care.  His favorite comment was; *Great Case!* The time in surgery flew by and thus began the fastest year of my schooling.

The benefits of accepting the student internship were already proven and yet they went well beyond what I had imagined.  My first thought was free lodging and no commute each morning.  Both of those were huge perks.  However, the intimate knowledge of the inner workings of the small animal clinic and the access to the professors whose offices were just down the hall were of incredible benefit to a student.  Having keys to almost everything helped, too.

Most of the emergency calls came from the surrounding community.  Some required immediate attention while most involved simple advice over the phone.  However, I did have several occasions when I got an in-house 'emergency'.  A professor would call late at night and ask me to go downstairs to check on a patient, administer treatments or update a treatment plan.  I was always sure to remind them of who was helping them out just in case they didn't recognize my voice.  "This is Gregg, I'd be happy to do that for you." Of course, you always made it a point to notate the time and initial the updated medical records, too.

There was one case in particular that created a bit of a stir. A beautiful golden retriever presented with severe vestibular disease. Vestibular disease is a disruption of the balance mechanism in the inner ear. He was so dizzy that he would roll across the floor until something obstructed his progress. Then he would continue to try to roll and hit his head repeatedly against the impediment. He was diagnosed with *otitis interna*, an inner ear infection. The medical staff put him on antibiotics and sedation. Two days later he was just as bad as he was on arrival. The neurologist wanted to start him on steroid therapy to reduce the inflammation of the nerves, but the medical staff was fighting him because steroids are contraindicated during infections. The debate raged all day. That night, the neurologist called just after midnight. On the second ring he was greeted by, "U of I Small Animal Clinic, this is Gregg. How can I help you?"

He seemed a little hesitant to speak, but said; "This is Dr. Petry, were you awake?"

"No, I was sound asleep. Is there anything I can help you with?"

"Yes. I'd like you to go downstairs and give that poor dog with vestibular syndrome a shot of cortisone." He proceeded to give me the particulars since I wasn't on that rotation. I knew that this was going to be controversial, but at least I was just the messenger. When he finished his instructions I reiterated, "This is Gregg, I'd be happy to do that for you."

The next morning the students arrived to find the dog sitting up. He was still dizzy, but he showed a marked improvement. Unfortunately, they didn't see my notations until after the medical people had been spouting off about how they knew the antibiotics would eventually work and how wrong the neuro people had been. My classmates on the rotation reported that flames can actually shoot out of someone's eyes. The only repercussion I suffered was the gratitude of Dr. Petry. That was payment enough because he could be quite intimidating to the students, but I got along famously with him.

It is fun to look back on the reputation that each professor had developed. Most of them earned their reputation and they were well aware of it. A tough reputation was used to good effect. A softer personality resulted in a more friendly association with the students. I'm sure that they had the same types of professors to deal with when they went through vet school and they were determined to pass the torch to us. The residents and interns that were still lacking a name for themselves simply needed to ask us seniors. We had names for all of them. Some were fun. Most were less than flattering. You certainly didn't want to be known as the swine professor or the stuttering sturgeon, but if the shoe fits....

The surgeons always seemed a bit overenthusiastic so we had slogans for them. To cut is to cure. Heal with steel. If you get bored, suture self. Take it to the table, Mable. Don't ignore it, explore it. They felt that they were the top rung on the referral ladder. If they couldn't help a pet then no one could. That was often the case, but there were times that I questioned whether some of the patients should have ever been put on the table even though the teaching hospital was their last hope. There often comes a time when nothing can be done.

Small animal medicine is the busiest of the rotations. The cases were assigned on a voluntary basis. You were expected to take the next case in line without being selective. You worked up the case and went on to the next one. That is an effective system in theory. However, in practice there are always students who are less motivated than others. I was very enthusiastic because this was what I hoped to do for many years to come. This is what Dr. Hagenburg had been preparing me for, and *I had keys to the clinic!*

There were certain protocols that had to be followed, but if you knew the system you could get things done very quickly and do the paperwork later. The ten students on this rotation varied greatly in their abilities. Some had never even placed an IV catheter! I had been doing this stuff for five years. The inequities in case loads became glaringly apparent at morning rounds.

Each case was presented to the entire group of professors, residents, interns and students by the student assigned to each case. You had to present the signalment (species, breed, age, sex and reproductive status), history, physical exam findings, lab results, radiographs, etc. along with your differential diagnoses and plan of action. Everyone on the rotation had 0, 1 or 2 cases at any given time. I always had 4 or 5. I was on the floor early every day. After finishing my treatments I would often help my classmates. That was the only time in four years that I was considered a 'gunner'. Other than that rotation I was pretty non-competitive with my classmates.

Sometimes the slackers get away with avoiding work, but that wasn't to be the case with this rotation. A nasty German shepherd dog presented with megacolon, a condition in which the colon becomes distended with feces. I would have a nasty disposition too if that were my colon. Before shipping the dog to surgery it had to be cleaned out with enemas. The three students who had been avoiding cases were assigned to this dog.

They gave enemas to that poor dog for *hours*. Over thirty pounds of feces were removed! They were miserable. So was the dog and anyone within the vapor cloud surrounding the ward. Sadly, when the dog went to surgery they found that he had no functional nerve endings in the colon and he was euthanized while still under anesthesia. All of their efforts were in vain.

Speaking of odors, ambulatory medicine was quite an experience. It convinced me not to do production medicine. I didn't mind the work. I loved the farmers and their way of life. They are the salt-of-the-earth kind of people. However, I didn't like the down time traveling between calls. It seemed like such a waste of time in which you had to spend money traveling instead of earning money working. I enjoy the faster pace of clinic work.

Equine medicine was very intimidating to me. I had never been around horses and my inexperience gave me a few scares. One horse in particular had my number. He would turn his rump towards me no matter which direction I approached from. I knew that he knew he was in control. That's bad; very bad. I had to get one of the good old boys to get him out for me. Then the horse was fine. I didn't think that I could present a very professional image in equine medicine. I also didn't like the idea that I may not be going home after work....I might end up in the hospital with a hoof in my head or spleen.

The best part of equine medicine came when the circus was in town. They had a tiger that needed some work done on a front foot. They brought him to the clinic in a huge rolling squeeze cage. It was too large to fit into the small animal clinic so they brought him to the equine clinic. One roar from that big cat and every horse in the place was in full fight or flight mode. Who the heck wanted to work on a crazed horse when a 400 pound cat was around, anyway?

The white Siberian tiger looked very confident in that cage. He knew he was at the top of the food chain and he could sense the nearness of the horses. As I stared at him from a respectable distance of about five feet, he met my gaze. He stared me down and then pulled himself up and roared right at me. I could feel his breath blowing my hair (I had some then) as I stood there frozen in place. Actually, I was melted in place. My legs turned to gelatin. I couldn't have lifted a finger to help myself. The two classmates that stood to either side of me slowly leaned away as if to tell the tiger 'Take him, just leave me alone!' Certain people might be willing to take a bullet for me, but there are very few people that would have stepped in front of that tiger.

Once he was sedated I was able to get close to the tiger. The base of his tail was twice the width of my wrist! His feet were huge. He had four-inch long nails. It would have been over for me in a jiffy. Of course, if you are ever eaten by a tiger there is one avenue of escape: run around and around in the stomach until you're all pooped out! I know that's old, but I'm not apologizing for it.

The reason for this visit was that the tiger had calluses on his feet from the rough surface on the training platforms. The professors were using a circular sander on his feet like we would use a pumice stone on our calluses. Taking advantage of the sedation, routine blood testing and a thorough physical examination were performed on the sleeping predator. The students weren't allowed to be involved in treating this magnificent cat. We were interested observers for the most part, but I can honestly say that I have grabbed a tiger by the tail and lived to tell about it.

Food animal medicine was an interesting rotation. We had to treat the usual cases of mastitis and reproductive problems, but we also inherited a case from the previous students on the rotation. A farmer was driving his daughter to a 4-H competition. The young bull to be shown was in the back of the pickup truck when the bed gave way. The bull scraped his legs down to the carpal bones. There wasn't enough skin to close the wounds so 'second intention' healing was in order. We had to keep the wounds clean and bandaged while Mother Nature did the rest.

After a few days of treatment the bull knew what was coming. He was very good natured (thank heavens), but he had become difficult to catch. Every morning you had to play his game of catch-the-bull-by-the-nose-ring. I found the best technique was to lean into his flank with your rump, slap his butt with one hand and when he turned to see what hit him you needed to immediately dive for the ring with the other hand. It helped to position him away from the land mines he had deposited in the stall overnight. Despite several botched attempts that ended with me on the floor of the stall the bull never stepped on me. He was very cooperative for the treatments once you caught him. I could see why they put so much effort into saving him despite the fact that his show days were over. He went on to heal completely and he was left with only a few unsightly scars.

*Graduation picture taken in April, 1982. Not bad for a pullover tuxedo top.*

A friend was doing a research paper on dolphins. She asked me to proof read it. I found a great typo that the computer missed on spell check. Instead of a caudal (tail) fin, dolphins had a cadudal fin. With this in mind, I checked the anatomical charts she had included with the paper. Although cadudal sounds like a great word, it was incorrect. However, I happened to notice that there was no pancreas on any of the charts.

Knowing that dolphins are mammals, I asked her where the digestive enzymes and insulin came from in lieu of a pancreas. She didn't know. We checked several different anatomical charts and none of them showed a pancreas. I finally called the Shedd Aquarium and spoke with the veterinary team on staff there. They assured me that dolphins have a prominent pancreas. They were as baffled as me by the absence of the pancreas on the charts (they confirmed it) and assured me that they would spread the word of this oversight to their colleagues. That is my one and only contribution to marine medicine (other than occasionally surveying a few ocean fish for abnormalities when I am fortunate enough to catch anything).

If you marry a gal who is a dental hygientist, would she be considered to be a prophy wife?

*A client allowed her eight year old child to attempt carrying their cat from the car into the clinic. They came into the clinic in tears. The child was scratched and the cat was missing.*

*It was a beautiful, sunny Saturday. My staff kept taking turns going outside to help look for the missing feline. This went on until after our two o'clock closing. When I finally finished my calls it was nearly 3:30 and the family had still not found the cat. I spent some time assessing their search process and it occurred to me that they hadn't checked under the hoods of the vehicles.*

*I recalled the time the mechanic shop next door had us rush over because the unusual sound coming from beneath a car turned out to be a parrot. It was quite nice and we found the owner with little difficulty. It was not the owner of the car, but a neighbor down the street.*

*I was also aghast at the prospect of the cat being in my fan belt as I started my car in front of that little girl. Therefore, I opened the hood of my car and looked around. No cat. But, the oil fill cap had rattled off and was dangling by the antipollution hose. As I carefully pulled it up I literally saw one glimpse of one eye of the cat!*

*I slowly closed the hood to prevent another escape. I motioned to the family to quietly surround the car. I slid underneath and noticed that there was only one way out; past the fan! I grabbed that cat like a rattlesnake grabbing a rodent. She seemed incredibly relieved to be found. No struggle at all.*

*We went into the clinic for a quick clean up and the annual visit that she tried so hard to skip out on. She went home in a borrowed carrier!*

# CHAPTER 11

# *Testing. Testing. One. Two.*

Amidst the work of rotations there loomed the culmination of your education; the state and national veterinary board examinations. These would be the last big tests of vet school. Your license hinged on passing these tests. Paranoia was rampant despite the fact that we were given a reduced work load in order to prepare for the tests. Copies of old tests were floated around in order to give us a feel for the national boards. The Illinois Board had just developed a new type of board exam, the Clinical Competency Test. There was no preparing for this one which made the angst that much more acute.

My attitude was that I should already know all of this stuff. Realistically, only one or two people failed the exam from each class every year. I estimated that I was at about a third of the way down from the top of my class and that they would have to fail an awful lot of people to get to me. That line of reasoning carried over to enough classmates that we had a core of card players that were ready to shuffle off to the break room at a moment's notice. Board exams were about the least stressful part of school for me.

There would be no grade. It was pass/fail. A score of 99% was the same as 70%. The test was administered at the vet school a short walk from my room. I knew I had passed the exam before I left the room. Only one more test to go….the CC test.

The Illinois Clinical Competency Test turned out to be quite fun to take. The aim of the test was to assess your ability to think through clinical cases. A case scenario was presented. You had to make a list of differential diagnoses, select tests to run and treatments to administer. You had a list of answers from which to select your options. A yellow highlighter was provided. As you marked selections lettering would appear that told you that you were correct or that you should select another answer. You knew immediately how you were doing.

I breezed through the CCT in record time until I encountered a herd of swine with pneumonia. I had worked up the case and diagnosed it correctly. The final question involved selecting eight managerial changes that could be made in order to help the herd recover. I highlighted seven answers, all of which were correct, but I couldn't find an eighth answer that seemed reasonable.

I finally highlighted an answer…wrong, please select another answer. So I did. Again, wrong. So I selected another. *Still wrong.* I couldn't see an answer that made any sense to me. At that point I started highlighting all of them. There wasn't another correct answer! They had shorted us on correct responses. I couldn't believe that I had just spent 40 minutes on a problem with no solution. However, it did come as quite a relief. At any rate, I walked out of the room knowing I had scored 100% on a test designed to test my clinical competency. All I needed was that piece of paper and I was ready for my career to start. Only a few months to go and it would be official.

Since half of the summer was spent in rotations at vet school there was time allotted for a senior externship. You were expected to work at a veterinary clinic in exchange for a summary and evaluation of your work. Some of the students were paid for their time and others weren't. I made it a point to find a paying internship. I applied to several clinics near home and took an assignment about 35 minutes away with an easy commute through the farmland southwest of Chicago. New Lenox was considered to be out in the boondocks back then, but the suburbs have since sprawled out to meet it.

I had a great time at my externship. We worked hard and I got along well with all of the staff. However, there was one big drawback: no appointment book. All of the cases were walk-ins and it drove me nuts! There was no flow to anything. You went from sitting around with nothing to do for half an hour to a full waiting room in a matter of minutes. Even surgeries could walk in.

"Can you spay my dog today?"

"Sure, when did she last eat?"

"Oh, about an hour ago."

"That's OK, we'll induce vomiting before surgery."

I decided that I would never put my staff, my patients or myself through that type of stress. I was given great supervision and I was allowed to do lots of surgical and medical cases while in New Lenox. However, despite my enjoyment of the externship I would take a job elsewhere. I was honest and frank about why I had made my choice to leave. It wasn't long after that decision that an appointment calendar was adopted at the clinic.

One of the things I learned there was that you could still have some fun being a doctor, despite the added responsibilities. A client found a stray cat with its head stuck inside of an empty glass jar. She was panicking as she felt the cat would soon suffocate and she couldn't get the jar off despite the liberal use of corn oil as a lubricant. The staff had picked up on the anxiety of the owner and they were all becoming more and more concerned as the seconds ticked by. It was immediately obvious that just pulling on the jar wasn't going to accomplish anything. I paused and thought for a moment. Then, very seriously, I asked if there was a hammer available. Two of the nurses ran off to look for one. The remaining staff members were sharing concerned looks with each other in obvious distrust of my plan. With their attention diverted I cocked the jar to one side, pulled out one ear and then the other and the jar was off. It would have been a nice touch to have a towel on hand. I could have thrown it over the jar and hit it with the hammer and then pulled out the rescued cat. However, the client immediately grabbed the cat and started hugging her and me. The nurses returned with the hammer just in time to see the tears of joy and the look of mischief in my eyes. They had been had and they remained on guard for the rest of my internship.

Graduation was a glorious event. There was a lot happening all at once. I had been going on job interviews on weekends when I didn't have emergency duties. Most of them were in the Chicago area, but some of them were in southwestern Michigan. Dr. Hagenburg had arranged most of the interviews around Chicago. He did too pursuasive a job in talking me up to the prospective employers. I was usually given a tour of the clinic and introduced to some of the staff. The tour would end with what amounted to; "What's good enough for Dr. Hagenburg is good enough for me. You can have the job."

With six standing job offers, I became the one doing the interviewing. The clinics in Michigan were disappointing to me. When I questioned them about where difficult surgeries or medical cases could be referred for help the answer was always the same: Michigan State University. That was a several-hour ride from the area I was investigating. When questioned about closer clinics they all answered with the same concern. The local vets would steal their clients. They were definitely seen as competitors rather than colleagues. If I worked in the area, that would make me a competitor, too.

The final straw came at a clinic that I was really beginning to like. I had stayed for a couple of hours. The staff was friendly and competent. The doctors were willing to be mentors and let me share the interesting cases. During the interview an elderly farmer carried in his 15 year old Doberman. The dog was virtually comatose and was dying of a combination of cancer and liver failure. The vet went into the exam room with the farmer and closed the door behind him. I knew what they were discussing and decided to let them have their privacy. A few minutes later the doors opened and I saw the farmer carrying his dog back to his truck.

"Isn't he going to put that poor dog to sleep?" I asked.

"Yes." The vet replied, "He's going to take him home to do it."

"Excuse me?" I stammered.

"Yeah, he's going to take him out behind the barn. He just wanted to be sure that there was nothing more we could do and that it was time."

That was genuinely his final act of love for the dog; take him out as if he was Old Yeller. I guess that's alright if you grew up on a farm and had become accustomed to raising and harvesting your food. Not me. That was the end of my interviews in Michigan.

My next interview proved to be the best. It was in the western suburbs of Chicago. Burr Ridge Veterinary Clinic. I had never heard of the town despite living in the area for my entire life. It was near an ice arena where I had skated a few times so I had a general idea of where it was. I was invited to come in early and stay late. I did, and I was invited back for a second interview.

Dr. Velders seemed to be and proved to be the nicest veterinarian to interview me. He was very concerned about the quality of my character as well as my professional abilities. He had me see clients with him. I scrubbed into surgery with him. He wanted a letter about my personal life, interests and professional goals.

Most of the previous clinics had very limited surgical equipment. It was usually in a single drawer or perhaps two: major pack, minor pack. Dr. Velders had three major packs, a minor pack, knee pack, eye pack, orthopedic pack and a whole wall with shelves filled with additional equipment. I discovered that BRVC was a referral clinic for surgeries despite a lack of board certification. His credentials were experience. That was good enough for me. A surgeon without the attitude!

I called five of the six standing job offers and told them I wasn't interested. I called the sixth, New Lenox, and informed them that I might be interested but that I was waiting to hear from Dr. Velders. I knew I was making the right decision when I heard their reply; "Oh. Velders, huh?" They made no effort to dissuade me as each of us knew that I had to do what I felt was best for me. We remain on good terms to this day, which is good because the practices are within twenty miles of each other, and we are all colleagues now..

Back at school, I was walking through the halls of the small animal clinic late one night when the head of the clinic, Dr. Irwin Small, called out to me with his gravelly voice; "Hey Greiner, you got a job yet?"

I turned to see the cherubic face on his bulldoggish body and replied, "I think I have two of them!"

"Oh good!" he answered. "Give me one. I have someone that needs it!"

Dr. Small knew details on every student that had graduated from the U. of I. vet school over the past twenty years. It was joked that the small animal clinic had been named after him and that there had been a Dr. Large at the university some years before.

I was happy to pass on the information for the New Lenox clinic when it became available. I was honored that he attended our graduation despite his administrative role that gave him limited interaction with our class.

Our final class party was a picnic prior to graduation. We roasted a steer and had a keg of beer. We discussed our job opportunities with bittersweet emotions. We knew that we would be scattered across the country and that many of us would probably not meet again except perhaps at reunions. Tomorrow was the day we had all worked so hard and so long for. The good-byes were long and sorrowful with promises to stay in touch.

Graduation was touching. The room was packed with relatives and friends. Dan got his standing ovation. One of our professors was a professional singer. His voice filled the room as only an operatic soloist can do. We later discovered that some of his research money was diverted to pay for expenses incurred while traveling to perform...oops, there went the professorship.

My family is so large that it could have filled the hall. Therefore, their attendance was limited. Of course, Mom and Dad were present. My great aunt and uncle on Dad's side, an aunt and a cousin came to the university to witness the ceremony. My siblings would wait to attend the graduation party at home. It was too far away for Gram and Gramps to attend, but their pride showed in the wonderful card and sentiments they had sent for my graduation party.

To my knowledge, this is the only party my father has ever hosted of his own accord. Entertaining was Mom's forte. However, this time Dad planned the event. We had a barbecue at the house and it seemed that everyone was invited. Few people failed to attend. Dad was tending bar behind a makeshift countertop that he had set up under the patio. He seemed very at ease there despite the fact that I had rarely seen him drink anything alcoholic in my 24 years living under his roof. As I walked past the bar he offered to make me a drink. When I asked what kind of poison he was pushing he responded, "Daiquiris."

I figured, correctly, that he had bought a mix and that I couldn't go too far wrong in trying one. Besides, there was a softball game starting and the drink could always fall victim to a stray ball or foot. As he finished his alchemy I took the glass and tasted the concoction. I fought back the brain freeze and complimented the paternal unit, "Not bad, Dad!"

As I turned to walk away he stopped me and said, "Oh, wait. I forgot something." I started to hand my glass back to him thinking it was the alcohol (I had attended a rum party in school once and it was difficult to even taste the mixers). Instead, he dropped in a hickory nut. In my confusion I stared at it and said, "What the heck is that?"

He replied, "A hickory daiquiri, Doc!"

Ouch. The punster victimized by his own father. Dad grinned

and walked away from the bar. The whole thing was a set-up for that one pun. I had no doubt, if any had existed before, that I was indeed my father's son.

The party was an enchanting mix of the old and young. The children played games in the backyard. The teenagers and adults who thought that they were still teenagers played softball in the vacant field one lot to the north. The more dignified sat in lawn chairs or milled about in the kitchen/ dining room area. Despite the fact that no presents would be accepted, ('your presence is sufficient' was included with the invitations), there was some work to be done.

My dearest, oldest aunt, Lucille by baptism, 'Sis' by moniker, gave me my first graduation gift. It was large, flat, square and heavy. Since today was all about me, I thought that she had framed an enlarged facsimile of my diploma or made a collage of college pictures she had coerced from my mother. My mouth fell open as I tore open the wrapping and realized what I was holding. The portrait of my Great Great Grampa, Dr. George Greiner!

He was a physician in Indiana and he was the only other doctor in the family going back as far as anyone could trace the family tree. Of the myriad branches currently alive on that tree, I was the one she wanted that portrait to belong to! She trumped any other gift that I could be given. Who could top that?

I was humbled beyond words and I have worked hard to justify her decision these many years. Dr. George was well respected by his hometown community and I pray that I can walk in his shoes for many years to come. I am still the only one in the family with a postgraduate degree and there are no prospects on the horizon for another as of this writing. My family gave me a mission as I embarked on my career with both feet firmly set on the ground: be as good as you can be to everyone you encounter.

*I was losing a lot of sleep over one of my upcoming surgeries. It was during my second year of practice. A large, aggressive German Shepherd dog was coming in for surgery on Friday. I was worried about handling the dog. I was worried about performing the surgery. It was a large mass and it was situated adjacent to the anus; it would be a challenge to remove it. Friday finally came. All of the other surgical patients were checked in. The shepherd was absent.*

*I asked my nurses to call the owners. I was concerned for their safety as they seemed eager to get the surgery done. My staff informed me that they had called the day before to reschedule it due a minor family emergency; he was coming the following Friday.*

*I lost all that sleep for nothing! Worse, I had the following week to worry about it all over again. I learned to stop checking my schedule ahead of time. Whatever comes in to the clinic gets my full attention. The schedule can look empty, but one or two emergencies later and you're suddenly running behind.*

*Mr. Daniels rushed into the clinic with his one year old female shih tsu lying in her padded basket. She was calm as can be. He was in full panic mode and the staff immediately ushered him into an exam room. As I entered he said, "Doc, I came home from shopping and Lily didn't greet me at the door. I found her in her bed and when I went to pick her up there was blood!"*

*By the calm demeanor and wagging tail of the dog I immediately surmised that this wasn't a chain saw accident. I gingerly lifted her out of the bed and saw not only a few drops of blood, but a newly born puppy as well. So did the mister. He stepped back, horrified and gasped, "But, that's.....that's impossible!"*

*I suggested a cause for the problem, "You do have two dogs, you know."*

*"But....but...that's her brother!"*

*He was mortified. That was the only puppy in the litter and with her full show coat Lily didn't 'show' she was pregnant. The pup was healthy and Mr. Daniels is now the proud owner of three <u>neutered</u> shih tsu dogs.*

INTERLUDE

## *Rich Beyond Words*

Since my paternal grandparents lived in the north woods of Wisconsin I have had the opportunity to wet a fishing line on a fairly regular basis. Dad loves to fish and he either enjoyed spending time with us kids or Mom needed intermittent sanity breaks. At any rate, I had my first chance to do some real fishing at the tender young age of twelve. Dad invited me to go to Canada with him (on *his* fishing trip).

I had seen pictures and heard some tall tales from his previous trips. The fishing was always great, the weather was always bad and the food was always sandy or burnt. There were bears and wolves and moose and mosquitoes the size of hummingbirds. I felt that I was being invited into manhood. It would be a sure sign that I had arrived if I made it back alive.

We would be accompanied by Dad's uncle, Arlo, and his son Bradley, my second cousin. Both of them were veterans of previous excursions into the wilds of Ontario and Uncle Arlo owned the tent we needed to borrow. They were a likely choice. Brad was old enough to drive the car if the need arose and he was already a pretty fair hand at the tiller of a boat. We had fished together many times at Gram's house and our history of good behavior was about to pay off. Arlo insisted I was only coming as bait for muskies.

It was a long drive from Chicago to Ely, Minnesota back in 1970; the roads have improved considerably in the past four decades. However, much of the trip was at night and I was able to get a few hours of sleep despite my fears of the unknown.

There would be two firsts for me on this trip before I would even get into a boat. It would be my first time in a foreign country and it would be my first time in a plane. Uncle Arlo ensured my good behavior by telling me stories about illegal fisherman getting caught by the Mounties and being dragged to jail from the middle of the woods because they had kept too many fish. (In later years I would be checked by officials from the MNR, Ministry of Natural Resources, literally in the middle of nowhere…and they would take you back to town if you were illegal and failed to come up with the fine. They carried nothing on the portages and there were plenty of them between the lake and town.) I was also expected to behave because I was representing my country and the president himself would be embarrassed if I caused trouble.

The plane ride was a mixture of fear and excitement. The canoes were strapped on to the pontoons beneath the plane. The fishing gear, tent, food, back packs, motors and gasoline went in the plane with us. Dad, Arlo and Brad went in the back of the plane with the gear while I got to ride in the copilot seat.

I pictured us taking off right from the dock, but we had to taxi all the way across the lake in order to take off into the wind. I also envisioned myself asking the pilot about a million questions about what we were seeing from the air, but the plane was very loud and the pilot was wearing a head set to maintain radio contact with the base camp.

After a short hop over some hills and small lakes we landed on the Canadian border to purchase our fishing licenses and face inspection, if necessary. It wasn't on this trip, but in future years we often had to unpack everything in order to get through customs. It was quickly back up in the air and we were off to Beaverhouse Lake.

About fifteen minutes into the half hour flight the pilot took off his headset and half-shouted to me: "Do you want to fly the plane?"

I was a little disturbed by this as it seemed to be more of a demand than a request. I don't think I surprised him by replying: "Sure, but you'll need to teach me how!"

I got a quick lesson on the steering wheel. A gauge would tell me if the wings were out of level. A few slight adjustments of the wheel would have them back to level. I got the feel of it quickly. He didn't point out our exact altitude on the altimeter, he just told me to keep the nose of the plane pointed at the horizon. I just knew that we were high. I didn't care how high so long as I didn't run out of oxygen and I couldn't see any chipmunks on the ground. Any place in between was alright by me.

Once the pilot felt some confidence in my steering he let go of his steering wheel and I was 'flying' the plane! It was exhilarating. The sky was clear and the early morning sun cast a warm glow on the lakes and trees below. Life was good. Or was it?

I noticed the pilot unfolding a large map. He kept staring at the map and then he would look intently out the window at the landscape below. He did this several times and then he slowly turned the map clockwise ninety degrees. We were lost! Oh my God! Doesn't this guy have to make it home every night? How could we be lost? We're lost!

He looked out the window a couple of more times before folding up the map and retaking control of the wheel. He must have seen the panic in my eyes as he smiled and pointed to a large lake ahead of us. He gave me a thumbs-up. I hoped he could find it the next week when he would fly out alone to pick us up at the end of the trip.

Once we had landed and the gear was safely stowed in the canoes we began the last leg of the trip. Quetico Provincial Park is a large nature preserve in south western Ontario. We were there for the fishing rather that simply camping and canoeing. Therefore, we had a six hour boat ride ahead of us to get us off the beaten trail.

The third portage we encountered was unlike the first two. The landing was rocky rather than sandy and the trail looked like it had stairs carved from the granite next to a small waterfall versus the grassy hills of the previous trails. The edges of the black granite stairs were covered with aluminum from the many canoes that had been dragged over the portage. As we approached the landing, which was at the edge of the known universe to me, I thought we had discovered a lost silver mine. However, I didn't want to appear greedy (or stupid) so rather than crying 'Eureka!', I asked Uncle Arlo what kind of rocks they might be.

He told me that it was a rare mineral found only in Canada and Argentina. It was called leverite. It was illegal to take it, but if I wanted to put a chunk of it into my backpack he wouldn't tell anyone. After going through customs and hearing all of those stories about the Mounties I wasn't about to take any. He kept trying to get me to put a five pound chunk into my pack. When I kept refusing he finally confessed that the ore was actually 'Leave-er-right' here. He just wanted to see if I would carry it back across all of those portages.

To make a short story long, we had a wonderful trip. I caught a 39 inch northern pike on the second day of the trip. It was the biggest fish I would catch for nearly thirty years although I always felt the next bigger one was just one cast away. Dad caught the biggest fish of the trip, a 42 incher, the following day. I can't say that I blame him for not allowing me to net it for him. Those canoes were a bit tippy and I was way more excited than he was. I was hooked on fishing up north for life.

Over these many years we have taken only one break from Canada to fish in the Ozarks twice. Catching fish that allow you to stick a thumb in their mouth and pick them up isn't nearly as dangerous or fun as catching those crazy pike. God willing, I will embark on my fortieth trip to Canada this summer. All of those have been with Dad. Many others have joined us off and on. The best fisherman of them all was Richie Hoz.

He was employed at the oil refinery where Dad worked. He was younger than Dad by about 15 years. Rich actually worked at fishing. He always had a line in the water. If he lost a lure and had to re-rig a pole he would have a jig hanging over the side with the handle of the pole under one cheek of his butt. He could fix any broken piece of equipment and be fishing at the same time.

Four years in a row Rich caught the biggest fish by stealing them at the boat. Dad or I would have a northern follow a lure up to the boat but not hit it. We would immediately figure 8 and jig the lure trying to entice the fish to hit. In the meantime Rich would finish his retrieve, notice the level of activity at the other end of the boat (Dad hollers for help while I tend to keep quiet about it!), drop his lure back in and catch the big one! I wouldn't mind so much, but we have bets riding on the biggest northern and walleye.

When Rich's son got old enough to go to the wilderness he eventually started his own family trips. On the first year of separate trips Rich and his group flew in on the plane that was picking us up. At this point Canada had banned motors from Quetico and we were going to a fly-in camp on the Ogoki Reservoir north of Thunder Bay. I had marked up a map with the best fishing holes that we had found. By one of the points a large X marked the location of a stick-up that I had identified by tacking a silver gum wrapper to it. I told Richie to tie off to that stick-up and he could catch all of the walleye he wanted. He did.

Upon returning home he called to thank me for the map. He ended up catching a ten pound walleye while tied off to that tree! For Ontario that is a huge fish (Lake Erie walleye are routinely larger) and, therefore, Rich had a taxidermist mount it for him. He brought it to my house to show it to me about nine months after his return. Less than a month later, Richie died from a heart attack. He was right around 50 years old.

I went to his wake and his son, Jay, had placed a picture of Rich holding up his ten pound walleye in the casket with him. He had a big smile on his face and the stick-up with the gum wrapper was in the background. I said some prayers and left the wake; I couldn't stay and face that picture without losing control of my emotions.

A few years later we were preparing for a return trip to the Ogoki. Two weeks before the trip I had a vivid dream about catching a big northern pike. No, it was THE big northern pike. Not only did I dream that I caught it, but where I caught it. And I told everyone that I was going to catch it and where I was going to catch it. Of course, that set me up for a good ribbing about it. One of my staff told her husband, Dave, about my dream. He drew a cartoon fish with big lips and long eyelashes with a thought bubble that said "Go for it, Big Boy". I took the cartoon with me to Canada and pinned it to the bunk with two fishing lures. I was going for it like I did every previous year, but this year I knew where to look.

On the fourth day of the six day trip I ran the motor for Dad. He hadn't had good fishing up to that point while my boat was the hot one. I guaranteed him a nice fish and around 11:00 in the morning we hit pay dirt. I trolled his line as close as I could to a drop off at the edge of a narrows in the flowage. My line was out in deeper water to keep it out of trouble. I knew Dad was about to hook a fish or a tree; I wasn't sure which would hit first. It was the fish, a beautiful 39 inch northern. I backed the boat into the deep water to give Dad some room to work with. The fish was hooked in the lip so the lure was easily removed, the fish measured and quickly released.

Dad was excited and felt he had just caught the big fish for the trip. I looked him right in the eye and said: "No, Dad. I'm catching the big guy tomorrow right down there by the big rock at Moose Crossing." It was just visible at the edge of the lake to our north. I was pointing at it and I was certain that the fish was waiting for me. Dad wished me luck.

The next day we awoke to a steady drizzle. The temperature wasn't bad for early September in Ontario....probably upper 50's judging by the color of my knuckles. There was a light chop on the water and the fishing was insane. Geoff's father-in-law, Buddy, was in the boat with me. He is the same age as my father and is also named Glen. The two of them are peas in the same pod. We couldn't go five minutes without a fish on. Whenever I asked Buddy where he wanted to fish next he would answer: "Wherever the front of the boat goes." It was going to Moose Crossing.

About one o'clock the rain stopped and the wind died down to nothing. The lake became a sheet of glass and the fishing just quit. We had finally fished our way to Moose Crossing. The other three boats had motored straight to it and had fished it heavily with great success. All three boats were at the big rock. Buddy and I decided to motor down and circle the wagons to see if they were ready to go in for lunch. As we approached I shut off the motor and coasted in between two of the boats. I knew that they had practically beaten the water to a froth around the big rock and I was resigned to just call it quits for the morning.

As we slid into position I thought to myself: "Big fish Rich would never just sit here without a line in the water." I picked up the first rod that my hand encountered and cast into the shallows next to the big rock. Even though Bob had just fished there a few seconds before, the lure hardly touched the water when the big one hit.

If you have seen the movie 'Pirates of the Caribbean' you will recall the seen when the gold coin hits the water and sends out a shock wave. That is what it looked like when this fish hit. I immediately recognized the scene as my dream. I knew exactly how to play him and he never had a chance to get away. I looked up as I set the hook and thought 'Thanks, Richie.' I'm certain he sent me that fish. I just know that he was thanking me for his big walleye and it was his way of telling me that he is OK up there. I had some doubts.

Unfortunately, the fish hit so hard and fast that he was hooked in the gills. I tried for half an hour to revive him, but he was belly up from the outset. I now have a 43 inch northern on my wall. It is over the desk in my new office despite the objections of our interior decorator. There is a plaque beneath it, a gift from Dad, that reads:

Ogoki Reservior
Sept. 2005
43 inches
25 pounds
Thanks, Richie.

I had a picture of me with the big fish in my exam room. It disappeared for awhile. I thought that it had been misplaced and thought nothing more of it. For my birthday I received a T-shirt with a silk-screen of the picture and a caption that read *I had a dream!*

*Me at 3 years of age with my big catch.*
*I never was afraid to touch a wild beast.*

*At my grandparents house in northern*
*Wisconsin. I was lying about the size*
*of the fish that got away.*

*The big boy that took me 35 years to*
*finally haul in. I can stop lying about the*
*size of my big fish.*

*Dave Mondo's cartoon fish with the*
*'Go for it Big Boy' attitude.*

GO FOR IT BIG BOY!

# CHAPTER 12

## *Light at the Start of the Tunnel*

The Monday after graduation found me at work. I was eager to get started for a variety of reasons. Mostly, it was because I was finally ready to play in the big leagues. I had paid my dues in the minors for long enough. Casey was ready to bat. Now, where do we keep the bats?

Fortunately, Dr. Velders was very organized. Or should I say that the staff kept him organized. The handful of nurses and receptionists had been with him for a number of years. They knew him and his foibles and he knew theirs. They kept pointing me in the right direction in order to get me (and them) through the day in a timely fashion. My schedule was fairly light and routine. Nobody wants to see the new grad with a sick pet!

I have always been terrible at remembering names. Therefore, I try to associate names with a physical characteristic of the person or some other place or thing that might trigger the production of useful brain waves. I asked Sue if she was married to a lawyer. When introduced to Carol I shook her hand and said, "I'll probably remember you around Christmas." With her motherly charm Carol looked at Dr. Velders and said, "This is going to be a sassy one!" I do declare that she was correct.

I was treated to a crash course on the workings of a busy clinic that day. The nurses acted as receptionists and vice versa. Everyone seemed capable of doing everything which was good because there was a lot to do. There were no emergency clinics at the time so it behooved us to get everyone taken care of during regular hours. Afterwards, you would be coming in alone to get the work done.

One of the most rewarding aspects of working at BRVC was the mentoring I received. The veterinarian that I was replacing stayed on for the first week of my debut to help me get my bearings. Dr. Velders loved to perform and teach surgeries. He would always be willing to share his cases and answer questions about mine. He also seemed genuinely interested in what I had learned in school and if it conflicted with what he had been taught or experienced then the debate was on…you needed to support your ideas with sound science.

He was also willing to buy new toys, oops, equipment, for the practice. If you could justify the expense of new technology he was very willing to purchase it. One of my professors was fond of telling the students that you should never be the last kid on the block to throw out an old toy, but don't be the first to buy a new one either. Let someone else work out the bugs and learn from their experience. Very often, I discovered that certain new treatments weren't so desirable to have around once some long term data was published. The word spreads quickly if adverse events are associated with a product, especially if you attend continuing education meetings and talk to colleagues.

With everyone interested in molding me into a useful member of the practice the time flew by. Within a week I was holding my own in the exam rooms. The clients seemed to accept me with open arms despite my youthful appearance. With my lack of years (only 24 of them), facial hair and poundage I looked like I had just graduated from high school. However, I had no problem with clients doubting my abilities. They appreciated my listening and communication skills. I have always been able to explain complicated medical conditions in simple terms. That is due in large part to my blue collar heritage. I tend to understand things in simple terms so that is how I relate them back to others. I am sincere in my feelings and beliefs. People tend to appreciate simple and sincere in this complicated world we have built.

By the end of my first week of practice everyone agreed that I really didn't need another doctor holding my hand every moment of the day. It was time to be on my own. Dr. Velders was available by phone if there were any adventures in the making. I was determined that wouldn't happen. The man deserved his personal time. They denied it, but I suspect that the staff was keeping him updated on my progress behind my back.

Wednesday was my first day alone. The morning surgeries had been carefully scheduled so as not to put a lot of stress on me or the staff. Melinda, the most experienced of the assistants, was very self assured. She ran a tight ship for me for the same reasons I was determined to do a good job for my clients and the clinic… she loved animals and the people that own them.

The surgeries went well. No emergencies popped up that might have distracted me. We stayed on schedule and we even had time to eat lunch and discuss a few things.

Melinda was just a bit younger than I was. She had been working with Dr. Velders since shortly after he opened the practice. She was in high school at the time. Her credentials were experience. She intended to go to veterinary school, but she just couldn't take tests very well. I would discover that one of the flaws in our system is that it excludes people like Melinda. She could diagnose illnesses better than half the vets in the area. Her technical skills were outstanding and she was great with people and pets in any circumstances. Although she isn't a veterinarian, 'Mindy' continues to work with animals and has been very successful in life. She currently runs animal control for a major metropolitan area.

The afternoon was humming along until a case presented that

seemed at first blush to be a routine case of dietary indiscretion. Two sisters, a spinster and a widow, lived together with their little mixed-breed dog. The dog was acting normally, but had vomited several times after eating a variety of table foods. What wasn't written in the history was the vitriol directed at the front desk because Dr. Velders wasn't there. They had followed him to Burr Ridge from his previous clinic. They had known him since he was a new graduate and they had *trained* him through their previous dogs' illnesses. They were adamant that he should be summoned from home to come in and evaluate their dog. They were *Velderites*!

I quickly learned that Velderites come in a wide variety of tones. Most were very accommodating towards me as I always commiserated that I liked to see my own doctor whenever possible, but in an emergency I would trust his associate to care for me. However, I also trusted that my concerns would be relayed to my primary care physician as soon as possible. I was always careful to alert Dr. Velders to their pets' problems (and shift the responsibility for them to him as quickly as possible). My first experience would prove to be one of the toughest. They were hardcore.

Everything I said was questioned. They would openly debate each other as to whether or not 'Dr. Velders would do that'. Invariably the answer was no. Thankfully, the dog was wagging his tail and licking my face. He wasn't seriously ill. He had no fever or abdominal discomfort. He still wanted to eat and drink. We decided that he could survive the night with conservative treatment and see Dr. Velders in the morning if he was still sick.

To my surprise, they took the medication and dietary instructions I had prescribed and followed them meticulously. They came back the next day for a recheck with Dr. Velders. Actually, they felt that this was the REAL office visit. Their dog was back to normal, but they wanted to be sure that I had prescribed the right medicine and had not missed anything important. Dr. Velders assured them that I had done the right things and then told them very seriously: "I won't be here forever and it's a good thing that you got to know Dr. Greiner with a minor problem rather than a big one." They were still wary of me for a long time and they made no effort to hide it. They were very intimidating to me and it seemed that their dog only got sick on Wednesdays!

Twenty years later those same clients give me a big kiss on the cheek before leaving from an office visit and they tell me that they love me. I give them a hug and genuinely return their love. Last year I went to Kelly's wake after visiting her in the nursing home several times. I was relieved to see so much family support for her surviving sister, Jackie. Their puppy graces the cover of this book (well, it's body does at least). I worry about and pray for my clients every day; especially the sick and the elderly. They don't prepare you for that level of attachment in vet school, but you learn it pretty quickly on your own if you have an open heart.

At the end of my second week of practice I received my first paycheck. My head was swimming with ideas. I had never collected a paycheck that wasn't going towards necessities…mostly tuition. I would spend it on baseball equipment, hockey gear, fishing tackle, a nice meal. Wait a second, forget that last one. I was really enjoying Mom's cooking after seven years of eating mostly college food.

When my next check arrived two weeks later I still hadn't cashed the first one. I was $1500 dollars in debt with my student loan, but I still had $1000 in the bank. I didn't want to be one of those people who pay interest so I paid off my student loan with my first two paychecks. Also, I wanted another student to have the same chance at a loan that I had. It meant a lot to have that cushion in case some unforeseen need arose. Sadly, today there are few students that leave college with a degree and less than five-figure indebtedness. Many are well into six figures. Imagine starting your career with a house payment and no roof over your head!

I felt that the many years of hard work had finally paid off. More importantly, the good decisions I made over the past ten years had left me in the driver's seat. I was able to turn down a position offering more money in favor of one that would offer more professional satisfaction. The facts that I am still at the same clinic 25 years later and that the other clinic has gone through a new associate every few years certainly prove that I made the right choice.

One of the more challenging aspects of my first year in practice was being on call at night. There was nowhere to go for emergencies except to your usual vet. That meant that the two doctors in our practice would be on call half of the time. Two nights a week and every other weekend were spent by the phone (no cell phones back then). That wasn't so bad at first, but as we neared expansion to a third doctor it became burdensome. Not only were we insanely busy throughout the day, but the call volume at night had increased proportionately.

Most of the calls were just that, calls. You could answer most of the concerns and make recommendations over the phone or call in medications to the pharmacy. However, there were many times when I would get home and need to get right back into the car and drive back to the office.

Despite the long hours, emergency work is very rewarding. I did many surgeries with no help except that offered by the owners. That even included caesarean sections. I would first try to deliver the puppies or, rarely, kittens vaginally by giving oxytocin to induce contractions of the uterus. If we met with no success or if the reluctant mother was in obvious distress we would go straight to surgery. I would prep the abdomen for surgery and have the owner stay with her pet while I set up the surgery room and scrubbed in. I would then have the owner administer the injectable anesthesia through the previously placed IV line per my directions. As quickly as possible I would get the newborns out and hand them to the owner who would immediately start drying and reviving them.

Things got pretty hectic if it was a large litter or if the new arrivals weren't coming around very well. I would scrub out and help the owner stimulate breathing in the newborns as I continued to monitor the mother as she slept on the table. I would then scrub back in to finish the surgery. I think my liability insurance carrier would have a coronary if that went on today. With the litigious society we have now, I would be afraid of a lawsuit if an owner dropped a puppy. That is a shame because having someone help deliver his or her own pups builds a phenomenal bond between them, their dog and their vet. They also see how much effort and emotion goes into the procedure on the part of the vet....especially if any of the pups die or must be euthanized due to congenital defects. It also gives the vet an opportunity to showcase his or her knowledge a bit as the owner is given a crash course in what they are doing to help and why.

With the proliferation of specialty and emergency clinics we no longer take our own emergencies at night. That is mostly due to the excellent level of care given at these facilities. They are fully staffed all night long. Our patients get immediate help by well trained vets with a lot of support staff. We are no longer maintaining the standard of care in our area when we come in alone to care for some of these critical cases.

I must admit that I don't miss coming in to the office at 3:00 in the morning, but I am very glad that I had the opportunity to do so. I feel that our new graduates should all have the same experience. Heat and pressure applied to the carbon of inexperience turn it into the diamonds of the profession.

*During my first week in practice Mrs. Harrison brought in her intact male Chow dog for a routine visit. He seemed very manageable, contrary to the reputation his breed has. He was licking my hands as I drew his blood for a heartworm test and his tail never missed a beat as I administered two inoculations.*

*When I turned his records over to make some notes I noticed the big red letters warning WATCH BITES MUZZLE that had been underlined at the top of the page. Mrs. Harrison started telling me that Dr. Velders always muzzled him and Dr. Nancy had to take him in back for the staff to hold him. "You handled him very nicely, doctor." My only explanation was the liver-scented aftershave I splashed on each morning. Whatever it was, I could have done anything to that dog and he wouldn't object at all. However, if he even saw Dr. Velders he would go right at him, teeth bared. No one was happier than Dr. V. that I took over that patient.*

*I was called to the clinic to attend to an emergency one Thanksgiving evening. Pixie, a five year old miniature schnauzer had gotten into the garbage while the family went out for an after dinner drink. Upon returning home they found Pixie lying on her side with a distended abdomen. She could barely breathe and she was nearly unresponsive. I thought at first that she was suffering from bloat, a condition in which the stomach twists and becomes distended with gas. However, when I gave the stomach a plunk with my index finger it didn't ping like a basketball. It sounded solid.*

*A radiograph confirmed that Pixie had gorged herself. She was so full that there was food filling the last one third of the esophagus; there was no room in the stomach for it. The stomach was so distended that Pixie couldn't move her diaphragm; she was literally turning blue from the compression on her lungs.*

*I decided to weigh Pixie before I made her vomit. She went from 12 pounds before vomiting to eight pounds afterwards. She consumed the equivalent of 50% of her body weight! Her mom called the following day to tell me that Pixie went home and headed straight for the garbage can. A trip to the vomitorium and she was ready to party again!*

# CHAPTER 13

# Organ-Eyed Medicine

When interviewing for a potential position as a new associate you will need to concern yourself with perks. Besides the usual work schedule, pay and vacation time, there are other means of compensation. As a professional you will need time off for continuing education. Preferably, lots of it because your diploma is a passport to continue learning for the rest of your life.

In the state of Illinois we are required to attend 30 hours of C.E. every two years in order to maintain a veterinary license. As a practical matter, you need much more than that in order to keep up with the rapid changes within the profession. The doctors in our practice are expected to summarize important new information gleaned from meetings. By sharing it with the other doctors we hope to be approaching 100 hours of advanced learning each year.

In addition to keeping up with the medical, surgical and technological breakthroughs that occur with amazing speed and regularity in veterinary medicine, continuing education meetings also help you build and maintain relationships with colleagues.

Veterinarians are relatively few in number compared to our human medicine counterparts. This allows us to communicate more effectively on an individual basis and as a whole. We are very responsive to changes in the profession and we try to act in a proactive manner to head off potential problems before they create trouble.

Dr. Velders insisted that I enroll as a member of the Chicago **V**eterinary **M**edical **A**ssociation as well as the Illinois State VMA and the American VMA. The practice paid for my dues in each of these organizations, but I had to do my part by attending some meetings and by reading my journals and bulletins from the associations.

The state and national meetings were difficult to attend because they lasted several days and it was difficult for the doctor left behind to keep up with the hours and workload. However, the CVMA meetings were very easy to attend. The Tuesday-evening meetings were at a hotel located only eight miles from the clinic. There were eight meetings throughout the year and six of them were followed by an all day seminar on Wednesday.

The seminars were impressive, but equally as important I was able to meet many of the veterinarians in nearby practices. It seemed as though everyone knew Dr. Velders. He was active in the association for a number of years and he took referral cases from many of the member clinics. I felt confirmed in my decision to work with him when I saw the respect he received from the other established professionals. I was proud that he was my sponsor as I applied for membership in the best local association of veterinarians in the country. I can still say that after knowing many of the members for twenty-five years.

It seemed expected that I would be taking the same path as Dr. Velders. The other doctors were interested in my progress and often asked what types of referrals I would be taking. I had no answer for them at first. I was still treading water and looking for a lifeboat on many days. As I gained experience and confidence things slowly began to change.

There is always a lineup of challenging cases that are dancing on your brain at any given time. This is particularly true early in your career as you struggle to organize the information crammed into your brain and apply it in a logical manner to your cases. It became apparent to the other vets that I was paying attention at the seminars when I started to ask specific questions about particular cases of mine that were pertinent to the lectures. I was especially heartened to have my colleagues approach me before and after the seminars to discuss my experiences and share their knowledge with me.

There is an old joke in the medical professions that if you have seen only one case of an illness you start your comments with "In my experience…." If you have seen two cases of an illness you may state: "Over and over I've seen……" Once you are on your third case you can drop the façade and speak with some degree of authority. Despite starting many of my stories with "In my experience…." there seemed to be an interest in what I had to say. It was heartening to be taken seriously. We were becoming colleagues.

Since I was attending meetings with great regularity I became an obvious target for the executive board. After one of the seminars a committee member approached me. If this ever happens to you, run. Or fake a seizure. At least drool a little and pick lint off of your shirt. Do whatever it takes to avoid eye contact. I didn't. The long and the short of it is that I was volunteered to do committee work. I was now truly a part of organized medicine.

The Continuing Education Committee was the backbone of the organization. In addition to collecting dues, the main source of income for the CVMA is selling C.E. packages. Members got a break on the price over non-members (they were frowned upon as people that wanted the benefits of organized medicine but didn't want to contribute towards it). The meetings could be purchased separately or as a package at a much better price. Each meeting had a corporate sponsor that would help defray the expenses for the speaker. The topics for the meetings would be decided by the

C.E. committee and approved by the board as a whole. We kept track of the topics from previous years and made a determined effort not to repeat subjects too closely.

My mission, whether or not I chose to accept it, was to find a speaker for one of the selected topics. I had to contact the speaker to get a commitment from him/her and then set up travel arrangements and accommodations. The contact person was also responsible for transportation from the airport to the hotel, to the Tuesday meeting, to the hotel, to the Wednesday meeting, to the hotel, to the airport again. You also had to set up the equipment for the speaker (a mike and projector back then) and make certain that they got paid their honorarium before they left. Most important, you had to find a sponsor for that meeting (i.e. you needed to beg the corporations for help).

This sounds like an awful lot of work, but it turned out to be a breeze! Nearly all of the speakers had previous experience with sponsors that supported their work (usually with products used for that specialty). It was great fun to call on world renowned experts and offer them a free trip to Chicago along with an honorarium that was competitive with the national associations. After all, the CVMA represented the second largest constituency of all of the local associations in the country. We took great pride in the quality of our speakers and the quality of their experience in coming to Chicago. The contact person treated the speaker to a nice dinner before the meeting. Both meals were included on the tab as a reward for their time and effort. It was well worth the effort as I was able to rub elbows with some of the most respected experts in the profession on an informal basis. It turns out that they put their pants on one leg at a time, too. However, their professional britches seem much bigger than mine.

When I joined the committee we were under pressure to expand enrollment in the C.E. packages as sales had begun to slip. Many members felt that the quality of the educational experience was declining. This was due in large part to the set up at the facility.

The meetings started at 9:00 a.m. and coffee and doughnuts were served at the back of the room. At each break a large throng would form at the back of the room. Many people ran into classmates and longtime friends that they hadn't seen for years. They would catch up on personal matters while many others would discuss cases or business. When it came time to resume the conference it was difficult to get people to take their seats. It was often difficult to hear the speaker over their ongoing conversations. I felt embarrassed for the contact person, the speaker and the organization when this happened and it happened at almost every seminar.

Therefore, when I took charge of my first speaker I came prepared. I brought the whistle that I used when refereeing hockey games. It was piercing and loud. It was exceptionally effective at getting the immediate attention of anyone within earshot.

When the end of the first break came I politely asked people to take their seats. Over the next few moments about half of them did. I remained at the podium smiling at the cooperative attendants and twirling the whistle by its chain. They knew what was coming. I finally gave one short blast of the whistle. Dead silence ensued followed by some scattered laughs as the realization of what happened sunk in. I announced the resumption of 'class' (the double meaning was lost on them). At the end of the next break I simply stood there twirling the whistle. A murmur of scattered laughs immediately went through the seated participants. The people at the back of the room turned to see what was so funny. They took their seats without hesitation before I had a chance to blast them again. As I announced the resumption of lecture I thanked them for being even more trainable than Pavlov's dogs! From that point on pretty much everyone knew who I was...the guy with the whistle. I never had to use it again despite running many such meetings. In fact, I was doing such a bang up job that I eventually became chairman of the committee.

At the first committee meeting with me at the helm we decided that the CVMA needed to regain its reputation as a leader in C.E. Despite our limited budget I wanted to bring in a speaker from New Zealand. I had heard of Dr. Builford through a friend. He was a very progressive speaker and was very popular when he spoke at a national conference that this friend had attended. The cost of transportation from New Zealand would be a big issue for the board. The travel time might be a big issue for Dr. Builford especially for such a short seminar.

Since we were planning a year in advance and phone calls across an ocean were quite expensive, I wrote to invite Dr. Builford to Chicago. He contacted me from the university where he was teaching. He informed me that he would be in California for six months doing a research project and that he would be delighted to come to Chicago during his time in The States. He would take the opportunity to visit and stay with family in the suburbs of Chicago. That meant no hotel costs and a flight from southern California instead of New Zealand! He even suggested a sponsor that would pay his travel and stipend costs, and they did. Even better, his family picked him up from the airport which saved me two trips to O'Hare airport. Unfortunately, that also meant that I would have limited personal contact with a very interesting person.

Dr. Builford lectured on oxygen derived free radicals and their involvement with many disease processes. At that time no one had any awareness of oxygen free radicals or their role in the body. Many of us heard it first at CVMA. Of course, anti-oxidant therapy is now very popular in the treatment and prevention of many diseases.

The C.E. committee was blessed with a great lineup of speakers over the next few years. We changed venues to much nicer facilities and the enrolment expanded at a steady pace. Things were well organized and running smoothly. A bit too smoothly. I became a target again.

I was asked to advance to a position on the executive board of the CVMA. It was a three year sentence, er, term. As chairman of a committee I was already attending the board meetings regularly. There were some things that I wanted to change or improve, so I jumped at the chance to have more of a voice in the organization.

The installation of new board members takes place during the annual Installation Dinner Dance. This is a formal affair held at varying venues but generally located in downtown Chicago. This would be my first real black tie affair.

Knowing that I would be introduced to a rather large showing of the membership I wanted to look my best. I bought my first tuxedo. As of this writing it remains my only tuxedo. I needed some help from the staff at the men's shop. I was offered several options, but I wasn't satisfied with any of them. I finally took a good, long look around the store. I pointed at a rather smartly dressed mannequin and asked the salesman, "Can you make this dummy look like that dummy?"

He did. And I must admit that I looked rather dashing. A black tux with a white shirt was accented with a midnight blue bowtie and matching cummerbund. Shirt studs and cufflinks completed the ensemble. I even smelled great with the addition of some eau de toilet. I still have a problem wearing anything with the word toilet in it. Yes, it was still me beneath those new threads. You can dress me up and you can take me out, but you can't always get me back home.

The theme for the evening was magic. A magician was engaged to provide a show for the troops. Little foil stars, moons, hearts and other objects were sprinkled on the tables to enhance the mood. The problem at my table was the mood. I was rather upbeat about the festivities and so was my date. However, the other four couples at our table seemed to be incapable of having a good time.

Despite my best efforts at initiating a conversation there was none to be had. The couples weren't even talking with each other. It was comical at first, but as I realized that these truly were dead fish I became determined to revive them. I took a shiny gold star about the size of a quarter, wetted it and stuck it to my forehead.

My date was taken by surprise, but she remained composed and started to laugh quietly. This was, in fact, a formal and fairly staid event and she was trying not to draw too much attention to our table. After about a minute had elapsed she suggested I take it off. I insisted that it was going to stay put until someone at the table at least acknowledged it. No one ever did. So there it stayed even as the emcee began the program.

After several announcements of general information he began the introduction of the board members. The new members went last. As each member was introduced he/she went on stage and formed a line. I was third from the last to go up. I was so intent on not stumbling over my own feet that I completely forgot about the prominent star on my forehead. As I took my place in line, a wave of laughter passed across the room.

I discreetly looked down and was relieved to find that my tuxedo was in order. I ran through a checklist of what could have gone wrong. No food, drink or blood on my shirt. The tie was facing forward. The tux didn't appear to be see-through. It finally dawned on me that the star was still in place. Nothing to do now but go with it, smile and chalk it up to yet another memorable moment in front of the CVMA members. I got a good ribbing at the next board meeting.

Since this was a volunteer position and since I had made an impressive introduction of myself at the dinner dance I decided to exploit the opportunity to move things along at that next meeting. Besides, what could they do, fire me?

The meetings needed to be held at a time that made it possible for a majority of the members to attend. For many years the most effective time was 8:00 p.m. in the middle of the week. That wouldn't have been too bad if not for the fact that the meetings ran until after 11:00 most of the time. There was too much wasted time and I was losing my beauty sleep. This was unacceptable so I decided to speed things up.

When someone had trouble phrasing a motion I would politely interrupt them and make the motion for them. They would happily second it and the president would then open it up for discussion. When it became apparent that the discussion was becoming circular I would immediately make a motion for a vote......seconded and done. Let's move on. I think the longest meeting during my tenure ended at 10:30. We got things done.

One of the most frustrating discussions I endured at the CVMA was focused on the rescheduling of a board meeting. We had the perfect storm of national and state meetings heading our way. There were so many board members going to the meetings that we wouldn't have a quorum for that month. Unfortunately, our lawyer was in attendance that night and he suggested that we couldn't just cancel or reschedule the meeting. We would need to call the meeting to order, wait an appropriate amount of time, declare that there wasn't a quorum and then reschedule the meeting for the following week.

I didn't want to challenge a lawyer who had been with the association for twenty years (and he took the reins from his father who was with CVMA for a generation of vets before him). However, I also didn't feel it was prudent to spend the money for a meeting room and waste the time showing up just to reschedule the meeting for another night. I suggested we hold the meeting at one of our clinics. That opened Pandora's box!

The by-laws had to be examined to see if we could change the venue. While the expedition crept through the jungle of rules the discussion continued. Wouldn't we need more than one person to show up for the meeting in order to reschedule the meeting? If we held it at a clinic would that be unfair advertising for that clinic when it was published in the bulletin? It went to vets only.... were they worried that other vets would send their pets to that clinic? Was there prestige to be gained by hosting a meeting with no quorum? This was getting ridiculous.

I suggested that I take the gavel with me and call the meeting to order in the vestibule of the hotel in order to save the expense of renting a meeting room. I would bring a bag of walnuts. When they were gone or if the gavel broke while cracking the nuts I would declare that we didn't have a quorum, announce the date for the rescheduled meeting and leave. If someone else would like to show up that would be fine, but if we had a disagreement I would end it by using the gavel in an inappropriate manner. That got a laugh from everyone but the lawyer. He was determined to ensure the integrity of CVMA.

Finally, a solution was found in the by-laws. The meeting date could be changed by publishing the change in the newsletter one and two months before the change of date. Hurrah for us! It actually took over an hour to figure that out. Then someone had the nerve to make a motion that we review the by-laws. Was this because the by-laws worked or because he just looked at them for the first time? I immediately suggested that we needed to deal with that as new business at another meeting or simply hand it to the judicial committee for consideration. That was greeted with looks of relief from everyone but the head of the judicial committee. We moved on.

Half way through my tenure as a three year board member I was approached by the board president and asked to take over the treasurer's job. I had no experience on a computer at the time and all of the records were run on a software package. I agreed to look things over before saying no.

What a mess! The former treasurer had no idea what was what. She would pay bills twice, get a refund of the extra payment and record it as income. Thankfully, she never threw a single piece of paper into the trash. It was all there in a brown expandable file that ominously resembled an accordion without keys. The word on the street was that she had resigned. If this was a mafia job they would have been searching the canals for her. I had less than 24 hours before my first board meeting as treasurer and the president had just informed me that there were 'problems with the budget'.

I've never been able to solve problems late at night. A good night's sleep always makes solutions come easier. Therefore, when I showed up for the meeting the following day I had spent only an hour or so going over the mess I had inherited. It was already apparent that this would be the death of at least one entire weekend trying to straighten it out. I was not prepared for the impending level of wrath awaiting the treasurer. The former treasurer probably was; thus the status of being the *former* treasurer.

The entire board was in attendance. That never happens. Some committees have little to present to the board and some members get stuck at work and can't get to the meeting. The agenda looked unremarkable. After the meeting was called to order a motion was made to skip directly to the treasurer's report. Gulp. I thought I heard someone mutter 'Get a rope'. I was introduced as the new sacrificial, oops, interim treasurer and the questions immediately came at me in very unfriendly terms. I expected to be eviscerated. Is this what they mean by organ-eyed medicine?

Rather than run (the door was covered), I very deliberately stood up and requested order in the room. With some help from the president's gavel a silence came over the room. All eyes were on me as I calmly announced that I agreed that everything was a mess. I had stepped in it only yesterday and I didn't have time to even wipe my feet yet. Thankfully, I hadn't fallen into it and had to wipe something else. They seemed to appreciate the humor and, also, the fact that they hadn't been asked to do it themselves. I said that I would come to the next meeting with orderly finances and an explanation. I did.

In examining the finances the first thing I noticed was the exceptionally high income we had enjoyed over the previous year. That happens when you pay bills twice and record it as income (instead of a negative expense). The next thing I noticed was that almost all of our money was in a single signature account. I was responsible for it as my signature card had just been signed and filed with the bank. It was a considerable amount because dues and C.E. monies had just come in. I transferred all of it to a two signature account so that our bill payments would need to be seen and signed by a higher authority than me. This got yours truly out of a pot of hot water…the board quickly voted to make this a permanent set up. A second checking account with a single signature was made available for paying small bills. It was also used as a petty cash account if minor matters arose suddenly.

The term of office for the treasurer was two years, but since I switched hats in midstream it was expected that I would move up to the role of secretary at the end of my shortened, nine month term. That would be followed by a term as president-elect and then president. At the time I had become involved with human healthcare reform at the national level. Specifically, it involved medical savings accounts. I was a board member for Americans for Intelligent Healthcare Reform and it was taking up a good chunk of my time. Therefore, I decided to leave the board of the CVMA. I thank them for the very professional manner in which the meetings were conducted. My experience there bolstered my effectiveness in future endeavors on other boards.

I continue to enjoy the camaraderie of the CVMA members. It is particularly fun when I receive a call asking for advice or my opinion on issues before the board. In fact, I received a call asking me to rejoin the C. E. committee the day after I finished writing this chapter! I must have been sending out some good vibrations that showed up as a blip on their radar. I declined the offer for now, but once this book is out of my brain I will likely need to volunteer for some sort of duty again. Who knows what kind of mess I will encounter. When I jump back in it will be with both feet!

*My staff came to know my busy schedule with the CVMA as the nights that 'Greiner has to get out of here'. I had a particularly hectic day before one of the meetings. That was mainly due to a dog that was admitted for persistent, severe vomiting. He was a new patient and his owner was a new client. It was determined that he had a foreign body in his stomach and proximal small intestines. Dr. Rooney had admitted the dog and run the diagnostics so my exposure to the owner was through phone calls to introduce myself as the surgeon and to give updates postoperatively.*

*I performed a gastrotomy to remove a pair of bluish green women's underwear. It wasn't immediately clear if the green was due to the stomach environment or if they had started out as that color. As usually happens with such objects they left the room quickly (they smelled terrible). The owner knew where they came from and asked that we not save them for her. They did, in fact, belong to her and the mystery of their disappearance was solved.*

*I have a colleague that removed a set of underwear from a dog that turned out to belong to someone other than the Mrs. That one ended up in divorce court; uncontested….he was busted.*

*At any rate, when I got to the CVMA board meeting that night I was running a bit late. Everyone was seated around the table as I sat down and opened my briefcase to retrieve the agenda for the meeting. I immediately started laughing. Our board president at the time was a woman. Marla asked me what was so funny and would I care to share it with the board.*

*I reached into the briefcase and pulled out the largest pair of bluish green women's underwear I have ever seen. It was the largest pair of women's underwear I have ever seen of any color! To add to my embarrassment, along with the laughter came Marla's voice: "Why Gregg, you've lost so much weight!"*

*I didn't know what to say. Hopefully, the look on my reddening face said it all. I was too busy contemplating who it was that I would have to get even with to come up with anything resembling a witty reply. It turns out that it was the entire staff that pitched in to launder the underwear and get it into my, appropriately named, brief case.*

# CHAPTER 14

# *Hall Monitor*

During senior year of veterinary school you are required to present some cases from a review of the veterinary literature. This is done in order to help you become familiar with the literature that is available to you and to ensure that you are capable of presenting a formal case report should the need arise. For example, one such occasion would be during the process of seeking board certification as a specialist. Currently, there is also a certification through the Board of Veterinary Practitioners that wasn't available when I graduated in 1982.

One of my classmates presented a paper on hyperthyroidism in cats. It was thought to be somewhat of a curiosity. Three cases were found and reported in 1980. I attended a seminar in 1983. The presenter had found fifty cases since the initial cases were reported. At that time no thyroid testing was routinely done in cats. In fact, the thyroid was generally ignored because cats don't suffer from the low thyroid function problems that so often afflict dogs and people.

Cats with elevated thyroid values suffer from an array of

symptoms. Thyroid hormone is a general stimulating hormone that affects every system in the body. Cats with elevated levels of the hormone thyroxin suffer from rapid weight loss despite a normal or greatly elevated appetite. They drink and urinate excessively thus resembling a patient with diabetes. They may have behavioral problems associated with brain dysfunction; this can be severe in people with hyperthyroidism (Grave's disease). The heart rate and blood pressure are often very elevated. I remember scoffing at that last bit. I had never checked the blood pressure on a pet except in physiology lab with a central catheter placed into the aorta under general anesthesia. That was a major undertaking and it didn't tell you what a normal pressure was with the pet awake. I never suspected we would one day check blood pressures routinely using Doppler units.

The blood tests in cats with hyperthyroidism often show elevated liver enzymes. This was thought to be associated with liver damage due to high blood pressure. We now know that it is due to the elevated metabolic activity seen in the liver and that it is completely reversible with treatment. The kidney values tend to elevate. This can be caused by the high blood pressure creating damage to the kidneys. Without the benefit of knowing the status of thyroid levels many of these cats would be diagnosed as primary heart, liver or kidney failure patients and would be doomed to die because the underlying cause of the illness wasn't being addressed.

This disease was so new that appropriate therapies had not been developed. Radioactive iodine wouldn't be a viable treatment for years to come and there was too little experience with anti-thyroid drugs to make them a meaningful option. Surgery was considered to be extremely risky. Nearly half of the cats in the initial study died during the attempt to remove the thyroid tumors which cause the overproduction of thyroid hormone. The cause of these deaths was cardiac arrest shortly after induction of inhalant anesthesia.

Sure enough, with a few weeks of attending the meeting I was presented with a cat that had virtually every symptom of hyperthyroidism. Our local laboratory had to send the submitted serum sample to Michigan State University for the thyroid test because they didn't have enough experience to have normal values for cats. The results came back a week later and the levels were way above normal. My first case! Now what?

Fortunately, one of the optional rotations that I took during my senior year of vet school was advanced anesthesia. The students were introduced to some non-standard techniques for anesthesia and pain management. One of the cutting-edge drugs that wasn't generally available in practice was an inhalant anesthetic called isoflurane. We were allowed to go to the anesthesia lab and anesthetize one cat using "Iso". The induction period was very short and smooth. Our monitors showed that the cardiopulmonary function was maintained far better on Iso than on other inhaled anesthetic agents. The recovery was short and smooth. This stuff was great! However, we were told that it was so expensive that it would never be widely used by veterinarians. I decided to see if that was still true.

After a thorough review of the anesthetic properties and costs associated with using Isoflurane I made a pitch to Dr. Velders. I decided that the cause of death for the cats in the initial study was probably the use of the current gold standard in anesthesia, halothane. It sensitizes the heart to adrenalin which results in an extremely high risk of abnormal heart rhythms. Cats with hyperthyroidism are adrenalin machines. The halothane was stopping their hearts. Isoflurane, on the other hand, actually desensitizes the heart to adrenalin making it an ideal agent for anesthetizing these patients. It had become the agent of choice in human medicine which resulted in bringing down the cost considerably. In fact, with the current promotion (a free anesthetic vaporizer with the purchase of a minimum order of anesthetic agent), the added cost to the client would be about $10 per patient. Dr. V immediately approved the investment in the new equipment.

Thyroid surgery in humans is notoriously bloody. The

parathyroids are important little glands that regulate the blood calcium levels. They must be preserved by removing them from the very vascular thyroid gland. Also, people have an isthmus of tissue that connects the left and right thyroids. The surgeon is forced to go through this tissue to preserve as much normal thyroid as possible. Since there was little experience with cats in the literature I went in prepared for a long and bloody battle.

I was pleasantly surprised by the ease of thyroidectomy (removal of the thyroid) in cats. There are two distinct thyroids that are easily found by making a small incision on the midline below the larynx (voice box) and separating, rather than cutting, the muscles. The parathyroids are easily identified and preserved via careful dissection. There are only two blood vessels to deal with and they are easily identified. The closure is a breeze and the recovery is virtually pain free.

The key to doing feline thyroid surgeries back then was that you needed to have Isoflurane anesthesia available for your patients. Our clinic was the only game in town except for one or two specialists that practiced a fair distance from Burr Ridge. We took referrals from far and wide until other vets got on the Iso boat some years later. I had several vets continue to refer cats for thyroid surgery even after they had Iso available in their practice. Once they came to our practice to scrub in on a thyroid patient they each wondered why they had been so worried about attempting it.

One of our early hyperthyroid patients was a 19 year old grey and white female domestic shorthair cat, Midge, belonging to an elderly couple, the Halls. Howard and Irma weren't just elderly. They were downright old.

They ended up spending a lot of time at the clinic because Midge did so well that she lived to be over twenty years old. She eventually developed diminished heart and kidney function. She needed medication, fluids and a special diet. The Halls couldn't administer the treatments at home. Therefore, they drove an hour each way to the clinic three days a week so that Dr. Velders could treat Midge for them.  Of course, if he wasn't there then I would take over.

Howard always wore his blue pinstripe suit and cute little fedora.  Irma wore her light blue floral print dress.  They would stay for an hour after Midge got her pills because, "If she vomits in the car on the way home we'll have to turn around so you can give them to her again."

The main concern for all of us wasn't Midge; she was a trooper.  It was Howard.  He had narcolepsy.  When you spoke to Howard he would nod his head and give you a cute little smile.  When you turned to Irma for a moment and then returned to Howard he would have dozed off.  I once asked Irma if Howard was okay to drive and she replied, "I talk to him the whole time."  I would have, too!

As a cat, living with Irma was life under the microscope.  Irma always had a complete update available on Midge's behavior.  When she ate.  When she pooped.  When she drank.  How much she drank.  When she moved for an unexplained reason.  If it was a day off from driving to the clinic, Irma called with her report.  No detail was left out of the monologue…

"Midge got up about five minutes late today, at 6:35.  Then she ate about eight pieces of kibble and a teaspoon of canned food.  Then she drank some water.  I think it was too cold for her at first because she had a few licks and then left.  She came back a few minutes later to get some more.  She seemed to test it with a little lick.  I think she swished it around in her mouth and then she drank real well.  At 6:57 she had a BM.  There was a piece about an inch long then another two pieces about one half and three quarters of an inch.  It was dark brown on the outside, but light brown on the inside (wow).  It must have smelled a bit because she didn't bury it as well as usual; I think she wanted to get away from it.  She felt better afterwards because then she wanted to look out the window for awhile."

Irma was so sweet and concerned about her cat that you just couldn't cut her short despite having clients in the waiting room.

Midge managed to live to the age of 23! When her end finally came it was very peaceful for her, but incredibly stressful for the Halls and, subsequently, for us.

We were abruptly cut off from our daily calls. My nurses called to inform the Halls that Midge's cremains had been returned to the clinic. Irma sounded awful. She offered no information about Howard or herself....that was totally unlike her. We decided that they needed another reason to live. The Good Lord provided an opportunity within the week.

A beautiful five year old spayed female Persian cat was in need of a home. She had belonged to an elderly couple that moved into a nursing facility. Her black and white coat was second only to her bronze eyes as her most striking feature. She loved to be petted, but she wasn't an in-your-face lap cat. As an adult, she didn't need as much attention as a kitten. The pace of the Halls should suit her nicely. Her name was Teke (tee-kee).

We informed Irma of the situation and asked her if they could provide a temporary home for Teke. They were delighted to do so. They came out the next day to pick her up. Teke seemed to realize immediately that this was her new meal ticket. She was more aggressively friendly with Irma than she was with any of the doctors or staff. Off they went. We suspected this would be more than a foster home.

The next morning we received a call from Irma. "Our little Teke made herself right at home. She slept in Midge's bed all night, but I had to give her a different towel. She liked the white one best. This morning she got up at 7:15. Do you think that she'll be a late riser all the time or is she just tired from all of the changes?"

Ah, things are back to normal! Needless to say, Teke's temporary home was a permanent one. The timing turned out to be providential as Howard suffered a stroke a short time later. He lingered only a short time before leaving Irma. They had been married for 62 years. According to Irma, they had never had so much as a disagreement in all of those years. They even shared the same birthday being born exactly one year apart with Howard being the senior. They had never had any children because Irma had medical problems that necessitated a hysterectomy after several years of illness starting early in their marriage. Howard worked a full time job and took care of Irma after work for all of those years. Sadly, Irma never needed to learn how to drive. That wasn't going to change at the age of 87.

The only relatives Irma had were a niece and her family. They lived about an hour and a half away. After Howard's death her niece would visit Irma weekly and help with laundry and shopping. Irma was miserable without Howard; she wanted to join him. Her only comfort was Teke. One day the unthinkable happened. Teke became ill.

When Irma informed me that Teke hadn't touched her food in two days I hoped it was the stress of Howard's departure. When she described the large volume of water that Teke was consuming, I knew the underlying disease was much more sinister. Irma brought Teke to the clinic via taxicab. They both looked emaciated. Blood tests quickly confirmed my suspicions…..kidney failure.

We didn't have ultrasound available at the time, but we knew that Persian cats have an inherited form of kidney failure that result from cysts forming in the tubules of the kidneys. The filter portion of the kidney continues to slowly put more fluid into the tubules causing progressive expansion of the cysts. This kills the surrounding normal kidney tissue resulting in kidney failure. With the already high values of waste that Teke had in her bloodstream I felt that she had only a short time to live. Irma decided otherwise. We would hospitalize Teke until she was well enough to go home. I wasn't sure that would ever be the case.

Miraculously, Teke did beautifully. Her blood tests showed a significant decrease in the kidney values. While still elevated, they were just above normal. Her appetite improved as did her general attitude and strength. She was well enough to go home, but how would she get there and how would she get any continued treatment and monitoring? Irma's niece couldn't pick up Teke for several days and Irma was very anxious to have company in the house again. We needed a taxi service, but who would be willing to give a cat a one-way ride?

I was born on the south side and I once delivered mail to post offices for a mailing service so I knew that the area the Halls lived in was one in decline. I didn't want my staff driving to such a questionable part of town. Yours truly would have to be the chauffeur.

Traveling east-west on the south side of Chicago can be miserable. The Stevenson Expressway (I-55) angles north as it traverses east; too far north if you're going to Irma's house. It would be side streets the entire way. It didn't take forever, but it sure seemed like it despite the light traffic on a Saturday afternoon.

I wasn't prepared for how bad the neighborhood would appear. It was located two blocks southeast of 95th St. and Halsted Ave. The house that Irma occupied looked as if it might be haunted. So did the neighboring houses. The yards were unkempt. You could barely see Irma's door due to the overgrown bushes. I recognized the park across the street as the site of a recent gang-related shooting. I drove around the block three times in order to check out some of the activities going on before leaving the relative safety of my truck. I finally parked, but I made certain that the Ford remained within sight of the front door. A pickup in the city stood out as a target in my mind, but I never did encounter any trouble there. The gang bangers probably thought I was a red necked good ole boy. The stick shift and the ammo boxes I used to store my tools enhanced that image in the mind of anyone checking out the contents of the truck. Ironically, they were probably afraid of me.

Irma's front door would have made a great castle entrance. It was three inches of solid oak with a huge deadbolt and two additional locks. Irma allowed my passage into the foyer and that was it. There was a staircase up to the bedrooms to my left. To the right was a pair of closed and locked French doors which lead to the parlor. I'm certain that Irma would never have referred to it as a front room. The corridor ahead of me had a door to the basement on the left, a bathroom on the right and the kitchen door straight ahead. All were closed. That was as far into the house as Irma would allow me. As urban blight moved into their once upscale neighborhood the Halls refused to move. They dug in, deep.

I explained Teke's treatments to Irma. They would be limited to dietary changes and supplements because that was all that Irma would be able to handle. I agreed to stop by and check Teke again in a week. It would be on Sunday to avoid the traffic. The house was only ten minutes from my parish, St. Peter and Paul, on south Halsted St. That would also leave my time more open ended.

I never thought that Teke would live for very long. Happily, I was mistaken. She clung to life for another three years. During that time she had several near-death episodes. She actually died in my arms once. I was able to resuscitate her immediately and she lived another six months. I made many trips to visit Irma during that time.

The door opener came during my sixth visit. I was still limited to a chair in the foyer. Irma asked me to wait there while she went upstairs to get some notes she had written about Teke. As I watched, Irma leaned against the wall to support herself with both hands. She took one step at a time. She reversed the procedure to get back down. There was nothing for her to hang onto.

I suggested that she needed a handrail for safety and support. Irma replied that she had always gone up those stairs like that and that she was perfectly content to continue to do the same. When I expressed concern that she might fall and hurt herself, Irma brushed it off as nonsense. I finally said, "Irma, what would happen to Teke if you fell and hurt yourself?" That was it. She needed a handrail. I installed it the following week.

That was the start of my relationship with what would become my surrogate grandma. My actual gram lived 400 miles north in Wisconsin. I traveled there about every six weeks to help her and Gramps, but Irma became my local version. She allowed me to clean up her yard.

Howard loved roses. You could tell that his yard had been a showcase at one time. Now, however, it was like the briars protecting a princess locked in a tower. I donated a lot of blood trying to clean that yard. I never did tell Irma about the trash I picked up…lots of liquor bottles, needles, even prophylactics. The house to the north was a crack house with people coming and going at all hours. I started to wonder if it was such a good idea to beat down the thorns. I left the ones along the side of the house….it would have been a miserable job to get through them in order to break into the house. The fence was dilapidated. I replaced it with chain link. I left the edges well above the top rail to make it difficult to climb. I replaced the gate leading to the ally.

In the middle of the fencing job I was greeted by the tenant of the crack house. She was a single mother with twins in the oven. She was as thin as a rail. Her formerly beautiful dark face was wrinkled and drawn. She looked to be nearly double her twenty something years. She thanked me for fixing the fence as it would help keep the local teenagers out of her yard as well. She apologized for the appearance of her yard. The landlord came over only when the rent was late and she had no means of cutting the grass herself. She looked pathetic. You guessed it. I mowed the lawn.

The following month I was greeted by the south neighbor. He wanted to hire me to trim his bushes in front. They were nearly as bad Irma's had been. This poor old black man couldn't speak more than a sentence before taking a hit from his oxygen tank. He had what we would now call COPD; chronic obstructive pulmonary disease. The debilitated man couldn't leave the house without assistance. You guessed it. I trimmed the bushes and mowed his lawn.

I met some very nice people on Irma's block. One fine gentleman, Harold, was watching patiently as I finished mowing the front yards. He kept looking at me with a curious gaze as he

156

chewed on the unlit stub of a thick cigar. I finally asked if I could help him with something. He looked me right in the eyes and asked, "You a friend of Miz All's?"

After responding that I was he flashed a broad grin and introduced himself as the former block captain. He checked on Irma every morning as he put her paper on the front porch. He came back every evening to make sure her television had been turned on (you could hear it even if you couldn't see the light from it). We exchanged phone numbers and agreed to contact each other in the event of any mishaps with Irma. It came as a relief that I didn't need to mow his lawn!

You might think that I was running a landscape service at this point, but these were little bitty city lots. I grew up mowing half an acre every week from spring through fall. These lots together didn't make half of Dad's lawn so I didn't feel that I was doing much work. I rarely saw the neighbors. Irma would always offer to pay me. Each time I would reply that if I took money from a little old lady God would either strike me dead or strike my truck dead. I couldn't have either of those things happen so I couldn't accept any money.

Irma insisted that she wanted to do something for me. At the time, I was a board member for a small private school. As with most Catholic schools, Immaculata Academy was in constant need of funding. I asked Irma to do something for the kids in my name. Therefore, she would send a modest check to the school every once in awhile. That made everyone happy. Irma was especially excited when she received thank you notes and drawings from the children.

Eventually, Teke passed away. Her end wasn't as quiet as Midge's. She fought her disease to the end and Irma didn't want to part with her. Teke died at the clinic as we tried to stave off her illness one last time. I wish I had left her at home to be with Irma at the end, but we were all hoping for more time. Irma was alone again.

I kept visiting Irma; we were now fast friends and that

transcended Teke's passing. I would now get calls when things broke or if Irma simply needed help getting rid of her garbage and recycling. One day I got a call that a neighbor had brought a deformed kitten to Irma. The neighbor stated that she knew Irma was good with cats and she thought that Irma could 'drown it for her'! I think idiot is too kind of a word to describe someone that would think Irma could ever have done something like that... especially at the age of 92! Irma decided to keep the kitten and attempt bottle feedings. The kitten was accepting skim milk, but Irma felt that it was much weaker than when it was dropped off two days previously. I was on my way to rescue the kitten that evening.

When I arrived I found a dehydrated, malnourished little ball of fur. The kitten was white with some grey highlights. Her right hind foot was curled at the toes similar to the way a knuckleball pitcher would grip a baseball. The left hind leg was curled backwards so that the bottom of the foot was over the left hip. This was going to be a project!

I told Irma that I was certain that I could straighten the right foot, but I was very concerned that the left leg might not be salvageable. The lack of nutrition could be easily overcome as the kitten was doing her part by nursing vigorously. I felt that the worse that could happen is that we would have a three legged cat. Irma let me take the kitten to the clinic for treatment.

Despite her young age, around four weeks of age, the kitten accepted some pureed kitten food. She quickly regained her strength; so much so that she fought the physical therapy with some vigor. The right foot straightened out quickly. The left leg was another matter. I could only bring it halfway into a normal position and it was useless for locomotion.

A week had gone by when I received a call from Irma. "When can my Molly come home?"

'My Molly'? I was taken aback. In the past week I had become very attached to the kitten and I figured that she would be an addition to my home. I wasn't sure what to say so I stammered,

"Irma, I was going to call her Curly because of her curly leg."

"I like 'Molly' better. When can I take her home?"

Well, I'll be darned. I thought, if Irma is willing to take on this little thing then who am I to deny her. "I'll see you tonight, Irma."

That was it. Irma was back. She looked miserable after Teke passed on. Now she was on a mission. Irma was relentless with the physical therapy. Within six weeks I couldn't tell which leg had been deformed. Little Molly was a white blur in Irma's parlor. I could barely catch her to do her wellness exams and vaccines. She learned early on that I was going to do something to her every time I came over. She became very difficult to locate, but Irma knew all of the hiding places that Molly frequented. Every once in awhile she would surprise us with a new one, so Irma started closing her in the parlor before I came over.

Irma and Molly, now over two years old, were getting along very well. I made sure that I visited on Sunday because I was leaving for a Canadian fishing trip Friday afternoon. I was literally walking out the door to start my journey when I received a phone call from the Chicago police. Harold noticed that Irma hadn't turned on her television and she wasn't answering the door. He called the police and they managed to get Irma on the phone. She was speaking with slurred speech and she was refusing to let them in to her house.

I asked the officer what kind of presence they had on the scene. He replied that there were three squad cars, an ambulance and a couple of fire trucks. The street was blocked off and they had their emergency lights on. Poor Irma was scared to death.

I asked him to lose most of the help. Surely, one or two squads and the ambulance would be sufficient. As they turned off their lights I was patched through to Irma's phone. She was definitely not responding to me in a normal fashion. It was difficult to understand anything she said, but I managed to figure out that she was concerned that the police would let Molly escape. She was able to understand my directions to lock Molly in the parlor and open the porch door for the officers. Thankfully, they talked to me on Irma's phone before I left for Canada. It was the most miserable vacation ever as I was in the bush with no means of getting an update on the situation until I returned home.

Irma had indeed suffered a stroke. She had already been transferred to a nursing home on 95th street not far from her house. I stopped by the house before going to the nursing home. Everything seemed secure from the outside. I had no means of entry, but I could at least assure Irma that there was no sign of foul play.

The nursing home looked dumpy from the outside, but it had been in business for a long time so I thought that the conditions on the inside would be better. When I entered the first sense to be assailed was my nose. It smelled of urine and worse. My Gram's nursing home always smelled like popcorn. Well, I rationalized, you can't clean every mess immediately and heaven knows my kennel has smelled this bad for brief periods. Maybe this is an aberration.

Nope. The next affront to the senses was the appearance of the patients. Most of them were still in hospital gowns or pajamas in the middle of the afternoon. They looked as if they had not even had their hair combed. Everyone was dressed and pressed by nine in the morning at Gram's place.

Irma was sitting in a wheelchair in her room when I arrived. She met me with a blank stare initially. As the sound of my voice reached her I could see hope flash across her eyes. She thought I was there to take her home. In a slow, clear and firm manner I explained to Irma that she would need to recover at the nursing home at least for awhile.

Even though she had lost nearly all of her speech Irma very clearly uttered, "MOLLY!" That was her main concern! I assured her that Molly was at the clinic and being taken care of by my staff. Her niece had called the clinic and met one of my staff at Irma's house so that Molly could be brought to the clinic for safe keeping. Everything was being taken care of, except Irma.

She looked worse with each passing day. The blankets I brought for her were 'missing'. So were some of her clothes. By the end of the week Irma had pneumonia. She was put back into the hospital and managed to recover. We couldn't allow her to go back to that nursing home. Her niece made arrangements for Irma to be moved to a home in Crystal Lake, IL. It was close to the niece, but well over an hour from the clinic in the opposite direction from my house.

Irma lingered at her new care facility for many months. I stopped in to visit every time I went to and from my grandparent's home in Wisconsin. It was sad to see my two matriarchs in their dotage. Each had suffered a stroke and neither could speak in so many words. They spoke with their eyes and hearts. I could see each of them light up when I greeted them.

Gram had Gramps visiting her every day. Irma's niece couldn't spend that kind of time with Irma while raising a family of her own, but she did her best and did very right by Irma.

As tears well in my eyes I recall my final visit with Irma. She wanted so badly to be back with her Howard. How her 67-pound body managed to get up each day was beyond me. Irma would go through the motions of washing her fingers repeatedly when she was trying to communicate. During my final visit she was very animated. She was desperate to tell me something. This continued for about twenty minutes.

In my frustration at my inability to understand Irma, I thought back to a day when I had just finished giving Molly one of her kitten vaccinations. Irma was quietly crying. As a tear rolled down her cheek she said, "I think God forgot about me."

"God doesn't forget about any of us, Irma. You must still have some work to do" I replied.

"Well, what work could I possibly do at my age?"

"You never know, Irma. You might touch someone on your death bed or maybe you're just keeping me out of purgatory. Keep up the good work!"

As the thought that she was on her death bed filled my head,

Irma stopped fidgeting her fingers. She held her hands over her heart as she took a deep breath and looked me right in the eyes. As clear as a bell, she said; "I think about you every day."

You could have knocked me over with a feather! After a brief moment to collect myself I said, "I think of you everyday too, Irma. And I say a prayer for you. I pray that you're happy here and that you get to go see Howard soon."

I gave her a long hug. She left to be with Howard that week. It was as if she needed permission to leave. Her Molly is still with us and is living with my longest serving staff member. Sue is still with me these many years. Or am I still with her? She was there first.

I last saw Irma at her wake. One of the neighbors looked down at the casket and said the classic line, "Irma looks good, doesn't she?"

"No", I replied. "She looks like hell! When I die I hope people look in my casket and say what should be said of Irma....couldn't go another mile on that body, could he?"

Thank you, Irma, for that final mile! You helped me overcome a lot of prejudices as you taught me more than you knew.

*Irma's death gave me cause to reflect on my own. I announced to my family that I would like to have three caskets at my wake. I want to be laid out in the center casket with an empty one to the left of me. The one to the right I want filled with ice, pop and beer. When Mom asked me if the empty one was for the empty cans and bottles I explained to her that I have other plans for it.*

*I want my body rigged so that when someone kneels on the kneeler in front of my casket my arm will wave and a recording of my voice will thank them for coming. If they keel over we can make it a double ceremony!*

*I also have plans for my grave marker. I don't want something that people can step on. I want a classic rounded tombstone. I'd like a St. Francis with some animals on either side. Arched across the top I would like Gregg T. Greiner DVM. Beneath that I would like:*

*Born Oct. 26, 1957*
*Grad. Univ. of Ill.  May,1982*
*Retired from practice _____          (hopefully)*
*Uncle of  _____  (whoever can count this up is good)*
*Retired from life _____*
*And at the very bottom I would like:  LET LYING DOGS SLEEP*

*A good friend wanted to borrow my truck to go to Canada on a fishing trip. I had planned a trip to northern Wisconsin during the week of his trip and I questioned whether his truck would get me to my Grandparents house. Rich told me that I could take his Corvette instead of the truck. I tossed my keys to him and said, "You're on. You can take my truck anywhere if you're going to trust me with your vet."*

*I told my staff that I was tired of hauling stuff with my truck and that I was going to trade it in for something that was entirely useless. Two weeks later I told them that a friend was selling his Corvette and that I was going to test drive it. Of course, that was followed by my raving about how cool the car was. It was, in fact, cool. Brown metallic with a T-top, it was the first model year with the computerized dashboard. I told the staff that I had fallen in love with it. The following week I had 'purchased' it.*

*Everyone wanted a ride in my new car. Dr. Velders told me the story about his little spitfire that he owned when he was starting the practice. With a young family on the way and the financial obligations of the new practice he decided to sell it. He* was convinced that this was one of the best things I had ever done. It was.

The only one that didn't believe I had bought it was Mrs. Velders. She knew how pragmatic I was and that I loved my pickup truck. My girlfriend had the best reaction of anyone; silence. She sat in the passenger seat with her arms folded staring straight ahead. When I finally got her to speak up it turned out that she thought I was having a midlife crisis and that the car was my chick magnet. I fessed up about my plan and made her swear to silence.

The following week I pulled into the parking lot driving my truck. Kellie was walking a dog. The perfect person to see the end of my prank, Kellie is Miss Nascar. She stood there with her jaw dropped as I slowed down and waved. She could barely speak. It was unbelievable to her that I could dump a vet! This remains my best gag to date. I had them all and it continued for almost two full weeks! They were even discussing my Christmas presents for that year; Corvette car mats, keychain, pillow cases, etc.

As my brother and I drove to our Grandparents house, Dave asked if I was going to try to fool Gram and Gramps. I didn't think Gram would go for it because she knew me so well, but I decided to try it.

We arrived about 11:00 p.m. and they were already asleep. The next morning I awoke and went downstairs for breakfast. Always the early risers, Gram and Gramps had empty coffee cups already. Gram looked at me and asked, "Whose car is that?"

I couldn't lie to my Gram. I told her the entire story about my staff believing my story. She immediately asked if she could take it for a drive. I handed her the keys. She left midmorning and was gone for most of the day. When she finally returned I asked where she had been. She drove around to the local resorts and told her friends that it was her new car. I asked her how fast she had been driving. She told me that she never went over 40 mph. I looked at her and said, "C'mon Gram, fess up."

She had a twinkle in her eyes as she replied, "I did 80!"

She wanted to drive her age and she did.

CHAPTER 15

*Watch Your Back*

It didn't take long to feel at home at the Burr Ridge Vet Clinic. Dr. Velders was much more a mentor than a boss. His staff was caring and eager to bring me up to speed. I'm not convinced that this was to ensure that the patients were receiving the best care possible or rather that they simply wanted to get out of the office at a reasonable hour. I tend to think it was the former because no one ever complained about a late night at the clinic.

There tended to be plenty of those. There were no certified technicians in the practice. There were very few in the entire profession at the time. That meant that critical cases, especially complicated surgeries, were often put off until late in the day when both of us doctors could give the case our complete attention. Since we were a surgical referral practice (we accepted cases from other veterinarians) those days came fairly often.

It wasn't unusual to begin a surgery at 7:00 pm and not leave the clinic until well past my normal bedtime. In particular, our spinal cases tended to be at night. After determining that a patient needed back surgery, we often prayed that the radiographs would show a glaring lesion such as a completely collapsed disc space or mineralized disc material in the spinal canal. A good neurological evaluation should have determined approximately where to find the lesion causing the loss of nerve function. If there was no obvious lesion on survey radiographs then a dye study was needed to locate the problem.

Doing the spinal taps and injections of contrast material were a bit nerve wracking (mine, hopefully not the patients), but they proved to be technically simple. However, the processing of the films was another story. We were still in the dark (room) ages.

At the university we had automatic processors that cranked out a radiograph within two minutes. The quality of the films was excellent. They came out dry and ready to be stored in an envelope. This was particularly beneficial if the films were being taken while a patient was under anesthesia. The days of fancy equipment were behind me for the time being. Dip tanks were the standard equipment in all but the largest private practices. We weren't one of them.

X-rays are generated by a source over the table. The patient is positioned beneath the source in a manner designed to best visualize the desired part of the anatomy. This can be tricky because you're wearing twenty pounds of lead to protect yourself from the radiation and some of the patients fail to appreciate the importance of remaining in position long enough to capture the image. The exposure is much longer than it would be for a 35mm camera...about $1/30^{th}$ of a second for most cases. It is easy to get blurring of the image, particularly if the patient is panting.

The X-rays pass through the patient. The greater density of tissues such as bone causes them to absorb more of the X-rays. The lesser density of tissues such as air-filled lungs allows the X-rays to pass through unimpeded. Therefore the energy going through the patient has variable strengths when it comes through the other side. This energy, still in the form of X-rays, then passes into a cassette holding the film beneath the table. A chemical in the cassette absorbs the energy from the X-rays. As the chemical releases the energy back it does so in the form of visible light. This exposes the film which is basic photographic film containing a silver emulsion.

Obviously, the cassette needs to be sealed so that light from the room doesn't expose the film before or after taking the radiograph. It can still be ruined prior to being 'fixed'. Therefore, developing the film is done in a darkroom illuminated by a red light which doesn't affect the silver atoms in the film.

The first step in processing is to remove the film from the cassette. It is important to immediately put another piece of film in its place so that you don't have a blank cassette for the next shot. The patient and clinic information is then marked on the exposed film using light shone through an index card. The black ink used to print the information blocks the light and shows up on the film once it is developed. The film is then pinned to a rack and immersed in the developing solution. It stays there for a period of time. The length of time varies based on the temperature of the solution and the age of the solution. The more films that go through it the less potent the solution becomes. The time factor definitely had some guesswork involved.

The film is then rinsed and put into a solution that stops the chemical reaction, the fixative. After a couple of minutes in the fixative you can take the film out and look at it in the light. Up to that time you had to hold it up to the red light and try guessing at the quality of the image. It was often ten minutes before you knew whether or not the image was satisfactory. If it wasn't then you had to adjust the exposure technique or positioning (or both on a bad day) and try again. This adds to the stress level on everyone; doctors, staff and patient.

About ten years into practice we decided that we were big enough to justify the expense of an automatic processor. Wow, films in less than two minutes! That was living. As of this writing we have recently gone digital. No more films. The image appears on a computer screen in less than five seconds! I never could have dreamed that such a tool could exist. I really could not have imagined that it would one day be affordable, but there it sits. It is a quantum leap in image quality and patient care. A few clicks of the mouse and copies are available on DVD. The software to read and manipulate the images is downloaded on each disc. Need a specialist to view them? Each night the images are stored remotely and available on the internet using a unique patient code for each set. They can even be shared via e-mail. Where will it end? I'd like to have one of those tricorders like Bones used on Star Trek sometime before I retire. I would immediately start referring to the other doctors as Captain Quirk and Spec. I'd like a phaser and then a transporter booth, too. But, I digress.

One of the finer points that is beaten into the head of every vet student is the difference between X-rays and radiographs. The former being the wavelength of energy used to generate the image and the latter being the image on the film or computer. Of course, most people use X-ray to mean the film.

At any rate, if your films didn't turn out on a sedated patient in the dip tank days it was cause for concern. The anesthetics were not nearly as safe as they are now and each failure meant more time under anesthesia and consequently more risk. Late nights could turn into stressful nights if you let them. Therefore, you learned to do things right the first time. Watch those little details. It's OK to hurry, but don't rush.

Now let's return to our back patients. Once the offending disc was located, surgery was performed to relieve the pressure on the spinal cord. Just like any other tissue, when the spinal cord is damaged it swells. Since it is surrounded by bone it has nowhere to go. Therefore, the swelling causes an increase in pressure on the spinal cord. This is similar to putting pressure on your 'funny bone'; it causes the nerves to stop functioning. The nerves on the outside of the spinal cord get hit first due their proximity to the wall of the spinal canal. Rather like hitting your funny bone, they go numb. The other nerves tend to go in specific order based on their depth from the surface. The deeper nerves are hit last. This is helpful in assessing the level of damage based on that neurological exam mentioned previously.

You may notice your veterinarian playing some funny games with your pet's feet. We test the ability of the patient to tell where their feet are located in relation to the rest of the body. The dog's weight is supported and the toes of a foot are pulled backwards. The patient's weight is slowly put back on the up-side-down foot. They should recognize the abnormal position immediately and replace the foot into a normal position without hesitation. Patients that have lost this *proprioception* will fail to do so in a normal fashion.

The next function that goes is sensation in the skin: superficial pain sensation. These patients fail to feel a skin pinch and when their proprioception is tested they will make no effort to move their feet back to a normal position until they simply try to move on their own.

The next level of nerve loss involves voluntary motor ability. The patients that have lost this function are paralyzed in the affected limbs. This is the indication for surgical decompression. If voluntary motor function is lost the prognosis becomes poor without surgery and guarded with immediate surgery. Waiting a day to see if they improve is not an option.

The final nerves to be affected are the ones associated with deep pain sensation. The patients suffering this degree of nerve loss have no sensation even when the base of a toenail is pinched firmly. Although the foot may still be retracted involuntarily through reflex action, we are looking for a conscious response to the toe pinch; they should turn to look at it or at least display some level of discomfort. If this is lacking, their spinal cord is damaged throughout and their prognosis for regaining function is very poor and dropping by the hour. They need immediate surgery…no putting them off for after-hours! Even with surgery, the prognosis for these patients regaining function is very guarded.

The families that elect to go without surgery are not without hope. Especially if there is sensation, there is a chance that steroid therapy can reduce the swelling in the spinal cord enough to help regain function. This needs to happen quickly. Even a day or two of pressure on that funny bone can cause permanent nerve damage. Then you are stuck with trying to re-grow nerves….a lengthy and iffy proposition. If surgery is not performed in the first 24 hours then it is not likely to increase the chances of recovery. This is one of the times that we wish we had a crystal ball to gaze into. No one wants to perform a surgery that ultimately is unsuccessful, especially a major one like back surgery.

The surgery is called a laminectomy. Anyone who performs them will remember their early experiences clearly. I recall a very large 'pucker factor' simply acting as the assistant. An incision is made through the skin and muscles to expose a portion of the spine. The top of the vertebrae are removed at the affected area. The covering of the spinal cord is carefully opened to help relieve the pressure on the cord. Any disc material in the canal is carefully flushed and suctioned away. The damage to the spinal cord is assessed. Occasionally, the damage is so severe that the spinal cord is literally mush. There is little to be done at this point. The patient will not regain function.

What a horrible phone call to make. You keep telling yourself that you didn't make this disease, you're just reporting it, but that doesn't provide much comfort as you give the news to a now grieving owner. Perhaps it was only a few hours ago that their dog was playing in the backyard and now they are faced with the decision of caring for a paraplegic for years to come or deciding to end the suffering before their pet wakes up from a painful surgery.

The flip side to those cases are the ones that wake up with little discomfort and immediate improvement in their neurological function. I'll never forget the first little dachshund that Dr. Velders and I worked on; Frieda was her name. She was in for her suture removal two weeks after surgery. Doc called me into the room. The owner was sitting cross legged on the floor and holding Frieda on her lap. When I entered the exam room she let Frieda go loose. Tears of joy were in everyone's eyes as little Frieda walked over to me. I got down on the floor and she started licking my face. What a payoff for missing a bit of sleep!

I had to confront this disease on a personal level. Early one morning I was awaken by Mitts. She was having one of her seizures. It seemed to be a bit more severe than usual. She was doing her usual shaking, but she wasn't trying to walk. I held her close and comforted her. She was able to relax a little, but the seizure went through its usual routine. She finally vomited and that should have been the end of it. Several minutes passed and she still made no effort to move her rear legs. I pinched her toes; nothing. She didn't react at all. All of my training and experience couldn't overcome my denial. She must be in a post-seizure aura. I must not have pinched her hard enough.

I slowly came to realize that Mitts was paralyzed. Worse yet, there was no deep pain sensation. We left for the clinic. Mom was aware of my concerns, but I didn't have the heart to tell her about the poor odds of Mitts surviving this. I wanted to have Dr. Velders confirm my fears before I let the family in on the whole story.

When Dr. Velders arrived I had already treated Mitts with intravenous steroids and I had just finished processing her radiographs. The films showed six degenerative discs in a row. They were in the usual location; the junction of the thoracic and lumbar spine. We couldn't identify the exact location of the one that had ruptured. A dye study was contraindicated due to her epilepsy; the dyes in use at the time could induce seizures. Even if surgery was performed, her other discs looked to be problematic in the near future. No one dared to mention euthanasia to me. I was prepared to deal with a paraplegic if necessary.

Mitts regained deep pain sensation within the first twenty four hours; a very hopeful sign. She was the best patient ever. Each time I carried her outside to express her bladder she licked my face and thanked me. She wasn't fond of the physical therapy, but I made sure she got lots of treats as I put her legs through range of motion exercises. Her appetite was voracious due to the steroids.

I hadn't been bashful about the dosage! This was do or die time. She received the highest recommended amount.

The second day I thought that I saw a leg move when she tried to get up. It wasn't wishful thinking; she definitely moved both rear legs on the third day. By the fourth day she was resisting me as I tried to express her bladder. I supported her with a towel fashioned into a sling around her abdomen in front of the rear legs. She pulled me around the yard with her front legs. She couldn't use the back legs yet, but they definitely moved as she walked around. By the end of the week she was getting up on her own! She went on to a full recovery. She had beaten the odds despite her age; she was fourteen at the time.

Of course, the family couldn't say enough about my veterinary skills. I finally admitted that I had little to do with the fact that she regained her nerve functions. I treated her the same way that I treat all of my disc patients. What Mitts had going for her is that she had far more people praying for her to recovery than any other dog in the world. I can't take credit for God's work. I'm just there to help Him do His work. As one of my professors once warned us, "You don't cure your patients. You help them to heal. The day you think you're curing diseases quit being a vet and become a tele-evangelist. It pays a lot better."

As the years have passed there has become less need to stay beyond normal hours. Veterinary emergency centers have sprung up around most metropolitan areas. Board certified surgeons are widely available and very well equipped. They can do a laminectomy in a fraction of the time it took me. No more carving off a piece of bone one little chip at a time using a rongeur. They have power tools which are much more efficient and safer for the patient. They also have nursing staff around the clock making postoperative care easier, safer and more effective.

Another huge advancement in treating spinal patients has been the availability of magnetic resonance imaging (MRI) and computed tomography (CT or CAT scans). No more risky spinal taps and injection of dye around the cord. Also, the discs and spinal cord are clearly seen and can be evaluated for damage. It is now possible to more accurately know the chances of recovery before having the spinal cord in your hands.

All of these advances have diminished the need to perform laminectomies in our facility. Once you are out of practice the desire to do them diminishes. This isn't a surgery you can do once in awhile and feel comfortable with them. I must admit that I don't miss the stress of doing backs, but I do miss my Friedas. I will always miss my Mitts.

*When Mitts suffered her spinal cord damage I decided to keep a positive attitude about her chances of recovering. Since she had no skin sensation caudal to (behind) her last rib I decided to remove some skin tags and oil gland tumors. I brought the cautery unit home and burned off several growths. In the middle of the procedure Mom entered the room. Once she realized what I was doing she commented, "Why are you taking those growths off? What if she never walks again?"*

*I put my hands over my ears and started singing. "La, la, la. I can't hear you."*

*I eventually turned to Mom and said, "If she doesn't recover from this then she'll at least go to heaven with no growths from here back!" I don't think St. Peter would have cared either way, but those unsightly skin tags always bothered me so I took advantage of her situation.*

*Our imaging consultant, Dr. B, was at the office performing some ultrasounds. Being a former professor of radiology, he had the mindset of a teacher. His terms were precise. He was an imaging consultant rather than a radiologist because ultrasounds don't involve radiation and they are a major part of his business. I asked Dr. B if he could look at some X-rays for me. He very smugly said, "Oh, I'd love to. I've never seen an X-ray!" Pointing at the X-ray table I said "Lay down right here and look at the little light. I'll crank this sucker up. Let me know what you see." In all of his years of teaching I was the only one that ever had a reply to his attempt to teach the difference between a radiograph and an X-ray. I might have gotten extra credit for that had I thought of it in school!*

*A friend of mine has had chronic spinal problems. He often complains that his back is killing him. I reply that his front is killing me!*

One of my nurses came in to the office on her day off. She looked dirty and was scraped and scratched as she led a black Labrador retriever by its collar. She wiped her brow and said, "I saw this dog running loose in my neighborhood. I chased him for a mile and a half. I went through bushes, fell in the mud and almost got hit by a car. I finally cornered him in a yard with a fence. I had to drag him back to my car to drive him here. He seems really nice; I sure hope we can find his owner!"

Fortunately, the microchip scanner revealed that he had one. It was then a simple matter to identify and locate his owners. However, they weren't answering their telephone. Kellie recognized the street address and decided to drive to the house with the dog.

As she neared the address her mouth fell open in disbelief. It was the yard in which she had cornered the dog! She had chased him home. She quietly put the dog back in the yard, closed the gate and left. She later called the owners to let them know that their dog had escaped so that they could put a lock on the gate.

We teased her that she should have asked for a reward. "Hey, I found this dog in your yard, what's that worth?"

# CHAPTER 16

## *Is It Time?*

That is one of the most common questions asked of veterinarians. Put another way, "When is it *going* to be time to say farewell to my beloved pet? What will happen when we come for his final visit? What will we do with his remains?" The answers to these questions are often difficult to contemplate, especially when you are the one making decisions for your pet. Mitts lived to be eighteen years old, an exceptional age for any dog, but especially long for a lab mix. I probably euthanized her half a dozen times before she made the decision for me.

Most pets don't spare their owners from deciding when to end their suffering. We never want to let them go, but we must remain focused on maintaining a reasonable quality of life for them. We don't want to be in a position where we are keeping them around for us, but rather for them.

There are some situations in which it is obvious that the suffering is severe and that it is not going to improve. At that point euthanasia is the only reasonable option. However, the more usual scenario isn't so black and white. It is the duty of your veterinarian to help you with your decision. You will need as much information as possible about the illness afflicting your pet and the options available for treatment. The costs associated with the various treatments should be weighed against a best estimate of the prognosis (likelihood of a positive outcome). Ultimately, the final decisions will be up to you and your family. No one knows your pet and the circumstances at home better than you.

Sometimes, the age of your pet, the costs associated with treatment, the uncertainty of the prognosis, family situations and other factors will increase the difficulty of making a decision. There is no easy formula. Logic is often clouded by emotion. Although I have listed some considerations below, there will ultimately come a time when you look your friend in the eyes and realize that today is the day. There will be no doubt. The dazed, far-away look or the 'I'm in pain and want to leave' looks are unmistakable. Whether for the first time or for the hundredth time, when you see those signs you will recognize them in your heart. You may hear many opinions, especially from well meaning family and friends, but listen to the voice in your heart.

If your pet is still eating, drinking, moving and having regular bowel movements and urinations then it is probably not time to say good bye, especially if he is still responsive to you, wagging his tail and acting as a member of the family.

If he has been diagnosed with an expensive problem you should ask yourself several questions. Is there a good chance of recovering? Is the initial cost of treatment within my budget? Will there be ongoing costs of treatment? Are recurrences or complications expected down the road? Does the treatment hold the promise of improving the quality of life for my pet for sufficient time to justify the cost?

If costs are not an issue, but the decision rests more on quality of life then we are fully into the realm of subjective analysis. Some experts suggest that you should assign a number to the quality of life of your pet. Starting at one if your pet is near death and going up to ten if it is acting like a youthful puppy. If the answer is between six and ten then it definitely isn't time. One to three and it probably is. Four and five suggest you may want to seek out options for helping your pet. Hopefully, you've seen your vet way before your pet gets down to a level five! The problem is that your number selection will often vary from day to day. Even a progressively downhill course isn't on a straight line. Just like an ailing person, our pets have good and bad days. When are the bad days too bad? When are the good days over? Go back to listening to your heart.

I often came home to find that Mitts couldn't greet me at the door. Occasionally she would have soiled herself in her attempts to get up. She would push so hard that she would have a bowel movement and then push herself through it. She tended to go in circles so I dubbed this the S &S (**it and spin). This enabled me to keep a sense of humor about it. She always appreciated a bath when this happened. She showed her appreciation by licking my face and hitting me with her wagging, soiled tail. It's a good thing I followed my heart on some of those days…it was tempting to call it quits.

When the time finally arrives, what happens next? Call your veterinarian's office. When you make an appointment to bring in your faithful companion for euthanasia we will do our best to schedule a time when it is convenient for you and quiet at the clinic. That may mean opening the doors a little early or late or around lunch time at my clinic; others may not be so accommodating. We like to make sure that you aren't bothered by our usual busy-ness and that we have adequate time to spend with you. Many clinics have a comfort room with a separate entrance from the outside so that you don't need to enter or exit through the waiting area during stressful events. We hope to incorporate this into the plans for our new clinic.

One of the decisions you will face is whether or not to stay with your pet when the act of euthanasia is performed. Most people do. Although we encourage everyone to remain with their pets in their final moments, some people just don't have the fortitude to watch them depart. When that is the case, our nursing staff is very compassionate and eager to comfort them in their last breaths. No pet is allowed to be on 'death row'. They don't go into a cage; they remain in the arms of our nurses while the doctor prepares and administers their last injection.

The medication used for euthanasia is designed for one purpose only....the *humane* taking of life. It is a concentrated form of pentobarbital, an intravenous anesthetic which was the primary drug used for general anesthesia until a few years ago. Pets receiving this injection experience the same sensation that a person undergoing general anesthesia would feel. As you count backwards from 100 you rarely make it past 95 before you lose consciousness and peacefully fall asleep. The difference is that the dosage used for euthanasia is a massive overdose of anesthesia so there is no waking up.

Anesthetics are drugs that are highly soluble in fat. This is necessary because nerve cells are coated with a fatty insulation so that they don't short circuit each other during impulse conduction. Therefore, after IV administration, the anesthetic goes first to the brain and induces unconsciousness before entering the heart muscle (where it is less soluble) and stopping the heart a few seconds later. Some people report a warm sensation in the arm as pentobarbital is given to them. It is unlikely that animals experience this (we older doctors remember using pentobarbital as an anesthetic and the animals never seemed to react to the injection), but there is also a local anesthetic in the injection to ensure their comfort.

The doctors at our clinic feel very strongly that you and your pet should not have to suffer from anxiety or pain at this critical juncture. We will always do our best to comfort you. Many people don't like to watch their pet receive any kind of injection. To avoid that experience we will often have our nurses take your pet to the treatment room and place a soft latex catheter in the vein. They will then flush the catheter with heparin (an anti-clotting drug) and saline to be sure it is properly placed and that no clots will form to plug it. They will then wrap it with a soft bandage in order to keep it in place even if your pet should move around.

If your pet is very anxious we will administer an injection of sedation before performing euthanasia. That injection simply goes into the muscle in the back leg. It consists of a narcotic pain reliever and a dissociative agent which disconnects the mind from the body. We routinely use this combination prior to giving anesthetics for surgery. It will make your pet very relaxed and sleepy within a few short minutes.

As they receive the final injection of pentobarbital many pets will lick their lips. This is due to a faint taste of the drug as it passes by the taste buds in the bloodstream. That is followed by a deep breath or two, profound relaxation and then cessation of breathing and heartbeat. The reflex of blinking when the eye is touched is the last one to go and is a good indicator of brain death. Don't be surprised if the doctor touches the eyeball to see if a blink results. Some seconds (even a minute or so) later another series of deep but incomplete breaths may occur. This is a reflex of the diaphragm in response to the lack of oxygen the deceased body is now experiencing. There has been no brain activity for some time already when this occurs, so don't be alarmed. Your pet may also pass urine and/or feces at this time as well. This also is normal so don't be embarrassed. We don't mind taking care of a mess. We do it for a living.

The doctors and staff are all concerned about your wishes for the after death care of your pet so don't be upset with them if they inquire more than once about the disposition of the remains; they want to be certain that your wishes are followed down to the last detail. You will be required to sign a paper stating that your pet hasn't bitten anyone in the past ten days (a precaution against the spread of rabies) and detailing your desires for after death care.

Some people are able to bury their pets at home. If that is the case, we will help you to prepare the body for interment by wrapping it in a towel or blanket (bring it with if your pet has a favorite one you wish it to be buried in) and then placing everything in a body bag. This is a heavy duty, leak resistant bag that has no chlorine to pollute the ground and air. It helps to prevent odors from leaking out so as not to attract scavengers. Local ordinances may govern this activity so be sure to check ahead of time.

If you discover that your pet has died at home please call your veterinarian. We will guide you through all of your after-death care options. If it is after business hours, you may wrap your pet in a blanket and keep the remains in a cool place. It may be desirable to put a piece of plastic (e.g. a garbage bag laid flat) under the blanket it case there is any leakage of bodily fluids. You can bring the body to the clinic for after-death care or go straight to a pet cemetery.

Many people choose to inter their pets at the local animal cemetery, another pet cemetery in the region or even out of state. Your vet will be happy to help you with making arrangements with the cemetery of your choice. Most of the local establishments will provide pick-up services if you aren't up to driving at this sad time or if you are unable to move your pet without assistance.

Most people elect cremation for their deceased pet. This can be done either privately or in a group with other pets. When subjected to group cremation, the remaining ashes (cremains) are scattered on the graves of the other pets at the local animal cemetery; this practice is likely to vary among the available facilities so you may want to check it out ahead of time.

Some animal disposal companies are licensed waste haulers. They often use incinerators rather that crematories. They are required by the EPA to dispose of the ashes as *waste* in a landfill. Their incinerators are too large to do a private cremation so a partitioned cremation must suffice. This involves placing several pets in the incinerator at the same time. They are separated by low partitions. I consider partitioned cremation to be a form of group cremation and would never recommend it to my clients. This service is not available through my clinic. When a private cremation is performed at the animal cemetery that services our clients, it is your pet and your pet only placed in the crematory which has been completely cleaned ahead of time. All of the ashes are removed, processed, placed in a heavy plastic bag, sealed, identified, dated and placed in a small white plastic urn of the type used for infants. A special urn of your choosing may be purchased instead. Your veterinarian should have a catalog of available styles. If not, the cemetery surely will.

You may also buy a container of appropriate dimensions on your own. While I can't speak with any authority about the practices of other services, I can assure my clients that they will not spill the cremains when opening an urn from our cremation service. The tar seal can be broken and the bag containing the cremains easily removed.

I have a dear friend who has the ashes from her dogs in a vase with a dried flower arrangement over them. The vase is on the mantle over the fireplace next to a picture of each dog. When she dies the ashes will be put into her coffin and be buried with her. This is a perfectly legal act, but be sure that your family is aware of your wishes and the location of the ashes. By the time your will is read you may already have been buried and it will be too late.

When the time actually arrives that you part with a pet, many people feel worse than they do losing a family member. That may be due to the level of attachment you feel or the amount of care you have provided. Pets seem to return our love many times over and treating a severe illness for a long time may result in deep feelings of loss and emptiness. How you express those feelings is an outward sign of your inner self. I have seen some very strong people reduced to tears. I have seen some very emotional people remain stoic at the loss of their pet. The important thing to remember is that you should feel free to be yourself. I am not ashamed to admit that I cried on the loss of my Mittens after 18 wonderful years together. She was one of my best friends. She was in large part responsible for my veterinary career. I would be ashamed if I didn't miss her! Virtually everyone at my clinic has been in your shoes at some time in their life. We understand.

You may be surprised by your reaction when you return home after leaving your pet at the clinic for the last time. You will undoubtedly be expecting your usual greeting at the door. You may hear the usual whine, purr, bark or footfalls around the house for quite some time. You may even see your pet around the house, especially out of the corner of your eye when you least expect it. A tuft of hair wafting across the floor or the empty food dish may bring a sudden rush of emotion at fond memories recalled. It would even be nice to have one more mess to clean up! Many people are visited in their dreams by their departed pets. While these sudden emotions can be disconcerting they often bring comfort; especially as time passes and healing begins.

I am often asked about the disposition of the remains of my own pets. When I lost Mittens I had intended to bury her in my backyard. I have plenty of space and I live in an unincorporated area. However, she picked the middle of winter to depart and the frozen ground made it impractical to dig a hole for her. Therefore, I had her cremated privately.

When her ashes were returned home the family games began. Over the past 18 years we had become geographically scattered. My sisters had settled in Michigan and their homes were in a rural area. My brothers had their own homes in Illinois and they had big yards, too. Each of us kids had a great place in mind for Mittens' final resting place. We even considered scattering her ashes in the lake at my grandparent's place in Wisconsin.

That Easter saw the family gathered together for the holiday. We decided as a group that Mittens deserved to be in the yard in which she spent so many happy years. I dug a hole near the flower garden (and those dang bunnies she liked to chase so much) and placed her ashes into it. I planted a lilac bush over her. Each year I cut some lilacs and place them in a vase. As I do, I recall all the times I wrestled with Mitts trying to cut her toenails. Somehow that has become a fond memory despite all of her struggling.

It has finally become apparent to my profession that many people experience severe symptoms of grief, guilt and isolation when faced with the loss of a pet. Very often that pet has been a best friend and confidant who has been through many tough times with its master. In response to the many silent sufferers seeking closure after losing a pet the Chicago Veterinary Medical Association has developed a pet loss help line. All of the volunteers are associated with veterinary clinics in the Chicagoland area. We are there to answer any questions and concerns that people may have about a pet they have lost or are in the process of losing. We encourage people to call before the final act of euthanasia. There may be options still available for their pet or perhaps we may simply confirm that the time has arrived. The volunteers are there to help you through the grieving process in any way we can. You may wish to attend a group session to see how others have coped with the loss of a pet. A trained grief counselor runs the sessions which are held at the CVMA office. 'Wings' is held on the first Wednesday evening of each month. We were one of the first pet loss help lines in the country, but we have since been joined by many others. Your vet should have information on availability of such services in your area.

I hope that these few thoughts have helped you if you are currently in the throes of dealing with pet loss. Remember that you aren't alone. It is normal to miss a loved one while awaiting a happy reunion in the hereafter. May we all deserve to go where our loving pets deserve to go! At the end of this chapter you will find a copy of the Rainbow Bridge. I hope it brings healing if you are in need of it. I would also like to share with you a touching example of how our pets can help us heal even grievous wounds.

'Calico' Burns was a young adult female domestic shorthair cat when I first met her. As her name implies, her coat was mostly calico colored although she had a bit of tortoise shell mixed in. She not only inherited the red hair gene, but she also inherited the hot-head attitude to go with it. She was very difficult to handle. We could usually wrap her in a towel for wellness visits, but procedures that would involve anything that even remotely resembled handling required sedation. She would have killed us if she could have and you were very glad that you didn't understand what she was saying. It was unfit for print.

Despite her many problems Calico lived to the ripe old age of 21 years. By the time Miss Burns decided to part with her, Calico was virtually comatose. She had a combination of cancer and kidney failure. She was totally unresponsive to me. I was able to pet her without drugs in her system for the first time.

It became immediately apparent that Miss Burns was having an extremely difficult time letting Calico go. She was in tears and was unable to speak in answer to my queries about how Calico was doing at home. I quickly surmised that she was ready to send Calico on her way, but she wasn't ready to lose her without a final struggle.

I suggested that we give some sedation to Calico. Due to her prior outbursts with even minimal handling I didn't want her last moments to be spent in panic. I also didn't want Miss Burns to get bitten because she wasn't about to let loose of Calico. She had her wrapped in a towel and was kissing her unresponsive face.

Calico didn't even blink an eyelid as I gave her an injection of sedation into the hamstrings of her right hind leg. I allowed 15 minutes for the sedation to take effect even though she was so far gone already. The tears had stopped. I wondered if they had run out. Her mom held her lovingly as I gave Calico the final shot. It was difficult to perceive any change in Calico's facial expression. She was there in body only. As always, I checked for a corneal reflex; it was absent. No heartbeat. She was officially gone, but mom still wasn't ready to let go of her.

She held onto Calico, gently rocking her in her arms and softly talking to her for the next three hours! Of course, I had other clients coming in and out all afternoon. However, I spent as much time as possible consoling Miss Burns. I kept going in and out of the exam room with her. I made sure that the staff offered her anything they thought she might need....water, tissues, the bathroom. But she was only moderately aware of them. Her only need was more time with Calico. I couldn't hear her soft conversation with Calico, but I didn't need to. I knew it was deeply personal and meant for Calico only.

When I finally took Calico into my arms I could sense that Miss Burns had a tremendous sense of tranquility about her. She was OK with Calico's departure. No, it was more than that. She was OK with herself and the world.

Just two days later I received an eight page letter from Miss Burns. She recalled many tough times that she had survived. Calico was always there for her. She was so much more than a cat. She was a confidante; a best friend that always had the answers to life's difficulties. You simply had to pet her, enjoy her rumbling purr and look into her eyes. The answers always came. The comfort always came.

Miss Burns continued on. She had lost her father when she was six years old. In a misguided effort to spare her feelings, her mother wouldn't allow her to go to the wake or funeral. As an adult, she had been in therapy for over twenty years trying to separate from her father. When I took Calico into my arms, I took her father, too!

I had suspected that she was working out some issues, but I had no idea how deep the waters ran. I learned that you can never tell what kind of a load a person is carrying; you can only offer to help with the burden and take what they give you without reservation.

I was struck by the fact that Miss Burns hadn't felt healing during twenty years of therapy. She hadn't received what she needed so desperately; someone to put their arm around her and genuinely, from the heart, say "I am sorry for your loss". Perhaps they tried and the door was barred to them. Calico certainly unlocked it for me. I'm glad that I was able to open it wide.

Miss Burns never returned to the clinic. She may have felt some embarrassment at baring her soul. Coming into the building may have brought back too many memories. She may have felt that she could never replace Calico, a cat who filled a chasm in her psyche. I like to think that she didn't *need* another Calico. If she ever does I'm certain that one will be sent into her life at the appropriate moment.

# The Rainbow Bridge

*There is a bridge connecting Heaven and Earth. It is called the Rainbow Bridge because of its many colors. Just this side of the Rainbow Bridge there is a land of meadows, hills and valleys with lush green grass.*

*When a beloved pet dies, the pet goes to this place. There is always food and water and warm spring weather. The old and frail animals are young again. Those who are maimed are made whole again. They play all day with each other.*

*There is only one thing missing. They are not with their special person who loved them on Earth. So, each day they run and play until the day comes when one suddenly stops playing and looks up! The nose twitches! The ears are up! The eyes are staring! And this one suddenly runs from the group!*

*You have been seen, and when you and your special friend meet, you take him or her in your arms and embrace. Your face is kissed again and again, and you look once more into the eyes of your trusting pet.*

*Then you cross the Rainbow Bridge together, never again to be separated.*

*When I lost my first patient Dr. Velders approached me with instructions to send a condolence letter to the family of the pet. It was a very awkward moment as I had never heard of such a thing. I knew of one clinic that sent a condolence card, but Dr. V was adamant that it needed to be a hand written, individual letter. He coached me on what to say, but he wouldn't give me the exact words; they had to be mine.*

*Looking back on twenty-five plus years of writing condolence letters I can tell you that it is one of the single most important things we do for our clients. We have people tell us that they have saved the letters for years and still read them with fond remembrances of their pet(s). Each letter comes from the heart and is addressed to the heart.*

# CHAPTER 17

# *Which Doctor*

As a general practitioner I have the opportunity to meet with a lot of people in an intimate, one-on-one setting. This includes many professionals in fields other than my own. It was at a time in my life in which the realization that I was not immortal was being reinforced by the illnesses of friends and family members when I met Dr. Lent. That is not his real name, but that is what comes to mind when I think of all the lifestyle changes he recommends for me.

A close friend was suffering from persistent vague symptoms which included severe fatigue, tremors, mild depression, muscle aches and general malaise. She has a family history of multiple sclerosis and was very concerned that she also might be afflicted with it.

I spoke with several clients in the human medical field about her symptoms, but none of them seemed confident in their recommendations for an appropriate plan of action. When I know a client has medical training I will often go straight to medical lingo. It is a bit scary when it seems to be going over their head! I sometimes check to see where they work and make a mental note not to end up there. I was getting a list of where not to go for help as her condition persisted and her anxiety grew.

As often happens, my concerns were addressed by the well-timed introduction to just the right person; Dr. Lent. His visit to the clinic that day was a happy one. Their Golden Retriever, Ginger, was in for a wellness examination, heartworm test and vaccinations. I had met Dr. Lent the previous year, but the visit was short and we had not had an opportunity to talk about anything but pet issues. He wouldn't get off so easily this time.

I mentioned my friend and her problems. Bill (we became informal since we were talking shop) felt that her symptoms were stress related, but listed the tests she should have performed and the order in which they should be done. I felt a tremendous sense of confidence in him and made arrangements for my friend to see him for an examination and appropriate testing.

His initial sense of her illness proved to be correct. Her stress was determined to be mostly work related. She made adjustments to her lifestyle as best as she could in order to limit the work stress. The decision to have a good day when she woke up helped a great deal, but I think that knowing she didn't have MS was a good part of the cure. Your mind can make you ill. Your mind can help you heal. A holistic approach to healing can have great benefits.

Since Dr. Lent seemed to do such a great job with my friend I decided to check him out for myself. Or should I say I had him check me out for myself? I made an appointment for the dreaded general physical exam.

I tend to deal with stress by joking about it. In fact, my staff refers to me as the happy sick man because I react to being sick by joking around. Some of my funniest bits have come during an illness. My dear departed Uncle Paul used to tell me that I was so funny I should be on a stage....the first one out of town!

I filled out the forms necessary for enrolling myself as a patient with Dr. Lent and then took a seat in the reception area as I patiently awaited my turn. Perhaps not so patiently; everyone else seemed to be ill. I began to feel some concern for my continued health. I started to imagine all of the awful diseases that could be floating towards me and I recalled how many diseases I thought I had when I was in vet school. For practically every infectious disease we studied I could imagine that I was experiencing some symptoms. Mercifully, my musings were interrupted when the wait was unexpectedly short. I wouldn't need the reading materials I had brought for the occasion.

I was brought into an exam room where the nurse took my history and some baseline data (for Bill-ing purposes). After the blood pressure and temperature readings she handed me a flimsy little gown; the type with a back draft that removes any sense of protection from the elements or probing eyes. As she prepared to leave the room the nurse asked me to change into the gown and make myself comfortable. The latter would prove difficult. (The inability to feel comfortable at this time is unofficially referred to as Gowns Syndrome).

As I struggled to adapt to my new toga I looked around the room for some form of diversion. The charts of various self examinations made me fidgety. I figured Doc would be taking care of those things. I'd rather do it myself! The usual equipment was there; nothing appeared to be too invasive. The needle disposal unit was tamper proof, unlike the ones I use. I supposed that was to avoid litigation in case some one poked himself with a used needle. Thank God I don't have the same concerns with AIDS or hepatitis in my practice. That box of latex exam gloves looked ominous.

Suddenly, in walked Bill. I greeted him informally in the vain hope that it would make him less inclined to feel the need to use those exam gloves. I thanked him for the nice work he had done for my friend and related the improvement in her condition. He thanked me for the referral and asked if I had any concerns about my health. I replied that I was there to have the appropriate tests for any of the diseases that he felt I was at risk for. A lipid profile as part of a cardiac evaluation was foremost on my mind, but I also wanted a baseline PSA test. PSA stands for prostate specific antigen. It is a blood test that detects inflammation in the prostate gland. With feigned seriousness, I stuck my right arm out, palm upward, and said, "Bill, I'd like you to check my prostate."

He smiled and said, "Sorry, I still do the digital exam as well."

He did that as the last part of the general physical. He seemed very satisfied with the exam and said, "Wow, you have the prostate of a 30 year old man." I was 40 years old at the time and, needless to say, I was pleased to hear his assessment. In my excitement I decided to let Bill have it a bit.

"How did you know that?" I said. "I keep it at home…in a jar….on my dresser."

"You're sick" he laughed.

"I'm sick? Look where your hand was!"

We both had a good laugh and exchanged some pleasantries before he ordered some tests. He left the room and within a few minutes his nurse returned to collect some blood from me. She also gave me a tetanus vaccine. That is particularly important in my profession considering the many animal encounters I experience.

After reclaiming my clothes and regaining my dignity I stopped at the receptionist's desk to check out. Dr. Lent (I thought I should be formal in front of the staff) paused in passing to tell me that he would call with the test results. Since Dad had bypass surgery at midlife, he strongly suggested that I set up a stress echocardiogram to further evaluate my heart regardless of the outcome of the tests. Of course, I agreed to do so. As I turned to leave, Bill looked at his receptionist, nodded towards me and said, "After he leaves, check the waiting area to be sure he didn't mark his territory."

"Oh, Bill", I responded, "I just can't resist those potted plants!"

We are now on permanent informal status and it is my sworn duty to abuse the staff at Bill's office whenever the opportunity arises. They love me. I know it. I can feel it. No matter how they try to deny it.

All of the blood tests and the subsequent cardiac evaluation came back normal. In fact, the cardiologist did some genetic marker testing and gave me great assurances that, genetically, I don't have my Dad's heart. You could have tied a string to me and floated me around the room like a balloon when I received that bit of good news. I continue to have echoes done every couple of years just to err on the side of safety. That ounce of prevention may be worth tons of cure.

The upshot of all of this is that Bill and I have become good friends. A couple of years later he brought Ginger in for an exam because she had stopped eating, was vomiting and was producing large volumes of dark yellow urine. It was immediately apparent on examination of Ginger's mucous membranes that she was jaundiced.

Jaundice is caused by excess bile pigments in the blood stream. It freely moves into all tissues and causes them to turn yellow. The pigment is a result of red blood cell destruction. The jaundice can be due to excess production of pigment through excess destruction of red blood cells (hemolytic anemia), decreased processing of a normal pigment load due to liver disease or obstruction of the bile ducts which provide passage of bile from the liver to the intestines. I suspected primary liver disease because she didn't appear to be anemic (gums weren't pale) and the liver felt enlarged and bumpy on abdominal palpation. I was further concerned by the lack of a fever which would normally accompany a bacterial infection that would potentially be treatable with appropriate antibiotic therapy.

Her blood chemistry tests confirmed that she had severe liver disease. The complete blood count results showed no signs of anemia or response to an infection. We needed to determine the underlying cause of the problem. Cancer was at the top of the list. An obstruction of the bile ducts due to gall stones is rare is dogs, but we needed to look for them in the hope that there was a cure for Ginger.

At the time, ultrasound imaging was performed at the clinic

by a visiting radiologist every other week. It wouldn't be available for another ten days. Since Ginger wasn't eating we decided that she needed help sooner. Rather than traveling to another imaging center Bill elected to go straight to an exploratory surgery on Ginger. Her chest was clear of tumors on pre-operative radiographs. However, surgery revealed multiple nodules on her liver. I took a biopsy of some of the affected tissue. I had plenty to choose from because it involved nearly the entire liver. I prayed that the histopathology would reveal them to be regenerative nodules, a benign but dramatic healing process as a result of some insult to the liver (such as toxins or a resolving infection).

Ginger felt terrific after surgery. She had received a lot of fluid therapy as well as antibiotics. The latter were an effort to get a jump on any infection that might be found. The news from the pathologist was reported to me a few days later. It was hepatic carcinoma which is one of the most aggressive tumors seen in the abdominal cavity. I called Bill with the sad news and grave prognosis. I expected Ginger to live for only a few weeks. Two months would be optimistic. He told me that the resumption of Ginger's appetite was short lived. She wasn't vomiting yet, but I knew that would be in her near future as the cancer progressed.

I asked Bill if he felt Ginger was suffering and whether he felt it was time to think about parting with her. I could feel his angst over the phone. He took a moment to collect himself before telling me that his wife was diagnosed with MS just two days before. Ginger was her emotional crutch and there was no way that they could even consider saying good bye to her beloved dog.

There is little to do for liver cancer other than giving palliative care and waiting for the end. I suggested that we at least try Ginger on a moderate dose of steroids. I hoped to reduce some of the swelling in the liver and thus enable the bile to flow more easily. Relieving her jaundice would certainly help Ginger feel better. I also hoped to induce a big appetite as a side effect of the steroids. We have some other drugs available today that have fewer undesirable side effects (such as drinking excessively), but at the time that was all I had to offer. Bill appreciated that I could phone the prescription in to a human pharmacy near his office since he had his hands full at home. Veterinarians use many of the same drugs that physicians prescribe for people and we often avail ourselves of the convenience offered to our clients by pharmacies.

Ginger returned to have her sutures removed the following week. She was acting like a new dog! She was eating well. She had done no vomiting and her yellow membranes seemed less jaundiced. Her arthritis was relieved as a side effect of the prednisone so she was much more active. I did my best to discourage optimism because she had a bad cancer. We would continue to keep her happy for as long as possible. Bill promised to keep me posted on the progress of both his dog and his wife.

To make a long story short, Ginger lived for another three years! About four months after her surgery Bill asked me what I thought was going on inside of Ginger's liver. I even began to question the diagnosis from the pathologist despite the fact that a microscopic diagnosis of cancer is rarely wrong. We decided to do chest radiographs again. There were lesions, presumably metastatic tumors, throughout the lungs. I could also feel her liver getting larger and more firm and bumpy. I still felt the end was near for Ginger despite her wagging tail and licking tongue.

Another few months passed by. The liver continued to enlarge, but still no jaundice or other symptoms. The prednisone dosage had been gradually reduced and finally stopped several weeks ago. Ginger continued to feel great. I told Bill, "The only explanation I have for you is that your family, Kathy in particular, needed this dog more than God. Keep up the prayers because they apparently did as much or more for Ginger than my efforts."

Death came for Ginger very quietly one night. She didn't wake up in the morning and she had enjoyed a nice sun bath in the yard the previous day. Bill allowed me to do a post mortem exam on her body. You could actually see the nodules on her liver bulging beneath the skin of her distended abdomen. The entire liver was cancerous except for the little accessory liver lobe. She had lived on that small, unaffected portion of liver for three years! The lungs were filled with scattered firm nodules. I sent biopsies of the liver and lungs to the lab and awaited results.

I didn't have to wait long. The pathologist actually called me to personally give me an oral report. That has not happened before or since Ginger's case. I have occasionally called the lab for clarifications on a case, but a pathologist has never been so excited as to call me first. Each of the lung lesions was a spread of the liver carcinoma, but each one had a capsule of scar tissue built around it. He had never seen or heard of anything like it. I'm sure that there is a logical medical explanation for Ginger, but I know that I had nothing to do with her long survival. Miracles happen every day, but she was the beneficiary of a biggie.

Bill's wife continues to struggle with her MS. The family will battle it for the rest of her life. She was given a great boost by the care of Ginger; a dog who fawned over her; another living thing that loved her and needed her; some one to take her mind off of her affliction and encourage her to get up and move. As is often the case with pets, Ginger gave back in love and care as much or more than she received.

*An MD client was discussing her educational experiences with me. She mentioned that she had a master's degree before becoming an MD. I asked the topic of her master's thesis and she replied, "I was studying the effect of frozen bandages on cold cuts!"*

*When I developed an unusual rash on my neck and ear lobe I suspected that I may have shingles. When I called my doctor he had immediate concerns about it and insisted that I see him immediately. I went to his office at noon and was ushered into an exam room without a wait.*

*Dr. Lent examined my ear canals and seemed exceptionally relieved that he didn't see any lesions. I asked if that would have been a bad thing and he informed me that Herpes (shingles) lesions in the ear canal are often associated with hearing loss and Bell's palsy (paralysis of the face on the affected side). I looked a bit distraught and slowly tapping my face on that side I asked him, "Am I…am I drooling, Bill?"*

*"No.", he replied.*

*"Huh? What'd you say?" I said as I cocked my head and cupped that ear towards him.*

*He informed me that I was the happiest patient he has ever diagnosed with shingles. I just figured that there are a lot worse things he could diagnose and that if I did get Bell's palsy I would simply look a bit funnier than I normally do for awhile. If I got hearing loss, well God gave me two ears and He can take the hearing from one if He wants. If it hurt, there was always pain meds.*

*I decided to have some fun with my clients and staff as well. I had to avoid pregnant women that had not yet had Chicken Pox…shingles is caused by the same virus and it can result in the loss of a pregnancy. Therefore, I would ask all my female clients if they were pregnant…even if they were little old ladies. I would hum Jingle Bells and when asked why (it was mid-summer) I would sing Shingle bells, shingle bells…*

*I even wrote up the top ten reasons why it is nice to have shingles:*

1.  *You will have a roof over your head.*
2.  *It is easy to get people to move out of your way.*
3.  *You get to visit the pretty nurses at the doctor's office.*
4.  *You can ask your doctor for pain medicines.*
5.  *You can play connect the dots and look for Elvis.*
6.  *You can rub a violin bow across your head while singing songs from Fiddler on the Roof.*
7.  *If you're really sick they may name a syndrome after you.*
8.  *Post-herpetic neuralgia builds pain tolerance and character.*
9.  *It's the blight of your life.*
    *And the number one reason that it is nice to have shingles:*
10. *It's the OTHER herpes!*

CHAPTER 18

# *No MSG Please*

I have always had a curious disposition; some would say that it matches my appearance. When I saw an advertisement for a seminar on acupuncture I couldn't resist the chance to learn about Eastern medicine. An added bonus was the venue...Las Vegas! I had never been in a casino since gambling was still illegal in the Midwest. Nowadays there seems to be a riverboat at every bend of the Mississippi.

The seminar didn't disappoint me; it was fascinating. The Chinese think of the body in totally different terms than we do in Western medicine. I could see why it was considered alternative medicine. I had no training in or understanding of the theories of energy flow through the body. If my patients were to benefit from this therapy they would need an alternate source. It was beyond my understanding up to this point.

The teacher for this seminar was Dr. Beltman. He had been trained in traditional western veterinary medicine but became interested in Chinese medicine early in his career. In order to receive training in acupuncture he had to travel to China. There were no veterinary acupuncturists in this country. He lived and studied in China for a couple of years before he felt competent enough to bring his skills home.

The language barrier was a significant obstacle for him at first. About a year into his training he felt comfortable enough to ask his professor a question that had been bothering him for months. He had received copies of acupuncture charts for people, horses, cows, pigs and even chickens. Where were the charts for dogs and cats? His superior gave him a perplexed look and replied, "Why would you want to do acupuncture on a dog or cat? You're just going to eat it!"

Total culture shock. This would be more of a challenge than he thought. With no charts to follow Dr. Beltman would be mapping his own course. His mentors were kind enough to help with his endeavor and Dr. Beltman would go on to widespread acclaim.

In Chinese medicine it is thought that disease symptoms are a result of disruption of energy flow through the body. The energy travels through channels called meridians. The goal is to restore energy flow and enhance the total body energy, Chi. Some of this energy radiates around the body, thus the practice of aura massage. Some people feel that they can see this energy around people and claim that they can 'read' auras. It is regrettable that this isn't a more scientific field of endeavor. It would be interesting to put this information to use in a rational manner.

I was attending a party some years later. A tarot card reader was hired to entertain at the party. She picked me out of a large group of people and introduced herself to me; "Hi, I'm Zorka. You have a magnificent aura."

I might have said the same to her if she had been twenty years younger and I had been five drinks wittier. At any rate, she somehow knew that some creepy things had happened in my life. The time I divined Dad's heart attack was first and foremost, but I also related some other ESPish events that had occurred.

She was determined that I needed to go to classes to enhance my psychic abilities. (Do they give aural exams there?) I responded that ignorance is bliss. Why would any one want to know about future events that they are powerless to change? Not me. I have enough trouble handling the present moment. Although, it makes me wonder about those lotto numbers; why don't psychics win every week?

Pardon my digression; back to the seminar. The meridians pass through the main organs and were named accordingly; lung, liver, gall bladder, kidney, etc. I found it interesting that the gall bladder had its own meridian, but the adrenal glands aren't even acknowledged as a structure in eastern medicine. All of the meridians have multiple points at the surface of the body where the energy level can be checked. My immediate thought was 'yeah, right', but then Dr. Beltman demonstrated the location of the acupuncture points on his own body. He used an Ohmeter to demonstrate the areas of decreased electrical resistance which denote acupuncture points. Now I was hooked. You could find these points with a scientific instrument rather than by sensing them with your fingertips. Up to this time I thought it was closer to voodoo than medicine. During the laboratory sessions we were able to use the Ohmeter to find points on our own bodies.

I was assured that I would eventually be able to stop using a meter because I would be able feel the points with my fingertips. I had significant doubts about that!

It is interesting that we use pressure on our acupuncture points routinely without being aware of what we are actually doing. For example, if you bang your arm against something you instinctively rub the area. Very often you are rubbing a spot adjacent to the actual injury; the local acupuncture point. When your eyes are tired you tend to rub them. The acupuncture point for tired eyes is below the eyelids on the floor of the sockets. You don't need to rub your eyes for relief, just the base of the sockets. I routinely use pressure on my sinus points to alleviate congestion due to allergies. It works immediately!

Dr. Beltman showed photos of Chinese patients having surgery performed using acupuncture analgesia instead of an anesthetic. He was quick to point out that you can still feel the sensations of surgery, but it doesn't hurt. I don't think that would go over well in our society. We take pills BEFORE arthritis pain starts! We drink because our football team is losing. We don't like to even think about pain. Personally, you can knock me out and wake me up when the pain is over.

By the end of the week we were performing acupuncture on ourselves. The needles are very thin. They were surprisingly pain-free. A different effect on the point was expected with a clockwise rotation of the needle versus a counterclockwise rotation. The different alloys used to make the needle are thought to produce different effects. Different groupings of points are used to treat different diseases. Considering I was having difficulty in finding a single point, this was getting complicated.

The class had been limited to sixteen attendees in order to give each of us enough attention. I had become comfortable enough with Dr. Beltman to ask him, "Shelly, how long did you do acupuncture before you stopped feeling like a novice?"

His response was, "Ten years."

"I don't think that I'll be doing this in my practice."

Seeming a bit surprised he asked, "Why not?"

I explained that I worked in a surgical referral practice. I scrubbed in on knee surgeries for five years with Dr. Velders before I felt comfortable enough to take my own cases. And you better believe Dr. Velders was around for the first few in case anything came up that seemed out of the ordinary. I feel the same way about acupuncture. It is very complicated and I felt doomed to fail without an experienced hand to help me.

Although I still do not perform acupuncture I'm glad that I attended the seminar. I refer patients to an experienced veterinary acupuncturist for a variety of illnesses afflicting my patients. I have seen some wonderful results and I believe in it for certain things, especially chronic pain. Some even believe acupuncture can cure cancer in pets. However, that hasn't been my experience.

If it causes a delay in more conventional therapy then it may be detrimental to your pet's health. Like other modes of therapy acupuncture is not a cure-all, but it is a useful tool.

This introduction into eastern medicine opened my mind to other therapies as well. I attended a seminar on herbal medicine that was taught by a thirty-year veteran of eastern veterinary medicine. She gave us a list of the top 25 herbal formulas that she used in her practice. Each was made by an herbal pharmacist. The list of ingredients was followed by a list of what each one was designed to do in terms of eastern and western medicine. Finally, here was someone who was willing to acknowledge that both cultures may have some truth behind their philosophy of healing.

She gave us one piece of advice to take home even if it was the only thing we learned that day: Never, Never, NEVER mix your own herbs. You will get into big trouble. Herbs are considered safe because of their use in China for the past 3000 years. If practitioners gave their patient medicine that made their condition worsen it could be punishable by up to death! First do no harm is their mantra.

` We don't live up to that in western medicine. If you watch any television at all you will see ads for drugs that treat asthma, arthritis, erectile dysfunction, obesity, smoking addiction; the list goes on and on. Each commercial comes with a quick disclaimer at the end warning of potential side effects. My favorite is the fat blocking drugs that may cause diarrhea, cramps, flatulence, oily secretions, urgency to defecate, inability to hold it, etc. It sounds like they finally got chili into a pill.

One of the interesting formulas on her list is used to treat degenerative spinal cord disease. At the time, I had several patients with degenerative myelopathy, a progressive loss of fatty insulation around the nerves in the spinal cord. This causes the nerves to short circuit resulting in progressive loss of function. Western medicine treats these patients with long term steroids at high doses. This doesn't stop the disease and I often question whether it even slows the progression of nerve loss. The side effects of steroids commonly include weight gain and muscle loss; a really bad duo for patients having difficult ambulation to start with. Since we had nothing to lose and since the herbs seemed safe enough to try, we gave them a shot on several patients.

It is very unlikely that even human patients will crush up herbs, make a bad tasting tea and choke it down the hatch. Therefore, the herbal pharmacy makes the tea and then freeze-dries it into a powdery granule for administration with food. Alternatively, the powder can be put into capsules. Since the herbs were made for human consumption I decided to taste them. Not bad; a bit like cinnamon (a lot like cinnamon….some is added to improve the taste). The dogs accepted it very well. Three of the four dogs in the initial group regained most or all of their nerve functions. Not bad for an incurable disease!

As a result of my initial experience with herbs I have become a bit of a believer. I tried about 15 of the herbal formulas and I have eight of them that I now keep on hand for routine use. The most frequently used formulas are for treating arthritis and allergies. Both are long-term illnesses. The western medicines used in treating them can have very negative long term side effects. It is nice to have a workable alternative.

Nutritional supplements can help stop the progression of arthritis, but the results are often inadequate. Nonsteroid anti-inflammatory drugs (NSAIDs) help relieve pain and inflammation, often dramatically and quickly, but the long term side effects include liver and kidney problems. We require blood tests every six months for pets on these drugs in order to ensure that they aren't harming them. Steroids have a long list of side effects including diabetes, liver problems and heart problems to name but a few. Again, frequent laboratory tests are required to monitor these patients.

The herbal formulas have been very safe in my experience. They are considered nutritional supplements and require no long term blood parameter monitoring. I have also been pleased to note that there should be a dramatic response to the herbs within two weeks. If none is seen then they are unlikely to be the answer and it is time to move on to something else. Many nutritional supplements are designed to simply maintain function; if you're not any worse then they must be helping. Not the herbs; if your pet is not better then the herbs aren't helping and it is time to move on to another mode of therapy.

One of the recent changes in therapeutic intervention for orthopedic diseases has been the opening of centers dedicated to physical therapy and other modes of therapy designed to regain function of muscles and joints. Underwater treadmills are now available. Massage therapy is an option. I even have dogs undergoing chiropractic manipulation and kinesiology. I wonder if some of these patients would be better benefited by a structured walk on a regular basis. But, if therapy is helping without placing an undue burden on the family or patient then I'm OK with it. Whatever it takes to motivate the family to keep their pets moving can be a viable part of the treatment regimen. 'Move it or lose it' definitely applies to patients with degenerative joint disease.

The herbs used to treat allergies are in tablet form. They are traditional Chinese medicine pills which resemble large black BBs. Again, they either work or they don't. I would rank them ahead of antihistamines in their efficacy, but behind steroids. They rank well ahead of both in their lack of side effects.

When I was in vet school I was taught that there is a chemical in the body that was referred to as SRSA; slow reacting substance of allergies. It could be isolated from the skin lesions of allergic dogs and injected into the skin of non-allergic dogs where it would cause a hive-type lesion in about 24 hours. The reaction would persist for several days afterwards. This was in contrast to histamine which causes an immediate reaction that persists for a short time. Thus, the name, *slow* reacting substance of allergies. We now know that this is a family of chemicals called leukotrienes. There have been efforts to make anti-leukotriene drugs, but they have had too many side effects in animals to be marketable. There is one available for humans, but we have limited experience with it in dogs.  Cost and side-effects have been problematic.

The herbs for allergies, Pe Min Kan Wan, were presented to me as an herbal antihistamine.  They never seem to produce results in the first week.  Antihistamines should work immediately.  I have reason to suspect that the herbs may be blocking leukotriene receptors or production.  Anyone interested in doing a doctoral thesis?  I'd love to know how the herbs work in terms of western medicine.

The formulas for most herbs are closely guarded secrets.  You can't patent an herb so anyone can copy your formula.  Hence, the phrase 'ancient Chinese secret'.  Many of the formulas are family secrets and are passed on from one generation to the next.  I often wonder how many treatments went to the grave with their discoverers.

The names of the herbs can be somewhat intimidating if you don't speak Chinese.  The English translations are mostly phonetic spellings of the original Chinese.  One topical formula for treating skin lesions is called Zi Cao.  I always referred to it as the red stuff because it is very red.  It has the appearance of being staining, but by an apparent miracle it isn't.  My brother Keith is much more computer literate than I am.  When I gave him some red stuff for a skin lesion on the foot of his dog he decided to go online and find out the meaning of Zi Cao.  He found a Chinese-English dictionary after a brief (0.14 sec.) Google search.  The translation was quite simply *red stuff*.

When I was visiting my friends Don and Marsha in Sarasota I had the opportunity to go fishing with their Chinese physician, RJ.  Yes, RJ.  Sounds like a good old boy name, but it is simply easier to pronounce than his full name.  Our conversation eventually led to a discussion of my experience with Chinese medicine.

I often receive free samples of herbal formulas with my usual orders.  One of the formulas is used to treat cold symptoms in people.  After three consecutive successes in treating my colds I decided that I should keep some on hand at all times.  At the first sign of a cold I take zhong gan ling for a couple of days and my symptoms resolve. It doesn't seem to work for the flu. RJ shook his head knowingly, apparently familiar with the product. I asked for a translation of zhong gan ling thinking it was a particular herb or herbs. He thought for a moment, looking for the proper English words and said, "Very bad, severe. Cold. Remedy." Chinese medicine must be a snap if you know Chinese!

My clients are often curious about what is in the herbal formulas and so am I. Herbology is not my forte, but if there is a formula that can help my patients without side effects then I'm interested in it. They are also curious about the names of the herbs. The names are sometimes difficult to pronounce despite their phonetic spellings. Clients often get them confused…it looks like alphabet soup at times. My staff often comes to me for help in getting the correct herbs especially when the client is completely mispronouncing the name. My favorite was when a client came in requesting more 'Ho Chi Min Trail mix'. I refilled the Du Huo Ji Shen Tang for her dog's arthritis.

When I first ordered herbs for my patients it was met with a lot of skepticism by the staff. One of the nurses brought in Ham-Fu, a stuffed hamster doll wearing a karate outfit and holding nun chucks. When his hand was pressed he would sing Kung Fu Fighting and spin his nun chucks. KC even dressed up as Dr. G, herbalist for Halloween. She wore a smock with the Chinese symbols for peace and love along with a rice hat. It was very funny and very flattering to me. It was nice to have some support as I began to explore nontraditional therapies.

A paradigm shift has occurred in the attitude of western and eastern doctors. (See, I paid attention at some of those management meetings. I knew I could get the word paradigm into a sentence somewhere!) When I was in school, eastern medicine was *alternative* medicine. If you were interested in it you needed to go somewhere else to get it and we were not about to talk to 'the other side'.

About five years after graduation it became *complementary* medicine. It seemed to be helping some patients so the attitude became "Gee, that seems to be working. We'll talk to those people, but you still have to go to them for the therapy. We'll use it to complement what we're doing."

In the past five years it has become obvious that some of the eastern medicine works quite well and we need to work it into our repertoire of treatment modalities. Therefore, we are beginning to see centers for *integrative* medicine where eastern and western specialists are available under the same roof. They even talk to each other and consult on cases! Nobody knows everything, but perhaps together we will find more answers for our patients.

*I recently received an invitation to a lecture series sponsored by an herbal manufacturing company in California. The first lecture was titled 'The Best of Master Tung's Magic Points'. This seemed to be more than alternative medicine; it sounded like an alternative life style.*

*Actual name of a dog: 'Max' Pyle. I really expected to be greeted by a Great Dane. When I opened the door, I met a happy little Boston terrier. When I commented to his owner about my misconception I was assured that the dog lived up to his name when he left deposits in the back yard!*

*When you call a drug abuse helpline and nobody is there to answer you are unlikely to get an answering machine, but you may get addictophone.*

*If a mafia hit man gets an itchy trigger finger should he put hydroCorleone ointment on it?*

# CHAPTER 19

# *Make a Career of it*

One of the most rewarding ways of giving back to the community is through the education of children.  I'm not referring to their visits at the clinic with their pets, although that is one of my favorite things.  Baby on board, Greiner is on it.  I love to work with children.

Here I am referring to activities outside of office hours.  It started with a client who asked for a tour of the clinic with her cubscout troop.  I had them come on a Saturday just before closing time.  I thought that I would be giving the tour unassisted, but several of the staff decided to stay and join in the fun.  We had a blast.  They asked a lot of great questions about everyday things that I took for granted; do dogs get cavities?  Do you use Band-aids on dogs?  Do shots hurt?  They went on and on.  Of course, I helped instigate some of the fun.

I had a toy stuffed cat that needed a physical exam and a 'shot'.  I showed the pack (or is it a den?) the different instruments that I use during a physical.  They knew what most of them were used for, but they were a bit shaky on those big names, like stethoscope.

They all giggled when I showed them where the thermometer went, just like the doctor did to them when they were babies! They got very serious when I gave the 'cat' its injection (I used air in the syringe). I explained the difference between a vaccination (which helps to prevent a disease) and a shot of medicine (which helps to treat a disease). I then offered shots to all of the kids. "Not me!" came the replies.

I then explained that we carried only animal medicines and if I gave them a dog shot they would have to eat off the floor for a week. A hand shot up. "I'll take one!" said one little boy. That prospect sounded great to him. His mother rolled her eyes and offered to let him eat with their dog that night. "No way, Bruno's a pig. He'll eat all of his food and mine."

Sensing a loss of control over the giggling boys I decided it was time to move on to radiology. I showed them the machine and explained what X-rays are and how we use them to generate medical images. I explained the dangers of radiation and let them try on the protective lead aprons and gloves that we wear when taking images. The gloves are heavy and they covered the entire forearm of the little boy trying one on. His arm dropped under the weight. As he recovered and held it up he hollered, "Whoa. Look, I'm Iron Man!" Of course, they all had to try one on after that.

The den mother had to end their visit before we finished the entire tour because they had a schedule to adhere to and I was being a bit long winded as I am want to be. We all had a great time. I received a wonderful thank you letter about week later. The boys had drawn pictures of me and things that had stuck in their fertile little minds during the tour. Some of the pictures were less than flattering and I hoped that I didn't really look like that. We decided to entertain any future dens and troops that wanted to come for a tour and we have done so many times since.

A larger audience became available when I was asked to do a career day presentation for the DuPage County vocational training center. Bus loads of seventh graders are transported to the center for a series of career presentations. The groups at each session consist of 20 to 30 children. The presenters have 15 minutes for each group. The bell is sounded and off they go to their next pre-selected session.

The students have a list of questions that need to be answered at each session. What personal qualities are needed for the job? How much education is required? How many hours are worked each week? How much money do you make? I always saved that one for last. I didn't want anyone losing interest if they had already been to presentations to become a higher paid professional such as an M.D. or engineer or attorney.

My biggest challenge at this annual event is cramming everything into fifteen minutes. When I see some of the kids losing interest (it is a day out of the normal routine and many of them are out to party), I pull out my trusty radiographs. There is nothing like a broken femur or coins in the stomach of a dog to regain lost interest.

After giving the same presentation five times in a row you start to forget what you went over for the group you're talking to. Did I mention all the different specialties available to vets? Did I mention what classes they should take in high school? In college? Fortunately, the end comes soon since I am finished after presenting at the morning sessions. I can't imagine the presenters that stay for the full two days of presentations. They deserve a week off after that! I'd never make it as an army recruiter.

My favorite career day presentations have been for the third grade pet awareness program through the Chicago Veterinary Medical Association. I also talk to a third grade class that is taught by one of my former assistants, Tracy. She left the clinic for college, but continued to work for us while on semester breaks. After graduating, she landed a teaching job in a school just ten minutes from the office. She is a great educator and her class is always well behaved and interested in what I have to say.

I step things down a notch for the lower grades. In addition to showing off some instruments and doing a physical on a stuffed animal (the thermometer bit never gets old), I talk to them about why animals may come to my clinic for help. I discuss my daily duties.

My first duty is to attend to any patients that are in the hospital. This may include animals that are sick or recovering from surgery. We don't do any boarding of pets in our facility. When you go to stay somewhere you go to a hotel, not a hospital. You don't want to sleep next to a sick patient and the sick patient wants peace and quiet. Besides that, a full kennel might distract from the care for the sick patients.

Admittance of patients scheduled for surgery or medical work up comes next. Each patient undergoing anesthesia has a complete physical and blood is drawn to make sure that they are healthy enough to undergo their procedure.

I discuss some scenarios for surgical patients and stress the benefits of having their own pets spayed and neutered. I put the mechanics of surgery aside for the moment, but we return to surgery at the end of the talk.

In the afternoon I do outpatient work. I explain why animals may come in for an office visit. Wellness examinations are part of it, but ill pets may come in at any time. We provide emergency services throughout the day as well as routine appointments. You never know what your day will be like. The children always have stories about their own pets or family members. It's amazing how many children bring up their own medical conditions during a discussion of pet problems. Kids relate to animals at a very basic level. In fact, very young children relate to animals as equals. Allowing them to be abusive to an animal is teaching them that it is acceptable to abuse a person. Teaching them to be kind and loving and sharing with their pets teaches them to be kind and loving and sharing towards people.

I ask for a show of hands. 'How many of you own a dog....a cat...a guinea pig...a rabbit...a ferret...an iguana....a snake....a fish....a bird? I even get the occasional hedge hog. No tigers or skunks yet. I tell the children that I have had an opportunity to work on all of those animals as well as on a lot of wildlife and an occasional zoo animal. You never know what may come in the front door.

I discuss some of the maladies that afflict animals. The fact that a dog or cat can get allergies or something as simple as diarrhea is amazing to the kids. So is the treatment for the diseases. Animals take many of the same medicines that people take, but some common human medicines may make an animal deathly sick. For example, acetaminophen is very toxic for cats. So I reinforce that they should never give medicine to their pet without calling their veterinarian first.

After some medical conditions have been discussed I ask the children how a vet might go about discovering the cause of a problem if it is not immediately apparent. Most of them guess blood tests correctly. I've never had them get urinalysis, but it is always good for a giggle when you explain how to get a sample. (Tracy's class is always amazed when they learn that she used to go outside to try to collect 'pee' in a pan from a dog.) With a little prodding they eventually guess X-rays and I also mention CT, MRI and ultrasound to them. Then the real fun begins. Radiographs.

I bring a collection of films with some very obvious lesions. I used to show the radiographs of an iguana that had swallowed a coin as the first case. Just realizing that it is the skeleton of a lizard that they are looking at brings a sense of awe to the children. This usually manages to regain order if the kids are getting antsy at this point. The teachers in attendance also became very attentive as I explain the symptoms associated with the lizard swallowing the coin. The owner had noticed that the iguana had become quite pale. This was due to anemia resulting from the absorption of the heavy metals in the penny. We performed surgery on the iguana to retrieve the coin and he recovered uneventfully.

Next, I show them an assortment of obvious foreign bodies in dogs. Rocks are always good. Dr. Velders' dog, Moose, was usually the star of this lineup. His foreign body wasn't as unusual as his story.

Moose was a very active ten year-old American Staffordshire terrier; no one ever referred to him as a pitbull even though that is one of the pit breeds. He was a wonderful dog that loved everyone, squirrels excepted.

Doc's teenaged daughter had a friend at the house on Christmas Eve. They were threading popcorn to put on the Christmas tree. The friend put down his strand to get more popcorn and when he returned it was gone. Moose ate the popcorn; needle, thread and all! Not only had he swallowed it, but it had penetrated through his stomach wall and was in the abdominal cavity. This was truly an emergency.

The Velders' Christmas Eve was spent at the clinic doing surgery to retrieve the needle from Moose's abdomen. Since it was actually out of the stomach, Dr. Velders searched throughout the abdomen to be certain that it hadn't done damage to any of the other organs. During the search he discovered a small tumor on Moose's spleen. He removed the spleen and sent the tumor to the lab for histopathology to determine what kind of tumor it was and whether it was malignant or benign.

Moose recovered uneventfully. His tumor was, in fact, malignant (hemangiosarcoma, a tumor of the blood vessels, for those interested), but it was caught at such an early stage that it hadn't spread. The foreign body had actually saved Moose's life!

The next sets of radiographs showed dogs with varying degrees of pregnancy. I always show the single pup film first because it is so obvious in the bulging little Maltese dog. Most of the classes get the gist of it right away and ooh and aah over the skeletal puppy in the womb. One group of students, however, was mortified. They were stunned as one of them said, "That dog swallowed a puppy!"

I was dumbfounded. I would never have followed the logic. Dog swallows rocks. Dog swallows needle. Of course, that dog swallowed a puppy. I quickly explained that the dog was pregnant and ever after I have shown the pregnant dog radiographs before the foreign body radiographs.

Once we have decided that a patient needs surgery I explain anesthesia to the students. I bring an endotracheal tube and demonstrate to the students how it goes down the airway to maintain oxygen and anesthesia to the patient. I show them the inflatable cuff that ensures a good seal so that the patient doesn't aspirate anything into the lungs or inhale room air around the tube.

I then discuss germs. I explain that vets need to shave the area in which the incision is to be made so that we can disinfect it. It is better to prevent infections by preemptive scrubbing than to try to control an infection after a surgery. I instruct them in the preparation of the surgeon before going into the surgery room. We wear a cap and mask so that germs don't get onto the patient during surgery. We scrub our hands and arms twice. The hands are dried first and then the forearms, making certain that you don't re-contaminate yourself. I then have Tracy assist in my 'gowning in'; she ties the sterile garment being certain not to touch the front of the gown since her hands have germs on them and the gown may come in contact with the surgical field. Her students are again amazed at her versatility.

After skipping over the details of actually doing the cutting (there is always at least one little boy who wants to hear it all), I end the session by providing caps, masks and non-sterile exam gloves for all of the students. Regrettably, you have to ask permission ahead of time because I've actually had parents get angry. Not because their child might have a latex allergy (I ask) or might somehow choke on a glove (if they lived this long without choking on something I don't think the gloves will do it), but because I gave their child 'medical supplies'. Come on, the masks have puppy and kitten faces on them; they look great. I don't know where some people are coming from, but I know where I'd like to tell them to go.

One year I was tapped by the CVMA to do two pet awareness programs in one day. The first school was in the inner city; literally in a slum. None of the children knew the names of any of my instruments. Most of them didn't even know what they were used for. There was no semblance of order. I had to nearly shout to get their attention. When I finally did it was short lived.

Few of them had pets of their own. All of their animal related stories were violent. They started with "I saw a cat get its' head bit off by a dog." And it got worse from there.

Even the radiographs were a disaster. The boys kept pointing to an inappropriate area near the pubis and giggling, 'What's back here?' They did this even for the pregnant dog films. Their fixation on male anatomy at this age was disturbing to me.

That afternoon I went to a school in a somewhat affluent suburb. The children knew what my instruments were used for and most of them knew the names of the instruments. They were well mannered and attentive. They asked great questions. We connected with each other very well.

It later occurred to me that few inner city children go home to learn. They are simply interested in surviving when they leave school. I saw the problem facing our country head on. Parents are the primary teachers of their children. With 80% of our inner city children in one parent families it is no wonder that their crime rate and illiteracy rate are through the roof. It doesn't take a village to raise children. It takes two parents. I wish I had the solution to this problem, but without some profound societal changes I don't see one on the horizon.

I congratulated the suburban teachers on the job they were doing. They all spoke highly of the school administrators who made the effort to communicate with the parents of the children. Not only was homework assigned, it was finished and submitted for grading. They had a partnership with the families. That is a formula for success, but it seems sadly lacking through most of our educational system.

I will continue to try to make a difference one career day at a time and by continuing to pay attention to the children that enter my clinic. Validation by an adult can be a powerful force in the life of a youngster. Motivation can help, too.

A few of the statistics that I have gleaned over the years seem to strike a chord with many students, especially those in the upper grades. Only 5% of the people in this country like their job and look forward to going to it! One in twenty; that is pretty pathetic. What is the surest way to get into that 5%? Get your college degree. Do it in four years. Get that degree in an area of study that fulfills your passion. If you are able to work at your hobby you will never have to actually work in your life. You will be happy regardless of your pay level.

The average four year college graduate will earn over one million dollars more in his or her lifetime than a non-college graduate. High school dropouts do even worse. If the happy life thing doesn't get their attention then perhaps the extra million bucks will.

My youngest brother took a circuitous route through life. I plowed through obstacles. He avoided them like Walter Peyton avoided tacklers. I had my doctorate at the age of 24. He was still in college at the age of 29 when we finally had the big brother-little brother discussion. Dave looked at me and quite seriously said, "I'm really having trouble finding myself."

I put my left hand forward and rotated my palm upward. I did the same with my right hand. I then grabbed my left gluteals followed by the right. I looked him in the eyes and said, "There's your ass, move it! If you need me to point it out I'd be happy to mark it with a footprint." and at the same time I made a punting motion from my right foot.

I convinced him to finish his degree in English which was where he had started his long educational career. I assured him that writing ability is a rare talent in the business community. He finished his degree at the end of the next semester. He also had a minor in business. He is now working in marketing and is enjoying great success. The duck finally found some water and is floating about like a cork. He seems very happy and I've never seen him work so hard! There is hope for success for us all....find your dream and chase it. This is America after all!

*Shortly after writing this chapter I heard Dave Durand, a career coach, on Relevant Radio. He summarized life's options very well. After school you can do one of three things (besides doing nothing, which is likely to end very badly). You can get a job which is essentially trading your time for money. You can have a career which is a job that enables you grow and advance in knowledge and earning potential. Or, you can have a vocation which is following and fulfilling your passion and not actually working at all. If you look forward to work each day you probably have found your vocation.*

*An avid golfer brought his dog, Gimme, in for a wellness visit. He seemed more concerned about his golf game than the matter at hand. Trying to be polite, I informed him that I had just taken up the vile sport only two months ago. When he asked how I was progressing I told him that I was protecting my identity by not using my real name on the course. When golfing, I have my nephews refer to me as T. J. That stands for Turf Johnson. In turn, I refer to them by their golf pseudonyms: Creek Shindeep, Chip Putpar and Forest Onaventure. He informed me that his friends call him 'Where'd it go Joe' because of his habit of keeping his head down and not following the flight of the ball. I don't have that problem yet because I simply listen for the sound of tree limbs breaking or watch for the splash if I'm anywhere near water. Johnny Depth was in the running as my pseudonym for awhile.*

*A man came in for a Bordetella (kennel cough) vaccination for his dog prior to sending it to a kennel. When I asked why the dog was being boarded he replied that after thirty years of marriage his wife deserved a trip to Hawaii. I just had to ask him, "So, are you going with?"*

CHAPTER 20

*Staff Stuff*

The clinic has been blessed with an extremely dedicated group of employees over the years. I would like to claim some responsibility for this, but the truth is that my main managerial skill is that I don't manage. The doctors have no training in management. We are lousy at it, we lack the time to do it and we don't enjoy doing it. Our staff has evolved using a general set of guidelines which was adopted and approved by the doctors, but which is executed by the staff members themselves.

With any group of people working in close quarters there will be some moments of discord. This is normal. What matters is the way in which conflicts are resolved. Our system has evolved over time. It is quite simple and yet it can be difficult to implement. It involves honesty and mutual respect for one another. The simple version is: No third party conversations.

If you feel that someone has done something improperly you work it out with that person. Don't talk about it with other employees unless it affects them. Third party conversations aren't permitted. If a lesson has been learned and can be used to improve a situation or service at the clinic then it can be shared with everyone via a staff meeting or notice on the bulletin board.

If the situation can't be resolved between the employees then their area manager becomes involved. The office manager and doctors are the last resort. We have three 'teams' that work together within the clinic. The reception area is run by the client relations team. They are responsible for greeting clients, preparing their records for the office visit, checking them out after the office visit, ensuring the medical records are complete before re-filing them and answering the incoming phone calls.

The nursing team is responsible for getting patients into the exam rooms, getting their history and, if possible, some baseline physical parameters (TPR....temperature, pulse and respiratory rates) and preparing materials needed for the visit such as vaccines. In recent years our technicians have also been enabled to perform tasks formerly done only by veterinarians such as drawing blood samples, doing nail trims and expressing anal (scent) glands (God bless them!). This not only frees up time for the vets but it also saves the clients some money by allowing us to offer these services at more reasonable rates.

Of course, our nurses are also the right arms of veterinarians in the treatment area and surgical suite. They run routine laboratory tests such as blood chemistries, blood cell counts, fecal analysis, ear swab cytology and urine analysis. Since they have much more technical knowledge than their counterparts in the client relations team we had some competition developing over 'turf' in the clinic. Each team felt that the other was over-stepping their authority or work space.

Initially, these growing pains were addressed by the doctors stepping in to settle disputes. It was difficult to do so without the appearance of 'taking sides'. The crisis came to a head over a seemingly minor dispute. It was an argument over which team should go over the instructions on administering medications with the owners. Emotions ran over and festering wounds opened wide.

The heads of the two teams approached the doctors and suggested that we needed to leave them alone for lunch hour so that they could 'deal with things'. We left; quickly. Upon our return it was immediately apparent that a change of attitude had been achieved. The first clue was the lack of eye makeup on the faces of the staff and the pile of tissues in the garbage can. Apparently, everyone let loose with all of their pent up frustrations. After the anger subsided a compromise was reached and the session ended with crying and hugging all around. I gradually became aware of what a great lunch I had enjoyed. Confrontation has never been my forte and it was the main theme of the meeting. Thankfully, the staff all learned a great deal about each other and the reasons for the incursions into each other's territory.

The client relations team felt that they were under-appreciated by the nursing staff. It was made clear to them that we needed to be one complete team. The client relations personnel are the first and last impression that a client receives. We can do the best medical work in the world, but if a client is turned off on the phone or at the front desk, then we haven't done a good job. In football you can score 50 points, but if the defense gives up 60 you still lose. Appropriate cross-training took place and many of the overlapping duties are now shared by the two teams.

The third team at the clinic consists mainly of one person. She is the inventory team. What was once a duty scattered among many became organized inside of one brain. This was necessitated by the computerization of the clinic. As supplies were received they had to be entered into the computer. The computer tracks inventory and determines pricing based on the cost of the product. We could no longer have individuals ordering from varying areas of the clinic without computer training for everyone. We needed one person as a one-stop ordering and entry area.

The inventory team computer training proved to be more complicated than we had anticipated. We became worried that we would be crippled by the loss of our 'team' should she decide to leave. Therefore, our office manager and the head of the nursing team received cross training and are now able to step in to fill the void left by vacations and illness absences.

About this time an interesting concept, team fit, was introduced to us by a management consultant. It had been pushed to the background as we adopted many of the changes we now live with. As each of the teams was empowered to make changes in their work environment it became more and more important to have team fit among the members. Our current policy for new employees is that they have a 60 day trial period in which they can leave for any reason and we can ask them to leave for any reason. They aren't being fired; they are being de-hired.

Any one can make adjustments to fit into an environment for a month or so, but by the end of two months you get an excellent feel for their personality and learning abilities. Personality is the more important of the two. In our practice employees must like animals. They must also like people since they work with both every minute of the day. Our clinic is quite small so we rub elbows and bump butts with each other frequently. There are plenty of opportunities get frustrated with a coworker. We can teach you any technical skills you will need, but we can't change your heart very easily. We hire for attitude and that has held us in good stead over the years. Fortunately, the need to de-hire is rare.

When a member of our staff leaves the clinic it is usually due to family reasons. They go off to college. They get married. A spouse takes a job transfer. When a new person is accepted into our clinic he or she becomes a part of the family. Like all families, we have moments when we become dysfunctional. My personal coping mechanism is to eliminate the dys and emphasize the fun.

Stress is what you make of it. If you wake up and think it is going to be a bad day, it will be. I take each day, each hour, and each patient as it comes. If I sense that my staff is becoming stressed I try to lift them up by making it fun. A quick pun, a kind word or a sincere thank you can go a long way towards dissolving stress.

Puns have become reflexive for me. There is no stopping them.

Many people think that puns are intended to evoke laughter. Actually, I get more satisfaction from seeing a brief wave of nausea cross the face of my victims. There is nothing like a little sense of illness to make you forget about your work related stress.

Much of the stress at the office involves needing information on several ill patients at the same time. I am careful to sense the workload on the nursing staff. When they feel overwhelmed I try to step in and help. Just doing a nail trim or blood draw on a difficult patient can be a big help. Sometimes the cases simply need to be prioritized. Organizing the work not only gives them a sense of control, it also makes progress more apparent. This results in a significant reduction in stress levels. I also reassure them that they are doing a great job under difficult circumstances and that they are appreciated.

Stress at the reception area often revolves around the telephone. The bells, the bells, make them stop! It can be difficult for the staff to help everyone at the same time. Many of the questions coming in necessitate the use of a doctor's brain. I never complain about the number of phone messages on my bulletin board. I know that I am addressing genuine concerns from my clients and helping to alleviate stress at the reception desk. As in most businesses, if the phone is quiet then business is probably not good.

I use the words 'please' and 'thank you' frequently throughout the day. In particular, I thank each of my staff as I see them leaving for the day. They tell me what I need to be doing and where I need to be doing it as we go through the day. They are much more my boss than I am theirs. I don't think any job should be thankless, particularly that of being my boss.

I rose through the ranks of my profession starting at the bottom rung of the ladder. I understand the workload on each of my employees and I do my best to pitch in wherever and whenever I can. I still don't mind cleaning a dirty cage rather than walking past it and smelling it. I'll occasionally answer a ringing phone when things get crazy. That certainly shocks the longtime client who is expecting to hear a staff member answering the phone.

I'm certain that the nursing staff loves me for my body. They sometimes need help to move large dogs that have been sedated. I'm often asked to carry dogs from the prep area to the surgery table or radiology. I try to do whatever expedites their work and at the same time enhances the safety of both the patient and the staff.

Since I have been in the trenches for so long I tend to think that I have "seen it all". Of course, just as I think that my staff comes up with something unusual. This includes practical jokes. They have become very adept at taking candid pictures and then cutting out the faces and pasting them onto a different body. That may include the body of other species; you never know where your face may end up.

One of my favorite uses of this technique came as a result of an escaped pet. It had slipped its leash in the parking lot as the owner was trying to drag it to the front door. One of the receptionists saw it happen and ran out to catch the dog. We had never seen Donna run so fast or so far. She was successful and sweatily returned the lost pet to his owner as she tried to catch her breath.

Within an hour one of the nurses had downloaded and printed a picture from the internet. It was Forrest Gump running down the sidewalk. His new head was a cut-out from a picture of Donna. The caption read 'Run, Forrest, Run!' and that is now the title of the award given to anyone capturing a stray pet.

Paybacks are always in order, but there are some basic rules that must be observed. Nothing humiliating can be involved. Don't get personal. Don't disrupt patient care. If you generate a mess it is yours. No personal injuries!

One of our standard gags involves substituting samples in the laboratory. It is great fun to put some chocolate pudding into a container and submit it as a stool sample. At the appropriate time you manage to get some on your fingers. Sniffing it prior to actually tasting it is always a nice touch. The effect on a trainee is enhanced when an experienced technician doesn't bat an eye and asks, "What do think, roundworms? Boy, those things taste bad!"

Serendipity can be a wonderful thing when pulling off a practical joke; when something unusual happens, take advantage of it. I once submitted some juice from the peppers that came with my Italian beef sandwich as a urine sample. The color was perfect and there was just enough of an odor to suggest there was a problem but not enough to give it away as a sham submission. The history submitted with the sample was intentionally suggestive of problems. Maybe there was an increase in water intake. There was some urgency to urinate. The dog was middle aged and mixed breed; an intact female (so there would be some concern about uterine problems). Of course, the history wasn't in my handwriting; it is bad enough to be recognizable and I didn't want to raise suspicions right out of the gate. You need to pay attention to details when planning this sort of thing.

My intention was to accidentally splash some 'urine' on myself, but I was to discover a more insidious means of tasting it. The chemistry analyses actually turned positive for sugar. It was just a trace, but the technician was immediately concerned that the dog might have diabetes. I suggested that the dipsticks used to do the chemistry analyses weren't nearly as accurate as taste buds in detecting sugar. To her horror I placed a drop of 'urine' on my tongue. I slowly licked my lips, shrugged and said; "Hmm...not bad." I then downed the whole test tube full of juice, grimaced and said, "Whew, sure tastes like diabetes. We'd better call the owner and set up some blood tests."

Unfortunately, the other staff couldn't contain themselves. Their laughter tipped my hand. I would have gone so far as to let her contact the owner (I used my home phone number as the contact number). One further suggestion is that you should be sure to use mild peppers so you don't hurt yourself chugging the juice. Safety first.

It is definitely better to give than to receive when it comes to practical jokes. I know this to be true because I have been on the receiving end of many gags. Always the good sport, I try to go with the flow. For my birthdays I have been arrested (fur lined cuffs…no details on that episode), I have had a fairy god gorilla sing to me while clutching my leg in front of clients, I have had a twenty foot inflatable gorilla holding a sign which read "Lordy, Lordy, Look who's 40!" and an eight foot tall fly fisherman standing among 50 jumping fish in the front lawn. His sign read 'Dr. Greiner finally caught the big one….50'. At least I didn't get a wheelchair decorated with 'over-the-hill' balloons like Dr. Velders. I'm sure I'll get something similarly humiliating when I least expect it. Dr. Rooney had a belly dancer give him dancing lessons while he wore a coconut bra, grass skirt, wig and lei. I really hope I don't get to try my hand at that in front of the staff. I dance like I have three left feet!

My staff does their best to keep me busy through the day. Idle hands are the devil's workshop and some of our pranks got out of control. The water fights ended when two of the staff hosed each other down in the kennel. It continued outside and included a running hose going into a car window. Once the line was crossed it was apparent that a boundary no longer existed and that any future water wars would end in a liquid holocaust. Too bad, a little syringeful of water now and then wasn't so bad.

One day a few weeks prior to the moratorium, I happened to see a sizeable syringe filled with water on the counter in the lab. The staff had been acting a bit squirrelly that day and I suspected that the syringe might have my name written on it. I quietly squirted the water into the sink and refilled the syringe with air. I then positioned myself on the opposite counter and started writing in the medical records of my current patient. Two of the technicians came into the lab. The silence behind me was deafening. One of them pretended to do some lab work while the other was trying to drip water down the back of my neck. They couldn't understand my lack of reaction until they figured out the syringe was empty. Busted. This wasn't my first rodeo. In fact, I could be the rodeo clown.

Next, they tried placing a half cup of water on the doorknob of the bathroom. The door swings inwards so that the cup would fall on the feet of anyone who walked out. Be sure to use a paper or plastic cup if you intend to try this. I was still on high alert. I expected to be greeted with a shower as I left the bathroom so I was still standing behind the door when the cup hit the floor. Busted again, and this time they had to go get a mop.

My comeuppance came when I left for the day. I almost made it to the safety of my car, but I couldn't get the door unlocked in time. At least they had some pity on me. They used cups instead of buckets. It was a warm day and they made the ride home nice and cool after my long day at the office. How thoughtful of them.

Our office manager is in charge of maintaining the overall sanity of the clinic. She is Dr. Rooney's wife. (I suspect she sleeps with her boss.) Karen has been a wonderful addition to the clinic. She has grown into a thoughtful and effective manager over the past ten plus years. She handles pretty much anything thrown at her. She rarely allows clinic concerns to get to a point of requiring intervention by the doctors.

One of the secrets to her success has been regular meetings with the staff as well as with the doctors. We were reluctant to initiate so many meetings due to the expense. We buy lunch as well as pay the staff for the unproductive time. We discovered very early on that the time was unproductive only in the sense that we weren't generating income. The improvement in attitudes and procedures more than compensate for the little bit of down time. A successful practice is like a successful marriage; trust and communication are essential.

I have had the exceptional experience of never having had an instant of doubt about the moral character of my partners. Although we each attend different houses of worship we know that we all share the same core values. We work towards a common goal: provide the best care possible for our animal friends as well as for their families. Our clinic tag line is: Building relationships through healthy pets.

Those relationships include those between staff members, owners, patients, and veterinarians as well as our support services such as drug companies, laboratories and suppliers. We have created a reliable and effective team designed to serve. I would be nothing without my wonderful partners and staff.

*The best compliment I have ever received:*

*Our clinic was treated to a pain management seminar by the president of the International Association for Pain Management in Animals, Nancy Shaffran. She gave an excellent three hour program on advanced pain management techniques. At the end of the session she pulled the doctors aside and commented that she had been in hundreds of clinics throughout her career and that we had the best culture she had ever seen in a veterinary clinic. "Your staff genuinely cares about each other as well as their patients."*

*I didn't quite know what to say and I finally stammered, 'In spite of me?'*

*"Everyone knows it all starts at the top", she quickly added.*

*A member of my client relations team, Donna, found an ad in a magazine which depicted a beautiful blond woman holding a martini and apparently having a great time at a party. The ad was for vodka and the woman had hair that resembled Donna's. The ad was placed on my bulletin board with a note that read: Look....it's Donna on her side job. I added '(drinking)' to the end of her sentence and beneath it I wrote, "This is what she looks like after you've consumed a bottle of this vodka!"*

*One day I received a note from my client relations team to return a call from a long time client. I knew that Judy had worked at a doctor's office for many years. When I returned her call I was surprised to reach the 'So and So Mental Health Facility'. I thought that perhaps she had switched jobs or that her employer had changed the focus of his practice. I asked to speak with Judy. "There is no one here by that name.", came the reply. I gave the receptionist the number I had called. "That is the correct number. This is the So and So Mental Health Facility."*

*"Well, this is Dr. Greiner calling for a Judy Knutzle."*

*"There is nobody that works here by that name. Could she be a patient?"*

*The thought that perhaps she was having some difficulties crossed my mind. "I don't think so, but I would appreciate it if you would check." I spelled the last name for her.*

*After a brief pause came her reply, "No, there is no one here by that name."*
*At this point I felt that I should step things up a notch, "Well, she does have four or five names depending on which voice is in her head today."*

*After a lengthy pause the receptionist stammered, "Is this regarding a consultation?"*

*Oh, yeah. You couldn't pay for that kind of writing. When I suggested that it was in regard to a police investigation the poor girl started looking through their appointment calendar. I started to feel guilty about leading her on so I confessed that I was sure I had the wrong number (my dyslexic staff had switched two of the numbers).*

*I thanked her for the great time and wished her as much fun through the rest of her day as I had talking to her.*

*Joe and Elaine owned over twenty cats. They were standing in line at the grocery check out with a huge cart filled with cat food. They were taking advantage of some great sale prices. The man checking out ahead of them kept looking back and gawking as they unloaded their bargains onto the checkout counter. Finally, as he was getting his change the man looked at Joe and said, "My God, how many cats do you have?" Joe calmly replied, "Oh, we don't have any. We run an old folks home." The man had no response. He accepted his change and walked away.*

*Dr. Greiner with restraint pole trying to get a grip on his 40th birthday.*

*It was back to 'school' on my 50th birthday.*

CHAPTER 21

## *Open the Door and See All the People*

When I was young and foolish, as opposed to my current status of experienced and foolish, I thought that my desire to be a veterinarian stemmed from the fact that I could work with animals and thus avoid working with people. That was much more than mere misconception; it was totally misguided. It took quite a while for the idea to sink in, but I now know that the main reason I love my career is the people. It is the bond between people and pets that makes my job so fulfilling.

I was very uncomfortable working with emotional owners for the first several years of practice. Men, in particular, are supposed to be emotionally restrained. If something bad happens, buck up. Bite that upper lip. Pip, pip and all that rot. What a bunch of bull. If you can't cry over a best friend, then when can you?

As often happens, it was a little old lady who opened my eyes. Ruthie had been a client with Dr. Velders since his first days in practice. The time to part with her old Doberman pinscher arrived very abruptly. The heart muscle disease that Dr. V had been treating for the past year finally caught up to the dog in the

236

form of a stroke. It brought back memories of my final minutes with Mitts.

I had been helping Mitts deal with her Cushing's disease for a couple of years. For the past year she frequently needed help getting up and around. She finally blessed me with having a stroke. A big one. She went from licking my face and begging for breakfast to nothing. No blink reflex; no swallow reflex; no reaction to anything.

Mom called me at the office to let me know that something had happened to Mitts. It was immediately apparent to me that she was at the end of the line. I brought home the euthanasia solution as I prayed that she would bless me with not needing it by the time I got there. In the event that Mitts had any signs of life in her, I stopped by the grocery store and bought her favorite treat, chicken loaf.

There was no greeting when I walked in the door. Mitts was lying on a pile of blankets on the floor. I walked up to her and gently grabbed her front feet; her least favorite thing that you could do to her. No response. I then took some chicken loaf and pushed it between her teeth. Nothing; she didn't even move her tongue. I looked at Mom and sadly said, "That's not my dog." Mittens was gone. Only her body remained.

I asked Mom if she wanted to stay with as I put Mitts to sleep. "Heavens, no!"

She left the room as I prepared the last shot I would ever administer to my old pal. I didn't hesitate. I was able to hold back the tears for the moment, but I wasn't sure how long that would last. I wasn't halfway through the injection when she fell asleep. That old ticker was still strong as it rushed my final gift to her brain. I finished the injection over the next few seconds, removed the needle from her leg and called Mom back in.

"That was it?"

"Yes, Mom. It was pentothal. It's just like going to sleep for surgery."

"Gosh, she didn't scream or cry or anything."

"Mom! What do you think I do for a living, inflict pain?" Her words had cut me to the quick. I thought, if my own mother questioned what was happening, what do my clients think when they don't stay with their pet at the end? I also noticed that Mom moped around the house for weeks after losing Mitts. She regretted not staying for the finale and her remorse was very evident. I don't get to see that in my clients after they leave the clinic.

Even in her death Mitts changed my life. When I first started in practice I had perhaps one out of four clients stay with their pet during euthanasia. I am probably up to 98%. I encourage everyone to stay. I am particularly patient with children if the family thinks they can handle the experience. I give it to them straight. Children may take things literally, so it is important to make it clear that their pet is not being 'put to sleep'. They might worry that they will go to sleep and not wake up themselves one morning. It is a shot that stops the heart and (depending on their religious affiliations) sends them to heaven.

As I was comforting Ruthie through her loss she brought up the subject of getting another dog. I told her that there was no right or wrong amount of time to wait before getting another pet. It is rather like losing a spouse. Some people are dating within weeks and others never seek companionship again. Some want a carbon copy of the first pet while others seek one that is completely different. When I suggested that perhaps she may want to downsize to a smaller breed of dog Ruthie wouldn't hear of it. If it wasn't a dobie it wasn't a dog.

Sure enough, within a week she had picked one out. Another black and tan. Another female. Her sister, Joan, bought a littermate. She lived a few blocks away from Ruth and they always came to the clinic together. Even if one of the dogs was sick, the other came along for the ride. They came in for nail trims together at least every two months.

On one visit Joan brought both dogs by herself. Ruth wasn't feeling well. This would be repeated on several consecutive occasions. Nearly a year had gone by without a visit from Ruth. I finally insisted that Joan drag Ruthie along on her next visit.

A few weeks later I was greeted by an emaciated Ruth. She looked awful. She had been suffering from pain shooting across the side of her face for the past year. She had been to a dentist, an oral surgeon, a TMJ specialist and three doctors. Nothing was giving her relief. In fact, her symptoms continued to steadily worsen.

I said, "Ruthie, you just described the course of the facial nerve as it passes from the base of the ear and across the side of your face. You must have a lesion along that nerve." She agreed to a visit with my doctor. I gave Bill a call to let him know what was happening and he immediately suggested she might need to see a neurologist.

After her visit with him she was sent straight to a hospital for a neuro consult. An MRI was performed and Ruthie was diagnosed with a malignant tumor on the side of her skull near the base of the ear. It was compressing the facial nerve and thus causing her pain. Surgery was performed to obtain a biopsy. Sadly, it wasn't possible to remove it. Ruthie died a few months later.

I was very disappointed in the care she had received. If her tumor had been diagnosed months sooner she might have lived. I was also disappointed that I didn't learn of her death until a month after she had died. I would have attended her wake had I known. My current record for attending wakes for clients is seven in one year. Being a visual learner, it helps me to gain closure if I see a person I've known and loved laid out in their casket. Ruthie was especially dear to me. She was one of the first clients I've shed tears in front of. She was one of a handful of clients for which I have suggested a diagnosis for their illness and sent them to my doctor for help. (Bill just shakes his head and wonders what I actually do with my time in the exam rooms.) I've had many clients tell me that they wish I was their doctor. I invariably tell them that I might suggest euthanasia to put them out of *our* misery. Besides, I tend to pass out when I see a person suffering.

Loretta was a client for many years. She was a stout little

fire plug of a woman. She is memorable for her contributions to the war effort during WW II. She was one of only two woman pilots in the civilian air corps. She flew reconnaissance and supply missions along the eastern seaboard. After the war she continued to fly until she could no longer pass her physicals. As her health failed she was assisted by her daughter and son. She was finally admitted to a long term assisted living facility in her old age.

One day her daughter called with the news that Loretta had died peacefully in her sleep.

I went to the wake with the expectation of sneaking in, paying my respects and quietly leaving. I don't like to interrupt a family gathering, especially at such a sad time. Besides, Loretta was a bit of a celebrity in my mind and I assumed that the wake would be crowded. When I walked into the funeral parlor I was stunned by the silence. The only people present were her son, daughter, grandchildren and a couple of friends. She had outlived most of her lifelong companions. Her daughter excitedly said, "Hey everyone, it's Doctor Greiner."

It was heart warming, albeit awkward, to be greeted in such a way. Everyone knew about me, even the grandchildren. Apparently, all that Loretta liked to talk about was her pets and I was an extension of them. It was embarrassing and humbling that I had made such an impact on her life and that I was so totally clueless about it. I often wonder how many lives we touch with the smallest acts of kindness. They can generate a life changing impact with little effort. It makes you want to do more.

We have several clients who work with organizations that train assistance dogs. They adopt young puppies and provide care and training for them for about a year. The puppies go through a rigorous selection process which is designed to determine their eligibility for the type of service that they can best provide. This starts with temperament testing before they are even taken from their mother. It continues in puppy classes and through the increasingly advanced training. At a year of age the pups, now dogs, are sent off for their final training. The toughest training is reserved for the cream of the crop; Seeing Eye Dogs. The goal of every volunteer is to get a dog into a sight assistance program. The ones that don't make the grade are used as wheelchair assistants, hearing assistants or therapy dogs.

Before leaving for school, the dogs are spay/neutered and radiographed to ensure that they don't have genetic problems that might limit their serviceability. This could include such maladies as hip dysplasia, elbow dysplasia or other bone growth problems. Their eyesight is certified by an ophthalmologist. Their temperament is certified by a behaviorist/trainer. It is a long and arduous process. When the time comes to part company it is very difficult to let them leave.

One particular client, Arlene, was especially successful in training assistance dogs. She had several foster dogs that went on to do wheel chair assistance. She carried a picture of her pride and joy; one of her dogs that made it through the sight assistance program. You couldn't wipe the smile off of the face of his blind owner! You could tell that his life had been transformed by his newfound companion. Even the dog seemed to be smiling in the picture.

Arlene's latest recruit was a golden retriever, Amber, who was going to be trained as a wheelchair assistant. She would be trained to open doors, pick up dropped items, retrieve items from a counter, etc. Only one obstacle remained before she could enter the final training program; she needed radiographic proof that she had good joints.

Amber was sedated to ensure ideal positioning for the radiographs. All of her joints were palpated and no abnormalities were found. The 'X-rays' looked normal to each of the doctors at the clinic, but we had a radiologist look at them before sending them along with Arlene. He agreed that they showed no abnormalities.

Two weeks later I received a call from a very distraught Arlene. They were sending Amber back to her because their radiologist didn't like the appearance of the elbows. She set up an appointment for the next day, but I delayed it to a time when our radiologist would be at the clinic.

Reassessment of the radiographs still revealed no suggestion of problems to us. We were baffled that the dog had been returned. The program director wanted Arlene to continue fostering Amber and have the elbows and hips rechecked in six months.

About a month later Arlene was diagnosed with breast cancer. It was bad; very aggressive and it was not expected to respond to chemotherapy or radiation. Surgery was her best hope of beating it. She underwent radical surgery and follow-up chemo and radiation. Nothing helped. In the end, it took Arlene from us.

During her decline, especially after her surgery and therapy sessions, Arlene needed an assistance dog! Amber jumped in enthusiastically. She was there to help retrieve objects at a moments notice or simply sit and absorb grief and radiate joy. When we repeated the radiographs at the requested six month interval we found Amber's joints to be normal. Arlene wondered why they had rejected Amber in the first place. My explanation was that God allowed them to see a 'lesion' because no one would need Amber more than she did. She received much more than physical help from Amber. She was Arlene's constant companion to the end which came all too quickly.

When Arlene died her family entered the dog into the assistance program. God bless them for being able to part with Amber in order to help another needy person.

While I have visited many clients and their families after a death in the family, I was unprepared for a final visit from a longtime client. Bill came to the office to tell me good bye. I knew he had been battling lung cancer, but I thought he was in a complete remission. Hoping that he was moving to an area with a better climate, I asked where he was moving to. "Off of the planet," came his reply. "My cancer is back. It is in my liver and the doctors are telling me that I have two weeks to two months to live. I don't think I'll have the strength to see you again."

I asked if he intended to do anything crazy, like go sky diving before he departed and he quietly told me that he took his son fishing last weekend.

"Did you have 'the talk' with him?" I asked.

"Yes I did." Bill replied. "I told him everything I expect of him and where to find all of my papers. Everything is in order for the family. I made my funeral arrangements and I have hospice care set up at the house for when I get bad."

We both cried as we hugged each other knowing that it would be the last time we would likely spend together. I asked Bill to say hello to the Big Guy for me when he passes through the Pearly Gates. "Thank Him for everything He has done for me up 'til now. I have no complaints and I look forward to seeing Him one day, but not too soon. I'm having a ball down here admiring His work."

Bill is the only person I have sent a funeral card to before their passing. He thanked me for my prayers and assured me that they would be returned in kind. His death wasn't pleasant, but the entire family helped him live his life to the fullest right up to the end. He was loved by many; a testament to a life well lived.

Not all of my clients have such sad tales to tell. The other end of the human age spectrum presents a lot of opportunity to have some fun. I enjoy fostering a bond between little children and their pets. Since they think of them as equals I take extra care to show children how to be gentle with their pet.

You can tell when a child has perhaps a bit too much empathy for their pet. This is readily apparent when the needles come out. Some of the kids start crying for their pet with the experience of their own immunizations fresh in their mind. Unless the child is extremely upset I try to give the 'shots' in the room. I will have one of the nurses hold their pet if mom is busy attending to her child. Usually, if I give some treats to a dog they don't even notice that they are getting an injection. With cats, I usually give them a little push along the table as they are injected. They are usually more concerned about the sliding than they are the injection.

When the pets are done I make a big deal about how brave

they were and suggest to the children that they are probably just as brave when they get their shots, too. Most children are brutally honest and one little boy responded with, "Not me, I puke!" His mother smiled and nodded.

I keep candy at the clinic (for the children; honestly). One important tip to keep in mind is to always ask for permission from the mothers before offering candy to their kids. You never know what may be off limits due to allergies, medical conditions or current punishments they are enduring. Dinner may be coming, too. Whenever possible, I use candy as leverage towards good behavior.

One little girl had been very good throughout the office visit with her little puppy. She even raised her hand to get permission before speaking. She must have been about six years old because she was missing her two front teeth. After the business end of the visit was finished I asked her mother if C-A-N-D-Y was permitted. I got the nod, turned to her daughter and said, "You were an awfully good helper today. Do you know what I have for my good helpers? I have a basket of candy!"

She flashed a semi-toothless smile and said, "Oh, I know. And, you have dog biscuits out there, too."

"You didn't eat those, did you??" I feigned disgust.

"No", she said. "The lid was on the jar!"

I asked her mother if she fed her children on the floor. The answer was 'no', but if they would go for it, it would certainly save on doing dishes. We made certain that there was enough candy going home to share with her siblings.

I left the exam room after one particular visit with tears welling up in my eyes. Dr. Velders was in the laboratory when I walked in, drying my eyes. He asked what had happened. I replied that I had just seen a little Labrador puppy. His three year old 'owner' was sitting on my lap helping me with the puppy. In my first week at the clinic his dad was the three year old sitting on my lap helping with his lab puppy.

Dr. V had a knowing smile on his face as he said, "Wait 'til you see the grandkids!"

Try as they might, there is no way the vet school professors can prepare you for the level of attachment you will feel towards your clients. We are family. We laugh together. We cry together. We support each other through some very difficult times.

*A budding medical photographer came in with his St. Bernard complaining that she was very lethargic after having been through a heat period six weeks ago. When I diagnosed his dog with an infected uterus and recommended immediate surgery he seemed somewhat happy about it. He wanted to use the opportunity to take some pictures of the surgery. I agreed, but warned him that he had to be careful not to interfere with our protocols or out he would go. He was fine with that.*

*While we anesthetized and prepped his pet we had a constant storm of flashes and clicks. He captured everything he could on film. This continued through her transfer to surgery, monitor hook-ups and draping. He even got a few shots of me in the scrub room as I gowned and gloved.*

*As I made the incision the action seemed to slow down a bit. I paid no heed to him as I entered the abdomen. As I started retrieving the greatly enlarged uterus I noticed a distinct lack of flashes. On I went. The uterus seemed to be endless. It began to resemble a rather large, pink snake. I finally found the end of it and as I reached for a laparotomy sponge to pack it off I looked up to see a white face slowly sliding down the back wall of the room with a camera slowly being lowered to chin level.*

*Half an hour later the two of them were reunited. I commented that the dog had picked a heck of a way to lose 5 pounds. My staff took some pictures of the dog in the recovery room and returned the camera to the owner. He was done for the day. After he left my nurses told me that he sounded like he had lost 5 pounds while trying to regain his composure in the bathroom. I think he met a fork in the road of life and discovered another path to follow.*

*Dr. Rooney was working with a pet chicken that came to the clinic with a history of being lame in one leg. After detecting a swollen, inflamed hock joint he decided to take a sample of joint fluid for analysis and culture. He was the logical choice to work on the bird because he was already used to being hen pecked and he was in a fowl mood. Of course, we were full of advice for him:*

-Keep that patient warm...about 350 degrees for an hour should do.
-If she spends much time out in the field it is probably a pasture-ella infection.
-Boil that syringe when your done and you can make some chicken needle soup.
-If you have to amputate they'll have to change her name to Eileen.
-Can't fly on one wing, can she walk on one leg?
-Do an amputation, a chicken this good you have to eat  slow.
-Keep her quiet or we'll have to charge some big buck, buck, bucks.
-I wonder if she has caw-er I.D. on her phone.

A client that was relatively new to the practice was giving my staff some anxiety related to his use of language that would embarrass a truck driver.  I asked him to tone it down in front of my staff, but he seemed incapable of controlling his mouth. I finally sent him a letter and a copy of his pet's medical records.  I told him bluntly that he wasn't welcome back unless he cleaned up his act.

The following week my staff received a box of chocolates and a letter of apology from him.  He has become a model client for my staff, but he occasionally lets loose with the language in the exam room.  That's OK around me because I was raised in a blue collar area and I have developed a rather thick skin for such things.

One day, he brought in his dog, Star, set her up on the exam table and said, "Doc, tell me what you think of my dog's a**hole."

I looked him up and down and said, "You look like you're doing OK to me!"

"Oh, I handed that one to you, Doc.", he laughed.

And I took it.  I never thought I could have said that to him just a few months earlier.

# CHAPTER 22

# *The End is Near*

The amazing advancements in veterinary medicine over the past 25 years would seem to be ushering in a golden age of patient care for our pets. My predecessors who practiced only sixty or more years ago spent their days treating sick pets. With the advent of vaccines, good quality pet foods and parasite control the focus of practice gradually shifted to preventing many of the diseases that once paid their salaries. The practice of preventive healthcare has been so successful that much of a veterinarian's work is now aimed at increasing longevity and quality of life. However, there have been definite growing pains associated with progress.

Much of the technology available to veterinarians today involves a substantial financial commitment. There may be several companies competing with each other to obtain that commitment for a particular piece of equipment. Each sales representative is trained in effectively promoting his or her own product line. Choosing a product that will be effective in your practice for many years into the future can be a time consuming and challenging process.

For example, when our practice became computerized we looked at six or eight different software packages. The doctors had a totally different perspective on what we were seeking compared to the nurses and receptionists. A feature that looked great to us looked like a white elephant to the staff. We ultimately left the decision in the hands of the staff because they would be the ones using the new system. The doctors don't belong on the computer in my practice; we are sure to make mistakes with it.

In order to narrow the search for an appropriate system we sent groups of staff to other clinics to be introduced to three prospective software packages. They were able to speak freely with their peers in other practices. Their questions were oriented towards ease of use and making the transition into modernity as smooth as possible.

After a lengthy process of gathering information and debating our options, we purchased the system that was favored by the majority of the staff. This was fortunate because the package that most interested the doctors became unavailable within five years. The company went out of business and left no support network for its customers. They had to go shopping for another program or try to maintain the system on their own.

One pearl of wisdom that was tossed to us during our research was that the software and hardware packages should be purchased from the same company. Otherwise, when problems arose the software manufacturer would blame it on the hardware people and vice versa. If we ran into trouble there should be only one number to call!

Our computer is used for business records only. The trend in the profession is to go to paperless medical records. I have had the opportunity to examine the records generated by 'paperless' work environments. The computer generates page after page of checklists. It is difficult, almost painful, to wade through the pages. More importantly, it is difficult to follow the thought process of the clinician.

The information is entered through the same checklist each

time. It isn't ranked by importance. It is entered the same way each time. It is essential to have a mental checklist when writing up medical records. You don't want to omit information. The checklists help to ensure that a complete physical examination is recorded on each patient, but handwritten notes give a much better feel for the thought process of the clinician. It is very easy to check things off on a list without having done them.

To that end, a SOAP format for record keeping is taught in veterinary school. The S stands for subjective; that is the information gleaned from the history taken from the owner. What symptoms does your pet have? Is the water intake normal? How is the activity level? Are the stools normal? These are things that may involve opinion.

The O stands for objective; what observations are made on the physical examination. What is found to be normal and abnormal on this patient? What is the heart rate? Is the rhythm normal? Record the body temperature, pulse and respirations. This is tangible information gathered through the physical exam.

The A stands for assessment. What is the differential diagnosis? What do you think is happening with this patient? The list should begin with the disease of highest suspicion and go down from there.

The P means plan; what testing needs to be done to narrow the list or get to a definitive diagnosis. What course of treatment is being prescribed? What follow up is needed?

The computer programs follow this rough form, but I suspect that much of the data entry is done out of routine with the end result being a lack of thought behind the notes. Most of the large corporate practices use these programs in order to provide uniform service to their patients at each clinic in the corporate chain. Ostensibly, this is to offer the same great standard of service to each patient. However, it can also be used to provide the home office with feedback on the veterinarians.

For example, I have a colleague who worked for a corporate practice for a brief period. On her second day at the clinic an outdoor male cat was presented to her with a large draining abscess on its cheek. It was apparent by the spacing of the two punctures that it was a bite from another cat. The cat was very difficult to handle and the family had some financial constraints to consider. Therefore, she started the cat on antibiotics and encouraged the family to use warm compresses on the area several times a day. Since the cat was not very cooperative at home, a liquid antibiotic was prescribed so that the family wouldn't have to force pills into him.

The next day a call came in from the 'home office' a thousand miles away. There were some issues with the case. Why wasn't a blood count done? A physical was barely possible with this cat without sedation. With the added financial constraints it was out of the question. Why was medication prescribed and not dispensed? She explained the circumstances and the fact that there was no liquid form of antibiotic in the practice. She was told to fill out a request form for the pharmacy committee and perhaps she could get a supply of liquid medicines in the practice.

Her problem was that she didn't sell enough product to the owners. Corporate practices have shareholders to keep happy. That takes money. Therefore, the corporation needs to sell, sell, sell. They are good at it; lots of promotional displays and lots of non-medical pet products. In fact, most of the corporate clinics are associated with a pet shop which they may or may not own. This helps to get traffic through the door at which point a sale can be made.

Corporations attract veterinarians by offering good pay, short hours (a 40 hour work week is short by veterinary standards), continuing education opportunities and lots of time off. They are generally well equipped and the veterinarian isn't risking his/her own capital by starting a private practice. The practice is marketed by the corporation and no management duties are required unless the veterinarian has an express desire to do so. In return, the vet has to be willing to follow protocols for almost everything. Protocols are designed to promote health and well being by being complete and thorough. The same great quality of care is offered to each patient.

Does every patient need the highest level of care possible? No. Does every patient need blood tests, radiographs, urinalysis, EKG, ultrasound? No. I was taught that a good history and physical examination should give the clinician a sense of what is happening right out of the gate. Testing should be done to rule diseases in or out, to check the degree of illness, to get baseline values at certain key parts of the pets' life or, on some occasions, as a fishing expedition when the cause of the symptoms leaves the clinician stumped. That is not the current method taught in school. Baseline values should be taken on all patients. Radiographs should be taken on all patients. If an objection is made to the cost of these routine tests, the owners are often made to feel that they are bad people for not wanting the best for their pet. Tests aren't recommended; they are *needed*. Students are taught that it is good business as well as good medicine to run tests on everything. The practice must be able to pay for those expensive pieces of equipment and provide a good income for the investors.

Concerns over maintaining the ethical standards within the veterinary profession have recently arisen. A movement calling itself Protect the Pets was formed with the goal of uniting veterinarians under the banner of compassion. A code of conduct was formulated. The first item on the list is to not put profit ahead of care for the pet as a motive for being in practice. It is imperative to treat clients, staff and pets with respect. No animal will be euthanized for the sake of convenience to the owner. If the code of conduct can't be followed then the veterinarian should go in search of another livelihood!

As I read down the list it occurred to me that I had already taken this oath; at graduation from veterinary school. It saddened me to realize that there may be a need for an organization like this in my profession. I thought that most of the hustlers went into other professions and that vets were generally a good bunch of people. I still feel that way, but some of us have gone to a few too many management seminars. Worse than that, many have left the management of their practice entirely in the hands of non-veterinarians who may not have the same level of compassion for the pets. Big is not necessarily better.

Another problem with amassing a large practice arises when it comes time to sell it. Traditionally, veterinarians start out as associates in a practice. After they become established in the practice, an opportunity to become a partner should become available. Eventually, the original owner is bought out of the practice totally as retirement nears. The sale of the practice is designed to supplement retirement planning.

This doesn't happen in corporate practices because the corporation is owned by shareholders. In large private practices it often doesn't happen because of the high cost of the buyout. Therefore, corporations have arisen which buy only large private clinics and turn them into clinics molded into their vision of a successful practice. While this is convenient for the owner who is retiring, it may not bode well for those left behind.

It is a difficult situation for everyone involved. There is a large emotional investment in building a practice over many years. The selling veterinarian would like to see the legacy of the clinic continued. There is certainly some ego involved, but most vets are genuinely interested in maintaining continuity for their clients, patients and staffs.

The corporate purchaser would like to see the practice thrive. It hopes to facilitate that process via a thorough examination and upgrade of management strategies in every facet of the practice. The staff may feel uncomfortable with new management changing the way things have been done for years. They may need to learn new skills including mastering a new computer system. Even the clients may feel uncomfortable with change. Change is scary. And yet, if these corporations don't buy the practice, who will?

Private specialty practices have even more acute transition problems. Their equipment may be incredibly expensive. For example, CT and MRI imaging is now available from private clinics. Even used equipment that has been retired from human hospitals may cost a quarter of a million dollars. There is a much smaller pool of qualified vets who can take their place in operating this specialized equipment and interpreting the data it generates. However, the demand for these services is there and the rush to offer them has resulted in widespread expansion of facilities equipped to provide them. What was formerly limited to the teaching hospitals can now be obtained locally. Providing staffing, stability and continuity at these facilities can be a tremendous challenge.

The spread of technology has resulted in other difficulties for the veterinary profession. Because of the increasing costs associated with veterinary health care we are seeing a proliferation of pet insurance companies.

As in the case of human medicine, the widespread use of insurance results in an increase in overall expenditures. These companies have their own overhead costs. They are in business to make money. They usually have shareholders who like to make money. If you happen to have a claim for an expensive healthcare problem then you are likely to come out ahead financially. Insurance only pays off if, God forbid, you need it. Otherwise, it adds to the overall cost of healthcare.

I have a fear of pet health insurance. It is presented to veterinarians as a means of enabling us to provide expensive health care and get paid for it. However, even a cursory survey of the human medical field will show that most health care providers aren't happy working within the current system. Protocols must be followed to the letter. Forms must be filled out with no errors. Claims are denied. Managed care systems proliferate. Eventually, the government must pass regulations to control the actions of the participants. Veterinarians should be wary lest we follow the same pattern and become burdened by a large network of rules that control our actions.

If an insurance company becomes financially strained they can resort to several means of raising income and lowering payouts. Increasing the rates for the insured, especially for higher risk patients, may be limited by law or the marketplace. The deductibles can be increased. Pre-existing conditions may be ruled out by requiring extensive work ups before enrollment. Co-pays for medication can be instituted. Chronic illnesses may become non-insurable. Our experience with our own forms of health insurance should be enough to make us nervous about pet health insurance.

A more insidious effect of the spread of technology is that it has enabled veterinary specialists to leave the university teaching hospitals. They can still practice at the same high level of expertise in a private clinic setting with the same or higher quality diagnostic technology at their disposal. They no longer have to teach. They make much more money. They don't have to do research or publish articles in scientific journals in order to remain on staff. It is a wonder that anyone would remain at a teaching hospital!

As a result, many have left. For example, my alma mater has not had a neurologist for several years. How do the students learn neurology without an expert to teach them? There is book learning to be sure, but there is no substitute for a neurologist at your side as you examine a patient with neurological deficits. The University of Illinois has not had a cardiologist for several years as of this writing. At the teaching hospital we did cardiac monitoring on all patients under anesthesia. I'm sure that the anesthesiologists are picking up some of the load there, but what about the cardiac patients being admitted for a cardiac workup? So far, the internal medicine staff starts the initial workup and a cardiologist is borrowed from Purdue one day a week. Hopefully, those patients can wait for that day!

In reaction to this exodus there are programs at some of the teaching hospitals in which the students are sent out to private practices for experience in various rotations. There are some minimum criteria that must be met, but I have little hope that the quality of the educational experience will be uniform among those practices. I know that I would have little time to teach students in my practice. I am also unqualified to teach. I don't have a curriculum to follow and the student's experience would be limited to what walked in the door during his or her time spent at the clinic. I don't have the extensive library and facilities that are available at a university. I feel that the learning experience should be in an insulated environment with lots of help available and utilizing state of the art equipment. That way the students can learn what they are capable of. Once they leave the university, if they need to make compromises from that highest level of care, at least they will know that they are doing so.

I read an article in a prominent veterinary journal expounding the benefits of one such program at the veterinary teaching hospital of the University of Florida. The students were being sent to a large emergency clinic for their ER rotation. I have a good friend who lost a dog at that clinic. She had a lot of questions that weren't being addressed so she asked me to act on behalf of her beloved dog, Asti. He had experienced severe complications after gall bladder surgery. I was delighted to step up to the plate. I love consulting on cases and I'm not bashful about giving my medical opinions.

Based on my conversations with the clinician on the case and the lab values reported to me, it became apparent that the dog had developed peritonitis, an infection throughout the abdominal cavity. I begged them to go back into surgery because peritonitis is not a medical disease. You must go back in, clean up the abdomen and provide drainage for a period of time afterwards.

Their response was, "We're the experts. If we think it is indicated then we'll do it." I was taken aback by their arrogant attitude. It was obvious that they didn't want a lowly general practitioner questioning their authority.

I replied, "If you keep doing what you're doing, you're going to keep getting what you're getting; and that is a sicker and sicker dog." They didn't want to hear it; at all. A wall went up and it became difficult to communicate with them. The dog died a day or two later.

My friend was distraught. She received no comforting or condolence letter from the clinic. Instead, she received a letter from the in-house legal team that she needed to pay her bill or action would be instituted to collect it. They hit a raw nerve. The result was legal action in both directions. In researching the legal records it was discovered that this clinic was involved in over forty legal cases in the previous year. I would be appalled to be involved in even *one*!

Is this what we should be teaching our students as the ideal way of practicing? If not, how do we encourage more veterinarians to have a career at a teaching institution in order to train them properly? Obviously, more pay would help, but that is an issue to be addressed by the state governments funding the programs. Do we allow large corporations to provide subsidies in exchange for the studies done at the universities? What would they expect in return?

The universities are supposed to be our bastion of free thinking. There have been reports of clinical trials and other product studies being performed at universities with results that are disappointing. Rather than publishing the data, it gets buried in a file room at the home office. This is made possible by the company claiming the data as theirs because they paid for it. I disagree. All studies done at the university level should be published whether the results are good or bad. How else can we trust the information coming out of our centers of higher education?

The veterinary schools have also been harassed by animal rights advocates. This has caused many of them to cease live animal surgeries for junior veterinary students. While there were certainly some cases of abuse in animal care at the universities it was rare and it wasn't tolerated at the U. of I. during my years of education. The human medical programs, particularly those involving the psychological sciences, have a much worse animal care track record. The end result of limiting junior vet students to 'surgery' on models is that new graduates have very poor surgical experience.

As a senior student in the surgical rotation it is difficult to do much surgery. The difficult cases are given to the board certified surgeons. The interns and residents grab most of the other interesting or challenging cases. The senior students get what is left over. Interviewing prospective veterinarians coming in to our practice has been disappointing. New graduates have performed very few surgeries; often only a few spays and neuters. It is now up to private practices to finish their education. This isn't benefiting our patients.

The quality of education has been diminished by internal pressures as well. I was attending a continuing education meeting that was presented by a faculty member of the Western Veterinary College in Saskatchewan, Canada. I had the opportunity to speak with him privately after the meeting. He related an incident that occurred at the school. The students were feeling 'stressed'. They were very vocal about being 'stressed'. This resulted in a meeting which was attended by representatives from the students, faculty and administration. Unbelievably, the students were given Wednesday afternoons off in order to reduce that stress! What are these people going to do in practice? If they think they're stressed while still being insulated by the walls of the university then they will find it impossible to cope with the stresses of everyday practice.

Another issue facing the veterinary profession is a lack of male participation. The vet schools are currently enrolling and graduating approximately 80% women. It is an excellent profession for women. If you want to work part time in order to raise your family there are plenty of clinics willing to hire you. It saves them the costs associated with a full time employee and many clinics have a heavy caseload, but don't have enough business to justify another fulltime vet. The addition of women to the profession has definitely increased the level of compassion within the profession. Also, it has ended the practice of publicly starting meetings with an off-color joke which was apparently common through the 1950's. (Before my time; I'm not *that* old!)

However great their contributions, 80% of the profession as women is as bad as having had it 80% men. It was nearly 100%

men until the 1940's!  Most women are interested in companion animal medicine.  It is much kinder to your body than practicing food animal medicine, the hours are more reasonable and the pay is generally better.  This is happening at a time when emerging new disease surveillance and bioterrorism concerns are increasing demands for veterinarians in production medicine.  The Food Supply Veterinary Medical Coalition (FSVMC) did a $300,000 study in 2005-2006 to map the supply and demand of veterinarians within the food animal sector.  We hope that their data will give us some insight on ways to generate more interest in this important industry.  I hope that it doesn't result in a separate track for large and small animal programs in vet school.  Although I don't work with food animals, I'm still glad that I had that training.  And, if I am ever asked to go back to food animal medicine it will probably mean that I survived Armageddon and the nation is absolutely desperate.

The American Veterinary Medical Association published a manpower study shortly before my graduation in 1982.  It painted a bleak future for veterinarians.  By the year 2000 there would be a tremendous excess in veterinary capacity.  In response to that survey efforts were made to expand job opportunities for veterinarians.  This resulted in the proliferation of specialty clinics and other non-traditional careers within the profession.  The manpower study was repeated ten years later and their conclusion was that we need more vets!  A tremendous shortage was envisioned for about the current time.  Some of the schools have expanded enrollment, but the employment picture certainly looks bright for the foreseeable future.

I think that I will be able to look down from eternity and know that I practiced veterinary medicine at one of the best times ever in history.  I hope that it isn't *the* best time.  The next generation of veterinarians will be instrumental in determining if that will be the case.

*An ancient tomb was recently excavated in Egypt. Much to the surprise of the archaeologists a dehydrated but otherwise well preserved soft drink was found. It was estimated to be 2600 years old. It was the worlds' first carbon-dated beverage.*

*A friend of mine left private practice in order to go into practice management with a large corporation. I saw him at a meeting and asked him how he liked the new duties. He replied that he simply traded one set of stresses for another. I remarked, "Why, George, you cross-stresser, you!"*

*Kellie, a member of our nursing team, is an ardent Detroit Redwings fan. I have always been a Chicago Blackhawks fan. We usually attend at least one game a year at the Chicago Stadium, now the United Center. The Hawks always win, of course.*

*When the Redwings won the Stanley Cup, I can't recall which one because there have been sooo many, I received a gift from a classmate in Detroit; a Redwings home jersey. Rather than burn it or otherwise desecrate it I decided to have some fun with Kellie. I had my brother, Dave, sign Steve Yzerman's name on it. He was Kellie's favorite player. Dave even put Yzerman's number under the signature for good measure. I wore it to the office the next day. Kellie was speechless at first. She finally stammered, "Oh my god, a Detroit home jersey!"*

*I showed her the autograph; "Ohmigod! Ohmigod! Steve Yzerman!"*

*I let her go for a minute and finally said; "You know, when you look at it upside down it looks more like David Greiner."*

*She was so mad. She wanted me to wear it to the Hawks-Redwings game the following three seasons. I refused to do so as a conscientious objector as well as for health reasons if the Hawks happened to lose the game.*

*I had a bit of a dilemma on my hands. I had a gift that I had desecrated and left to die a lonely death. It was mocking me as it hung in the closet. I needed to do something with it. After a good deal of thought, I sent it to the front office of the Detroit Redwings with a letter explaining what I had done. They honored my request to have Steve Yzerman actually sign it next to Dave's fake autograph. They even sent a letter authenticating it. (Would I lie twice in one gag?) Only after seeing the letter did Kellie have an exceptional Christmas that year. [Let's go Red Wings clap clap clap] [Detroit *****] Chicago hockey fans know how to fill in the blank.*

## *Epilogue*

I don't want to scare off young readers as they consider a career in veterinary medicine. I can honestly say that I can't think of even a handful of days that I didn't want to go to the office. I enjoy what I do immensely and I can't think of a more satisfying career. Very few people can say that about their job. As a veterinarian, if you don't like what you are doing you have the power to change what you do.

I told Dr. Velders during my first month of practice that I would re-evaluate my life near the expiration of our one-year agreement (no contract…it was a handshake). If I didn't like small animal practice then I would move on to something else. He couldn't imagine changing careers himself so he inquired what kind of move I would possibly make. I had already put some thought into this and I informed him that I would look into fish medicine.

Well, he was thinking goldfish. However, I was thinking fish farming. It has become a fairly big industry over the past 25 years and they are hard pressed to find enough veterinarians to supply their needs. A great deal of regulation controls the interstate shipping of fish and vets are needed to perform testing for diseases prior to shipping. I lost interest when I discovered that most of the testing does not involve a fishing pole.

Veterinary medicine has changed tremendously over the past several decades. There are many avenues to pursue that were not even imagined only a short time ago. Many specialties have arisen that were unthinkable (e.g. oncology) a short time ago. As noted earlier, the main focus of general practice has gone from treating illnesses (largely unsuccessfully) to preventing them. This is particularly true of infectious diseases and parasitism. We have made great strides in both arenas with the advent of vaccines and monthly parasite preventives. Improved sanitation has helped tremendously also. There may come a day when the average veterinarian may have difficulty in diagnosing parasite infestations because they will be so rare. Old age no longer implies poor health. We are learning that diet and exercise are just as critical to healthy aging in pets as they are in humans.

The human-animal bond is now celebrated as a way for us and our pets to grow old well together. Healthy habits are important for both people and pets. Many people are motivated to care for themselves only through caring for their pets. Getting a dog out for a walk is not only good exercise for all involved, but it also enables otherwise isolated people to get out and make some friends. Some elderly people won't go to the store for themselves, but they'll run to the store if the pet food supply runs low.

There are many well organized programs for orchestrating interactions between needy people and pets. The Delta Society is dedicated to developing programs to enhance interactions between people and pets. They have great need of volunteers and I guarantee that you will be richly rewarded by donating your time, treasure or talents to one of their local affiliates.

As of this writing we are suffering one of the worst economies since the Great Depression. Veterinarian practices will see a modest level of scrimping, but they have been traditionally recession-proof as most people will provide care for their pets even if it means delaying care for themselves. I once read that no veterinarian was unemployed during the Great Depression. I hope that the same will be said of our current situation despite the fact that we no longer commute on horseback.

I was 'without a job' for a few weeks last year. I took some time off from the clinic without pay to finish writing this novel. That was the first time since the age of 14 that I didn't have a paying job. I kept calling the clinic every other day to ask if they had any messages for me. "No. You're not here." I was quietly devastated. I hated being away from the office. I resolved to die with my boots on by practicing as long as possible. If I lose my skills I think I will become a greeter like they have at the big box stores. Or, perhaps I'll go back to school and get another degree....I'd sure like to know more about a lot of different things. Being a lifelong learner has been one of the greatest benefits of my education.

If I could impart only one lesson to each person who blesses me by sharing in this book it would be this: love to learn and learn to love. Everything else will fall in place.

# Appendix

I would like to share with those who care to read it the eulogy I delivered at my father's funeral. Writing it was easy…I knew exactly what I wanted to say about Dad. Delivering it was much more difficult.

Despite having the friendliest audience I will ever have, I was extremely apprehensive about getting through it. Just before I went up to the podium I handed a copy to Dr. Rooney and asked if would step up to the plate if I couldn't finish the eulogy. I knew that no one in my family would be up to the task.

He thought for a moment and then said, "Yes, I would be honored. I'll introduce myself as your partner…Business Partner!!"

I knew he had my back and his humor was just what I needed to get me through. Ironically, the only part I didn't cry about when reading it at home was the only part that choked me up while delivering it. That was when I mentioned our mutual friend, Rich. I hope they're pestering Grampa at his favorite fishing hole in heaven where the water is deep enough for you to stand up and drink.


*July 27, 2009*

Most of you know me, but for those who don't I am Glen's eldest son, Gregg. I have three older sisters, one younger sister and three younger brothers. That is just the beginning of my father's legacy. He currently has 36 living grandchildren and 32 great grandchildren. While his life has ended he is still exerting quite an influence on our lives and through us, the world we continue to live in.

Glen persevered through a tough childhood. I never met his father; he died just prior to my birth. Dad never spoke ill of him though he easily could have. In fact, he rarely spoke of him at all because he had few fond memories of him to share with us. There wasn't much love in their household. To the day she died he always called his mom 'mother'. She never told us grandchildren that she loved us. Her favorite words were 'tough, tough' as in "Gramma, I don't like this venison." "Tough, tough. That's what I made for dinner. Eat more vegetables if you're still hungry."

Dad could have easily continued this legacy, but he chose not to. He was the greatest father any child could hope for. While he was always quiet and reserved, he was always there. And he wasn't just 'there'; he was a presence in our lives.

He truly enjoyed spending time with his children. He was our baseball coach, our hockey manager, our engineer. He kept the vacant lot mowed so we could play baseball close to home. He built an ice rink in the wetlands behind the house complete with boards and lights. He even made a Zamboni for us to resurface the ice. He erected a backboard and hoop in the driveway and put up floodlights so we could play basketball at night. But, the most important thing he built for us was character.

He didn't just make a play area and kick us out of the house. He was out there with us. He played hockey right up to his heart attack at the age of 49. He quit playing because he had to, but he continued to drive my brothers all over creation in order to watch them play. He also drove Lynn, his baby girl, to many baseball games. He was always an active fan when the coaching hat came off. I don't recall that he ever officially coached the girl's teams because he was a man's man. He had issues with yelling at the girls. He didn't seem to mind when it came to us boys. With inanimate objects he was merciless.

I have often told people that the DVM after my name is an abbreviation for the Latin translation of 'doesn't work on motor vehicles'. That is because I had the opportunity to watch Dad work on the family cars. He cussed out anyone that 'could have invented such a stupid thing' right down to the guy who invented the wheel. I walked into the garage one day to get my baseball mitt. Dad was sitting under the hood of his old Ford pickup truck where the engine once sat. Neat rows of labeled parts were lined up on the floor. He looked up at me and menacingly said, "Don't touch a thing." I shut the door and left. I didn't need my mitt that badly.

One of the greatest compliments of my life I received at my 30th high school reunion. Mike Kennedy came up to me and after saying hello immediately asked how Dad was doing. "Great!", I replied. "He is still shooting his age (75) on the golf course." Mike continued, "I want you to go home and tell your Dad that I said hello and thanks for the great childhood. All of the fun we had was due to him. He let us play baseball and basketball and hockey. He is the one that took us camping and fishing. I wish I could do half of the things with my kids that he did with me."

I could still see the respect and affection present after all those years. Probably even more so because Mike now realized what tremendous effort it takes to stay involved with your children. When Dad said no to any request for his time it was with reluctance. He had a lot of demands on his time, but he still managed to beat us at a game of Stratego before sending us off to bed. (I can still hear the yells of "I play the winner" coming from the rec room and I can still see the look of disappointment when Dad had lost the game (probably on purpose) and you had to play against a sibling…flush with success after beating the champ.)

One bad habit that Dad did retain from his upbringing was never saying "I love you." He felt that it was unnecessary because he showed us that he did every day. His 'I love you' was throwing batting practice or putting a worm on the hook. It was always maintaining security. Despite raising eight children we never felt that we were lacking anything. We certainly did without a lot of things that our friends had access to, but in the end it gave us the knowledge that stuff is not important. It all gets pushed to the side or broken at some point. That should never happen to a person. People are important, not things.

There are so many aspects of Dad's life that I would like to cover, but that would take hours. However, I cannot fail to mention Clark Oil. When Dad was sent to Chicago from the north woods of Wisconsin, Uncle Arlo was able to get work for him at the refinery in Blue Island. It was manual labor; digging ditches for a pipeline. He walked out of his interview and began digging while still wearing his suit! They talked about that at the refinery for years.

When that work was finished Dad was literally at the bus depot waiting to go back north when one of the supervisors at the refinery asked Arlo if that nephew of his was still around. "He was a good worker and I have another job to get done." Arlo drove to the station and brought him back. Dad retired from Clark 43 years later. He went to night school for years and became supervisor of operations. What a great role model for us kids....work hard and keep learning. Good things will happen as a result.

Dad was on call for most of those years. When the phone rang late at night you could bet it was the refinery. Dad never hesitated to go to the phone. He never looked angry or frustrated. He cared about what was going on at the refinery and he was always concerned about the safety of his coworkers. When there was a leaky pipe or valve Dad stepped in not only to supervise, but to get his hands dirty and help. When there was a fire Dad put himself in harm's way with the rest of his crew. We spent many nights praying with Mom that Dad would return home safely.

After Dad had his heart attack it became known just how much he was doing at the refinery. It took 3 trained people to do his job. Mr. Clark came to the hospital personally to thank Dad for all he had been doing and to apologize for not being aware of the amount of stress he had been under. I wish that corporate America still the heart of Emory Clark. He took very good care of his employees and they worked hard for him. All of us older kids remember the Clark picnics and Christmas parties! I also remember many of Dad's coworkers. Some of them had the unique experience of fishing with Glen....very often with his eldest son in Canada.

All who know me can attest to the level of excitement I have for Canadian fishing. I have had the honor of going on 39 trips scattered across Ontario with my father. The last two trips were drive-up camps. We wanted to have access to immediate help as Dad developed more medical problems. The first 37 were fly-in trips. At first we camped in the boundary waters of Quetico Provincial Park and later we graduated to fly-in camps and bases.

Most of the guys that joined us for their first wilderness experience were hooked for life. Special mention goes to Rich Hozelton, a good friend to Dad, a great asset to the refinery and the best fisherman I have ever been to camp with. Some, however, never wanted to return. Harry Firmiss comes to mind…if he thought he could have made it back to base camp he would have started walking out the first day. That plane ride was the worst experience of his life. His idea of fishing wasn't 12 hours in a boat. It was 3 hours, a nap, a Snickers bar and watch TV. The silence was so profound he couldn't sleep because he could 'hear his hair growing' and half of the mosquitoes in Ontario now had his blood type. One thing that nobody could seriously complain about was the food. We ate like kings and Dad was affectionately known as 'the cook'. That didn't make him immune to pranks, especially when Uncle Arlo was around. Then he was 'that rotten cook' as in "That rotten cook got two desserts." or "That rotten cook is nice and warm while we're out here cleaning fish." The only time it was considered to be impolite to insult the cook was when you had a mouthful of food. Dad's usual response to a ribbing was, "How do you want your eggs in the morning, sandy or burnt?"

Dad's stepfather, Emil, came on many of our trips. He always called Dad 'cook' on the trips, but went back to Glen or Glennie as soon as we left camp. All who met Emil immediately liked him. He was the salt of the Earth and I know that Dad was grateful that his mother was finally in good hands. I have a lifetime of memories from the dozens of trips that Dad and I took to help his parents in the north woods. Emil never had too much work for us to do. He always left some work 'for tomorrow' so we could go fishing today. Dad loved to tease him about that being a sure sign of a union electrician…always leave some work for tomorrow.

Dad's work on Earth came to a full completion. He managed to outlive his heart, but he could no longer deny that he had cancer. When he could no longer hide it, he took care of all of his unfinished business before going home. He even made certain that his library books were returned with no late fees. He made me return his time card to the Meadows Golf Course where he worked after his retirement from Clark. That was the most difficult thing for me to do. Golf was his passion and I knew that he would leave us when that passion faded. I felt his life slipping from my grasp as I returned that card.

He wanted my assurances that Mom would be taken care of and he insisted that his possessions went to those who needed them the most. I have taken on the solemn duty of executing my father's specific wishes, but in parting I wanted him to have one of my possessions.

The master angler pin he is wearing is mine. His friend, or rather our friend, Big Fish Richie Hoz, guided me to my 43 inch northern pike from beyond the grave (see Interlude). I love fishing, but I loved the time I had alone with Dad even more. I am not a master angler. If anyone deserves the award it is my mother. She had the greatest catch of all.

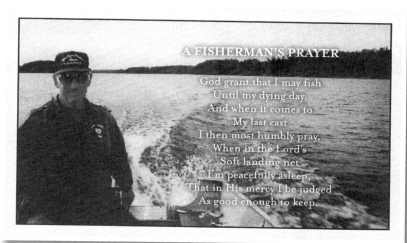

A FISHERMAN'S PRAYER

God grant that I may fish
Until my dying day,
And when it comes to
My last cast
I then most humbly pray,
When in the Lord's
Soft landing net
I'm peacefully asleep,
That in His mercy I be judged
As good enough to keep.